Hare-Hunting and Harriers

With Notices of Beagles and Basset Hounds, and a History of Hunting with Dogs

By H. A. Bryden

Illustrated from Photographs by R. B. Lodge and Others

PANTIANOS
CLASSICS

Published by Pantianos Classics

ISBN-13: 978-1-78987-131-9

First published in 1903

Contents

William Somervile - Author of "The Chace"

(National Portrait Gallery)

Editor's Preface

IN the following pages a keen all-round sportsman has given what may claim to be in the nature of an exhaustive account, both practical and historic, of hare-hunting. While he has not hesitated to draw on the works of such classic authorities as Somervile, Beckford and "Stonehenge," it is mainly to his own personal knowledge of a fine sport, supplemented where necessary by information generously given by living authorities, including many Masters of existing packs of harriers, beagles, or bassets, that his book owes its extraordinary interest.

What is likely, over and above the great pains which Mr. Bryden has evidently taken with his record, to strike the reader is the hopeful tone of his remarks. He could not, of course, blind himself to the prejudicial effect of the spread of bricks and mortar, or to certain conditions of modern agriculture, which tend to limit the opportunities for hunting hare. Like other wild animals, the hare has unavoidably retired from the environs of our growing towns. We no longer expect to see wild hares at large in the Regent's Park, where once they were so abundant that the Zoological Society had to erect a hare-proof fence round its Gardens, to prevent the park hares breaking through and eating the flowers. That would have been about the time when Queen Victoria came to the throne; and less than a century earlier snipe were seen in Conduit Street and wildfowl in Pimlico, while the bark of the fox sounded on moonlight nights from the fastnesses of Kensington Gardens. Those times are gone, and with them the wild creatures have in great measure passed. Even so, however, Mr. Bryden is hopeful, and his prophetic eye sees future generations of his hare-hunting countrymen, after the smoke from our manufacturing centres has stifled the last British hare, repairing, with the aid of some as yet undreamt means of rapid travel, for week-end hunts to Tierra del Fuego or the Asiatic tundras, in pursuit of merry hares that continue to flourish in purer air.

The author has certainly made out a good case for the strong appeal of his favourite sport to keen sportsmen and sportswomen of all ages, of moderate means, and of proficiency in the saddle or otherwise. He has also indicates how considerable tracts of suitable country in this island are still unexploited by harriers or other dogs entered to hare. The distribution of that animal is admittedly irregular, for whereas it is so plentiful in some parts of the country that even enthusiastic hare-hunters welcome an occasional coursing meeting as a check on excessive numbers, in others, owing chiefly to the operation of the Ground Game Act, it seems near extinction. Still, as Mr. Bryden shows, it should be no very difficult matter to establish hare warrens or turn down hares and thus restore a good show of game. If the plan of these volumes admitted of an Author's Preface, I feel sure that Mr. Bryden would take the opportunity of tendering his best thanks to the many Masters of Harriers and others who have so ungrudgingly helped with their knowledge and with their cameras to make the book what it is.

F. G. A.

Chapter One - Chiefly Historical

Hare-hunting can claim a more respectable antiquity even than the chase of the fox. It may be doubted whether Tickell, the poet, is correct when he designates that mighty hunter, Nimrod, a follower of the timid hare as well as of the noblest of great game, two thousand years before the Christian era. He says of that kingly sportsman:

"Bold Nimrod first the Lion's Trophies wore,
 The Panther bound, and lanc'd the bristling Boar;
 He taught to turn the Hare, to bay the Deer,
 And wheel the Courser in his mid Career.

Whether or not Nimrod occasionally descended to the pursuit of the hare, it is certain that this form of chase is a sufficiently ancient one. Xenophon, who flourished three hundred and fifty years before the birth of Christ, hunted hare with as much enthusiasm as our English squires of the eighteenth century, and has left minute accounts of the sport, describing the hare and her habits, the early morning trail, the find and the chase. He has some curious observations upon the hare and her ways. The scent of young hares, he tells us, is stronger than that of the full-grown animal, for the reason that the weakness of their limbs permits the whole body at times to touch the earth. He has a theory that, as the hare's tail is of no aid to her in steering, she employs for this purpose her long ears, laying down the ear upon that side from which the hound makes his rush at her and, turning instantly, leaving her pursuers behind. He has much to say concerning the treatment of hounds, and he recommends that the young entry should be permitted to tear their quarry when run into. There are also directions against straggling, and Xenophon seems to have had a particular objection to that bane of all masters, the skirter.

Kings, warriors, and statesmen have, from time immemorial, been enthusiastically devoted to all forms of hunting. That they did not despise sport with the hare is abundantly clear. Nor, considering the extraordinary resourcefulness of this animal, the sport she provides, the mazes she weaves in her flight, the extreme interest of the chase which she affords, and the fine qualities required in hounds which can successfully cope with so fleet and cunning a beast of chase, is this surprising. Edward III., during his campaigns in France, maintained sixty couples of harriers as well as the same number of staghounds.

The greatest heroes seem to have found sport with the hare acceptable to their natures. At the battle of Roncesvalles, when Charlemagne hears from afar off the distant blast of Roland's horn, he is eager to march instantly to his rescue, believing that the young paladin must be in sore jeopardy. But the traitor, Ganelon, to whom the Moors owed their victory on that fatal day, palters with him and puts him off. "For a hare," he says, "would Roland sound his horn all day, and at this moment he is most likely laughing with his twelve Peers over the fright he has caused us."

James I., although by no means an admirable king, had, to his credit, a real love of hunting in all its branches. He certainly kept harriers as well as staghounds, and among the expenses of his establishment are to be found the following entries:

Robert Rayne, Serjeant of the King's Buckhounds, received 50 per annum; in addition, as one of the Yeomen of the Privy Harriers, he drew 36 yearly.

	£	s.	d.
" To Sir Patrick Howme, Master of the Privy Harriers, for his fee 120*l.* per annum, and for keeping one footman, four horses, and twenty Couple of Dogs, 100*l.* per annum . . .	220	0	0
To Richard Gwynne, Groom of the Harriers to the Prince, 13*d.* per diem, and twenty shillings per annum for his Livery	20	15	0
To John Waters, Yeoman of the Harriers to the King, twelve pence per diem . . .	18	5	0

Queen Elizabeth kept "Buck Hounds," "Hart Hounds," "Hunting Harriers," and "Otter Hounds." Among her expenses are to be found the following:

Otter-hounds cost her, apparently, no more than £13 6s. 8d. per annum for Master's fee; probably servants of the

	£	s.	d
Master of the Harriers Fee	11	6	0
Yeoman's Fee	6	0	0
Officers and others serving under the same Master, Wages and Allowances . . .	79	1	8
Total . .	96	7	8

other packs were employed with otter in summer. Buckhounds cost £92 9s. 2d. and Hart hounds £38 is. 5d., so that it is apparent that Queen Elizabeth's harriers were reckoned at least as important as any other part of her hunting establishment. The hare, however, was always held from very early ages in a highly honourable estimation as a beast of chase; far more so, in fact, than the fox, which, until towards the end of the seventeenth century, was classed merely as vermin to be destroyed anyhow and anywhere.

Down to the time of the Reformation, not only the noblemen and gentry, but churchmen of almost every degree - save the poorer priests hunted. Many of the higher dignitaries maintained great state and devoted most of their lime to field sports. Walter, Bishop of Rochester, who flourished in the thirteenth century, and lived to the age of eighty, made hunting his sole occupation, "to the total neglect of the duties of his office." Becket, on his embassy to the Court of France, took with him hounds and hawks, and no doubt used them freely. The greater dignitaries of the Church saw to it that they had ample hunting grounds. At the date of the Reformation the See of Norwich possessed no less than thirteen parks, "well stocked with deer and other animals of the chase." Even in Charles I.'s time, Bishop Juxon was a keen follower of the chase; he maintained a good pack of hounds, "and had them so well ordered and hunted," says Whitlock, "chiefly by his own skill and direction, that they exceeded all other hounds in England." Parsons still hunt in England, but it must, one fancies, be considerably more than a hundred years since a Bishop went out with hounds - even with a quiet pack of harriers!

In the "Gentleman's Recreation," published by Nicholas Cox in 1677, there is much curious and odd information on hare-hunting, among other field sports, compiled, I believe, chiefly from authors before his time. Here are samples of the quaint Cox's lore. "We say the Deer is broke up. The Fox and Hare is cased." In those days it was the custom to divest the hare of her skin when killed, and, the gall and lights being taken away under the impression that they made hounds sick the huntsman, who carried some bread, cut up into small pieces, dipped these in the blood and gave them with the entrails to the hounds. The hare was after this broken up and given among the pack, and if any young hound was too timid to come in and take his share, he was presented with the head. The modern custom of giving hounds the entrails and handing the hare over to the farmer upon whose land she was found, is surely a much more seemly and profitable way of dealing with the dead quarry.

To return to Nicholas Cox. Among "Terms for the Footing and Treading of all Beasts of Venery and Chase," he says: "Of a hare, diversely, for when she is in open field she soreth; when she winds about to deceive the Hounds then she doubleth; when she beateth on the Hard Highway, and her footing can be perceived, then she pricketh; and in the snow it is called the Trace of the Hare."

Concerning tracking hares in the snow, by the way, there used to be a special Statute, 14 & 15 Hen. VIII. cap. 10, which provided as follows: "None shall trace, destroy or kill any Hare in the Snow, in pain of 6s. 8d. for every such Offence; which penalty assessed in Sessions shall go to the King; but in a Leet, to the Lord thereof." Whether this ordinance has ever been repealed I know not; probably it has. An earlier Act of Richard II.'s reign - 13 Rich. II. cap. 13 - set forth that "No man who hath not lands of 40s. per annum, nor Clerk who hath not 10l. revenue per annum shall have or keep any Greyhound, Hound, Dog, Ferret, Net or Engine to destroy Deer, Hares, Coneys, or any other Gentleman's Game, in pain of one whole year's imprisonment, which Justices of Peace have power to inflict."

The boar and wolf were in process of time exterminated in these islands, and wild deer, except on the moorlands of the West - Exmoor chiefly - and the fells of Cumberland and Westmoreland, became more and more difficult to find. Sportsmen were thus reduced to hunting the semi-feral deer of their own parks, a form of sport which, by the sixteenth and seventeenth centuries, French writers upon Venery already referred to with some contempt. With the decline of deer, it is certain that the chase of the hare assumed much more importance, and by the seventeenth century it is clear that hare-hunting was a sport held in high favour among English squires. During this and the eighteenth century it seems to have been the custom among country gentlemen to keep a mixed kennel of hounds, with which they pursued hare, otter, and occasionally fox, as it pleased them. By the early years of the eighteenth century the fox had emerged from its once low estimation and was beginning to be hunted regularly. The foxhound proper had now been evolved, and from the middle of the eighteenth century it may be said that fox-hunting increased more and more in favour until it had quite outstripped in popularity the chase of the hare.

William Somervile, the author of "The Chace," undoubtedly the finest poem on hunting in the English language, was a typical squire of his time. He flourished between 1677 and 1742, residing, after the age of twenty-seven, when he resigned his Fellowship at New College, Oxford, upon his own estate of Edstone, in Warwickshire. Edstone, in the parish of Wootton Wawen, lies in the very heart of Shakespeare's country, about seven miles from Stratford-on-Avon, and about four from Henley-in-Arden. Here Somervile, during many long and happy years, devoted himself, heart and soul, to the sport of hunting, rousing in turn hare, fox, and otter from their various lurking-places. "The site of his kennel," says a writer in the *Sporting Magazine* of February 1832, "was well chosen, on a little eminence erect, facing the south-east, with a grove of willow, poplar and elm at the back, to shield it from the north and west winds. The kennel was spacious, with a fine brook babbling through. He kept about twelve couple of beagles, bred chiefly between the small Cotswold harrier and the Southern hound; six couple of foxhounds, rather rough and wire-haired; and five couple of otter-hounds, which in the winter season made an addition to the foxhounds." In this passage "beagle" should read "harrier" and *vice versa*. The mating of the slow, ponderous Southern hound with the fleet Cotswold beagle would produce a first-rate harrier, and that, undoubtedly, was the strain cultivated by Somervile. The coupling of Southern hound and harrier would not produce beagle, but, conversely, Southern hound and beagle would produce harrier. This strain, by the way - Southern hound and beagle - is still plainly apparent, sometimes crossed with a dash of the foxhound, in most of the old-fashioned packs of pure harriers still hunting in the United Kingdom. For the chase of the hare there is nothing to surpass it. "The country he hunted," continues the same writer, "was chiefly woodland, except that where his beagles were generally thrown off; and every parish, being uninclosed, yielded excellent sport. To the feeding of his hounds, and the management and arrangement of his kennels, he attended himself...He conducted the chase himself; leaving a man in the kennel to prepare the food, who was in the capacity of earth stopper. His stud was small, four nags being the greatest number he ever had in the stable; employing his favourite, Old Ball, three times in the week. Old Ball was a real good English hunter, standing about fifteen hands high, with black legs, short back, high in the shoulders, large barrel, thin head, cropped ears, and a white blaze down the face."

These particulars were communicated to the writer of the article in question by a Warwickshire man, who had himself been entered to hunting by Somervile's old huntsman, John Hoitt, who survived his master more than half a century and died in 1802. William Somervile lies, together with two of his huntsmen, Jacob Boeter and John Hoitt, in Wootton Wawen churchyard. Until the year 1898 no memorial of him existed; but in that year, thanks to the exertions of the Rev. F. T. Bramston, Vicar of Wootton, a tablet was subscribed for and erected inside the church. On the tomb of his last huntsman may be seen the following lines, composed by the Rev. J. Eaches, a former vicar:

"Here Hoitt, all his sports and labours past,
 Joins his loved Master, Somervile, at last;
 Together went they, echoing fields to try,
 Together now in silent dust they lie.
 Servant and lord, when once we yield our breath,
 Huntsman and poet, are alike to Death.
 Life's motley drama calls for powers and men
 Of different casts, to fill its changeful scene;
 But all the merit that we justly prize,
 Not in the past but in the acting lies.
 And as the lyre, so may the huntsman's horn
 Fame's trumpet rival, and his name adorn."

The quiet country church of Wootton Wawen, the last resting-place of one of the keenest and best sportsmen that ever crossed a horse, sounded a horn, or cheered his hounds, of the man whose poem, "The Chace," will remain a classic so long as the English tongue endures, is surely worthy of a pilgrimage by any lover of hunting who happens to be within a score or two of miles!

Somervile's custom of hunting both hare and fox during the winter season was commonly followed by most country gentlemen of the eighteenth century. Somervile himself kept his hounds apart, and hunted hare and fox with harriers and foxhounds, reinforcing, as we have seen, the latter during the proper season with his otter-hounds, which were then unemployed. He says in "The Chace":

"A different hound for ev'ry diff' rent chace
 Select with judgment; nor the tim'rous hare
 O'er-matched destroy, but leave that vile offence
 To the mean, murd'rous coursing crew, intent
 On blood and spoil. O blast their hopes just Heav'n."

The poet seems to have had a peculiar hatred for coursing, a sentiment which in these days has largely disappeared, although, for obvious reasons, hare hunters are not over-fond of greyhounds and their masters.

Somervile may truthfully be styled the father of modern hunting. Before his time writers on sport employed an archaic and cumbrous style, now obsolete for centuries, and difficult and fatiguing of comprehension even by the most devoted student of hunting literature. Somervile inaugurates a completely new era. His spirit is largely modern, his style easy, clear and flowing; even at the present day it is a real pleasure to read his graphic descriptions and stirring pictures. To the hare -hunter, especially, his volume must always be invaluable; his instructions on kennel and hound management are sound and practical, and may be referred to with advantage even by the modern master or huntsman. We pass with him, as it were, from the Middle Ages to Modern England in the palmiest days of sport. It is a supreme test of Somervile's merit that Beckford, himself the greatest classic on hunting down to the present day, so frequently refers to "The Chace" and quotes so freely from it. There can be no doubt whatever that the author of "The Chace," although he describes with equal facility, spirit, and truth fox-hunting and the chase of stag and otter, loved hare-hunting beyond all other forms of sport. In the second book of his poem are to be found descriptions of a hare hunt which are destined, probably, never to be surpassed. I cannot refrain from quoting a few of his brilliant pictures. After some opening lines he leads his reader to the countryside:

"Now golden autumn from her open lap
Her fragrant bounty show'rs; the fields are shorn;
Inwardly smiling, the proud farmer views
The rising pyramids that grace his yard,
And counts his large increase; his barns are stor'd
And groaning staddles bend beneath their load.
All now is free as air, and the gay pack
In the rough, bristly stubbles range unblam'd;
No widow's tears o'erflow, no secret curse
Swells in the farmer's breast, which his pale lips
Trembling conceal, by his fierce landlord aw'd;
But courteous now he levels ev'ry fence,
Joins in the common cry, and holloas loud,
Charm' d with the rattling thunder of the field.
Oh bear me, some kind power invisible!
... to those spacious plains, where the strain'd eye
In the wide prospect lost, beholds at last
Sarum's proud spire, that o'er the hill ascends,
And pierces thro' the clouds. Or to thy downs
Fair Cotswold, where the well-breath'd beagle climbs,
With matchless speed, thy green aspiring brow,
And leaves the lagging multitude behind."

Somervile, in addition to his Warwickshire property, had an estate that of SomervileAston in Gloucestershire, and it is certain frequently hunted there. All his touches are lifelike and most natural, even to the casual reader of 1903. Hunters saddled up and rode forth earlier in 1735 the date of the poem than they do at the present day. They loved the long trailing of the hare to her seat, a part of the chase long since abandoned. He continues:

"Farewell, Cleora, [1] here deep sunk in down,

Slumber secure, with happy dreams amus'd,
Till grateful steams shall tempt thee to receive
Thy early meal, or thy officious maids,
The toilet plac'd, shall urge thee to perform
The important work. Me other joys invite,
The horn sonorous calls, the pack awak'd
Their matins chant, nor brook my long delay."

Now comes the meet:
                    "Delightful scene!
Where all around is gay, men, horses, dogs,
And in each smiling countenance appears
Fresh blooming health and universal joy."

They throw off, and presently hounds find a trail. The hare is put off gently
from her seat:

"Here huntsman bring
(But without hurry) all thy jolly hounds,
And calmly lay them on. How low they stoop,
And seem to plough the ground; then all at once
With greedy nostrils snuff the fuming steam,
The welkin rings, men, dogs, hills, rocks, and woods,
In the full concert join!" . . .

Here follows some sound advice:

"Huntsman! her gait observe: if in wide rings
She wheel her mazy way, in the same round
Persisting still, she'll foil the beaten track.
But if she fly, and with the fav'ring wind
Urge her bold course, less intricate thy task:
Push on thy pack."

The chase goes on:

"The puzzling pack unravel, wile by wile,
Maze within maze. The covert's utmost bound
Slyly she skirts; behind then cautious creeps,
And in that very track, so lately stain' d
By all the steaming crowd, seems to pursue
The foe she flies."
How true a picture is this, and this again:

"But hold I see her from the covert break;
Sad on yon little eminence she sits;
Intent she listens, with one ear erect,
Pond'ring and doubtful what new course to take,
And how t' escape the fierce bloodthirsty crew

14

That still urge on and still in volleys loud Insult her woes....
                    .....her fears prevail,
And o'er the plain, and o'er the mountain's ridge
Away she flies."

The huntsmen "smoke along the vale," the old hounds now begin to come to the front, as they will do when the chase is sinking; a check ensues, caused by a flock of sheep, the line is recovered, and away, after another slight check, they drive.

"Now the poor chace
Begins to flag, to her last shifts reduc'd.
From brake to brake she flies, and visits all
Her haunts."

The end comes, and the kill and obsequies are described. By Somervile's time, it is clear, the hare was not "cased," or skinned, broken up and thrown to the pack, but dealt with according to present methods the hounds being rewarded with the heart and entrails only.

No prose description of a hare hunt and the writer has read many hundreds in his time can possibly eclipse Somervile's blank verse. The whole poem abounds in the most faithful and minute pictures of hunting, and it ought to be in the hands of every sportsman, by whom it may still be perused not only with pleasure but with great profit.

Peter Beckford, whose "Thoughts on Hunting" are to this hour held in so great estimation by all concerned with the chase of fox and hare, was born in 1740, and succeeded to a handsome fortune and estate on the

HARE-HUNTING, 1798
UNKENNELLING

HARE-HUNTING, 1793
DRAWING

death of his father, Julines Beckford, whose forbears had gathered wealth in the West Indies. Beckford, a man of culture and attainments considerably beyond the squires of his day, was Member for Morpeth in 1768 and had travelled abroad. He was manifestly a first-rate sportsman, understanding thoroughly the whole process and economy of hunting, hounds, and horses. He lived in a fine old Georgian or Queen Anne Mansion at Steepleton-Iwerne, in Dorsetshire, and hunted for the most part in Cranbourne Chase, of which he was Ranger. The country in which he hunted is apparently identical with that now used by the South Dorset foxhounds. Mr. Otho Paget, in his excellent edition of Beckford, published in 1899, gives some interesting details concerning this classic author. He gives also some very interesting pictures of Steepleton-Iwerne (which is still inhabited by descendants of Beckford the Misses Pitt, his great-granddaughters) of Beckford himself, and of his favourite horses and hounds.

Beckford's great book was published in 1781. It was soon recognised as a standard work one may say *the* standard work - on hunting, and has retained its authority and its popularity down to the present day. Beckford, like Somervile, had a touch of the modern spirit, he wrote easily and well, with a vein of pleasantly caustic humour; and although it is one hundred and twenty-five years since his volume first appeared, he can be read with pleasure by the reader of the twentieth century, while his facts and inferences are practically as valuable now as when they were first perused. Many editions testify to the high estimation in which "Thoughts on Hunting" has always been held.

Beckford was by choice a foxhunter, and the greater part of his book is devoted to that branch of the chase. He had, however, at one time kept harriers, and his letters on hare-hunting are to the full as pithy and as informing as the rest of his volume. He devoted three chapters or letters to the sport of hare-hunting, and his remarks may well be pondered even by the present-day harrier-man. Beckford bred his harriers between the large, slow, hunting harrier and the little fox beagle; "the former," he says, "are too dull, too heavy, and too slow; the latter too lively, too light, and too fleet." The foxbeagle, it may be noted, was for generations employed, before the regular chase of the fox with foxhounds came into vogue; reynard being considered in those days as mere vermin, to be run to earth and knocked on the head as speedily as possible.

"The first species," continues Beckford, "it is true, have excellent noses and, I make no doubt, will kill their game, at least if the day be long enough; but you know the days are short in winter, and it is bad hunting in the dark; the other, on the contrary, fling and dash and are all alive, but every cold blast affects them; and if your country be wet and damp, it is not impossible that some of them may be drowned. My hounds were a cross of both these kinds, in which it was my endeavour to get as much bone and strength in as small compass as possible. It was a difficult undertaking. I bred many years, and an infinity of hounds, before I could get what I wanted; I at last had the pleasure to see them very handsome; small yet bony; they ran remarkably well together; ran fast enough; had all the alacrity that you could desire; and would hunt the coldest scent. When they were thus perfect, I did as many others do I parted with them."

Beckford is always amusing. Many of his anecdotes, with which the book abounds, are first rate. He describes, comically enough, the procuring of some beagles no doubt "the little beagles" already spoken of from the North of England.

"Having heard of a small pack of beagles to be disposed of in Derbyshire," he says, "I sent my coachman (the person whom I could at that time best spare to fetch them). It was a long journey, and not having been used to hounds, he had some trouble in getting them along; besides which, as ill-luck would have it, they had not been out of the kennel for many weeks before, and were so riotous, that they ran after every thing they saw; sheep, curdogs, and birds of all sorts, as well as hares and deer, I found, had been his amusement all the way along. However, he lost but one hound, and when I asked him what he thought of them, he said, 'they could not fail of being good hounds, for they would hunt anything.'"

In Beckford's time warren hares were often caught in traps and occasionally turned down before hounds and greyhounds, much as is a bag-fox with hounds at the present day. Beckford gives directions in his twelfth letter concerning the taking of these warren hares. Trap-hares are, thank Heaven, seldom heard of nowadays. Beckford himself, although he writes of the custom of his time, seems to have been averse to employing them for hunting. He recommended, if they were to be used, that they should be turned down wind, and the hounds hunted like a pack of foxhounds. A trapped hare almost invariably ran straight, made few or no doubles, and left a strong scent.

It has been said by many enthusiastic fox-hunters that Beckford took little account of hare-hunting. This is erroneous. He preferred fox-hunting, but he distinctly states in this letter (twelve) that he never meant to depreciate this excellent form of sport. "It is a good diversion," he says, "in a good country: you are always certain of sport: and if you really love to see your hounds hunt, the hare, when properly hunted, will show you more of it than any other animal."

Towards the end of the eighteenth century, even in Beckford's time - he died in 1809 - it was becoming the fashion to introduce a touch of foxhound blood into the old harrier strain. In fact the dwarf foxhound had certainly made his appearance as a harrier by the opening years of the nineteenth century. From that time there have been two schools of harriermen in England; those who stick by the old harrier blood produced, originally, as Somervile and Beckford produced their packs, by crossing the old Southern hound with the quick and nimble beagle - preferably the North-country beagle - and those who swear by foxhound blood, and will have it for hare-hunting, either pure, as in the case of the dwarf foxhound, or almost pure and but lightly crossed with the original harrier stock. These two schools of hare-hunters pursue and continue to pursue their quarry in widely different ways: the former content to hunt out, steadily but surely, the mazes and windings of the hare's natural flight; the later pushing their quarry so hard that she has no leisure and is too hard pressed to display her usual antics, and is burst up in a third or half of the time usually occupied by harriers of pure blood. Each school has its ardent supporters. Personally, I am one of those who like to see the hare hunted in the old-fashioned manner; and without the least wishing to return to the days of the seventeenth and early part of the eighteenth century, when followers of the old lumbering Southern hound spent half a dozen hours or more in running down their hare, I prefer a chase of an hour or more, with plenty of hound music - and your true harrier has a most beautiful and melodious voice - to a burst of twenty minutes, in which the quarry is completely overmastered and never has the faintest chance, which, in my opinion, she should have, of making her escape. Although many books have been written on hunting, it is astonishing how little learning is to be gathered concerning the chase of the hare. Somervile and Beckford to this hour remain almost our only masterpieces and authorities on this subject. "An Essay on Hunting," by a Country Squire, published in 1733, contains some useful information; and Stonehenge's "British Sports," the Badminton Library volume on Hunting, and an article in the "Encyclopaedia of Sport," also deal shortly with the subject. If I include a capital little volume on "Hare Hunting," by "Tantara," published in 1893, I have, I think, exhausted the list of authorities which may be consulted usefully by those desirous of informing themselves on the lore and lessons of this most excellent sport.

[1] A fancy name, one may take it, for his wife, a member of the Bethell family in Yorkshire.

Chapter Two - Hare-Hunters of the Past

OUR ancestors, as I have hinted, looked upon the chase of the hare as an operation to be conducted with what in these impatient days would be regarded as an unconscionable waste of time. Rising soon after the winter's dawn, they sallied forth with their big, deep-flewed, deep-voiced, long-eared, Southern hounds - standing some twenty-four or twenty-six inches at the shoulder - and, finding, after some trouble, traces of the hare in its overnight's wanderings, tracked it steadily to its form. They were not allowed to drive it from its seat; but the quarry, being at length discovered in its form, was pushed off and the hounds laid on, unless, as of course often happened, the hare had been already startled by the deep voices of its pursuers, drawing nearer and nearer, and had already slipped away. The Southern hound was what hunting-men of this day, and indeed of the last century, would consider far too much tied to the scent. Its sense of smell was so keen, its enjoyment of the scent so overpowering, that, instead of pushing along, as do the foxhound and modern harrier, and driving at its game, with the object of killing within some reasonable period say an hour or two - it would actually sit down upon the line and, lifting up its deep mellow voice, pour forth its satisfaction and enjoyment upon the wintry air. It never had much pace, and with such interruptions - and they were by no means singular - it is not astounding to find that the hunt, under such conditions, especially if, as sometimes happened, fresh hares were put up, lasted hour after hour. Three hours in those days must have been reckoned a quick hare-hunt; more often than not the solemn chase went on until five, six, and occasionally even more had been consumed. After having killed their hare, if they had the luck to do so, the jolly sportsmen wended their ways homeward, and wound up the day with a portentous dinner and a carouse thereafter.

These sport-loving squires, slow though their methods and tedious their style of hunting, if compared with the chase of our own time, were, after all, lineal ancestors of the present race of fox and hare-hunters and country gentlemen. If they had what seem to us defects from the modern point of view, they had, nevertheless, a score of excellent qualities. They were hearty, hospitable, jovial, full of the enjoyment of life; they stayed at home upon their acres and spent their money around them; they were good landlords, good farmers, great judges of stock and agriculture; and they had time and leisure to cultivate those domestic virtues which ensure pleasant homes and cheerful families. Some of them - by no means all - drank, it is true, more than was good for them. But, it is to be remembered, before the great French wars and the era of port-wine, the country gentleman, and especially those of the minor sort, drank ale for the most part, varied by claret and punch, and were not likely, therefore, to be so afflicted by gout and other ailments, as the three- or four-bottle men who came after them and drank the strong wine of Portugal. It will be, I think, not unprofitable to place before the reader one or two pictures of the hunting squires of the sixteenth and seventeenth centuries. Here is one, taken from the life, by Lord Chancellor Shaftesbury, in his memoirs of the Honourable William Hastings.

"In the year 1638," says Lord Shaftesbury, "lived Mr. Hastings at Woodlands, in the County of Southampton. By his quality, son, brother, and uncle to the Earls of Huntingdon. [1] He was, perad venture, an original in our age, or rather the copy of our antient Nobility in *hunting*, not in warlike times. He was very low, strong, and active, with reddish flaxen hair. His clothes, which, when new, were never worth five pounds, were of Green cloth. His house was perfectly old-fashioned; in the midst of a large Park, well stocked with Deer and Rabbits, many Fish-ponds, a great store of wood and timber, a Bowling-green in it, long but narrow, full of high ridges, never having been levelled since it was ploughed; round sand Bowls were used, and it had a Banquetting house like a Stand, built in a tree.

"Mr. H. kept all manner of Hounds that run Buck, Fox, Hare, Otter and Badger; Hawks both long and short winged. He had all sorts of Nets for Fish. A walk in the New Forest, and the Manor of Christchurch; this last supplied him with *Red Deer*, Sea and River Fish; and, indeed, all his neighbours grounds and Royalties were free to him, who bestowed all his time on these Sports." At his mansion were found "beef, pudding, and small beer, and a

House not so neatly kept as to shame him (the neighbour) or his dirty shoes, the great Hall strewed with marrow bones, full of Hawks, Perches, Hounds, Spaniels, and Terriers; the upper side of the Hall hung with the Fox skins of this year and the last year's killing, here and there a Martin Cat intermixed, and Game-keepers and Hunters poles in abundance.

"The Parlour was a large room as properly furnished. On a hearth, paved with brick, lay some Terriers, and the choicest Hounds and Spaniels. Seldom less than two of the great chairs had litters of *Kittens* on them, which were not to be disturbed, he always having three or four Cats attending him at dinner; and to defend such meat as he had no mind to part with, he kept order with a short white stick that lay by him. The windows, which were very large, served for places to lay his Arrows, Cross-bows, and other such accoutrements. The corners of the room were full of the best chose Hunting and Hawking poles. An *Oyster* table at the lower end, which was in constant use twice a day, all the year round, for he never failed to eat Oysters before Dinner and Supper, through all seasons. In the upper part of the room were two small tables and a desk; on the one side of the desk was a Church Bible, and on the other the Book of Martyrs. Upon the tables were Hawks-hoods, Bells, etc., two or three old green Hats, with their crowns thrust in, so as to hold ten or a dozen eggs, which were of a Pheasant-kind of poultry; these he took much care of, and fed himself. Tables, Boxes, Dice, Cards, were not wanting. In the holes of the desk was store of old used Tobacco pipes.

"On one side of this end of the room was the door of a Closet, wherein stood the strong Beer and the Wine, which never came thence but in *single* glasses, that being the rule of the house exactly observed; for he never exceeded in drinking, nor ever permitted it. On the other side was the door into an old Chapel, not used for devotion. The Pulpit, as the safest place, never wanted a cold Chine of Beef, Venison pasty, Gammon of bacon, or a great Apple pie, with a thick crust extremely baked. His table cost him not much, though it was always well supplied. His *Sports* furnished all but Beef and Mutton, except Fridays, when he had the best of *salt* as well as other *Fish*, he could get, and this was the day on which his neighbours of the first quality visited him. He never wanted a London pudding, and sung it in with 'My pert Eyes therein a!' He drank a glass or two at meals, very often syrup of Gilyflowers in his Sack, and always a tun glass stood by him, holding a pint of small beer, which he often stirred with Rosemary. He was affable but soon angry, calling his servants Bastards and Cuckoldy Knaves. He lived to be an Hundred, never lost his eyesight, but always wrote and read without spectacles, and got on Horseback without help. Until past Fourscore years, he rode up to the death of a Stag, as well as any man." A portrait of this gentleman, who may be styled something of an eccentric and a character, even in his own age, was, and I believe still is, at Wimborne St. Giles, the seat of the Earl of Shaftesbury. [2]

Here is another portrait, that of one of the lesser gentry, flourishing in the middle of the eighteenth century. It is given by Daniel, in his "Rural Sports," published in 1801. "It may be excused," says Mr. Daniel in his excellent book, "if the digression be continued for the purpose of sketching a Sportsman of the last age, as it may shew, that however we may have excelled in fashionable manners, it has been at the expense of abolishing a class of Men, who formed no inconsiderable link of the chain between the Peer and the Peasant in this Country. This Character, now worn out and gone, was the independent Gentleman, of three or four hundred pounds a-year, who commonly appeared in his Drab or Plush Coat, with large silver buttons, and rarely without Boots. His time was principally spent in Field amusements, and his travels never exceeded the distance of the County town, and that only at Assizes and Sessions, or to attend an Election. A Journey to London was, by one of these Men, reckoned as great an undertaking, as is at present a Voyage to the East Indies, and undertaken with scarce less precaution and preparation. At Church upon a Sunday he always appeared, never played at Cards but at Christmas, when he exchanged his usual beverage of Ale for a Bowl of strong Brandy Punch, garnished with a toast and Nutmeg.

HARE-HUNTING, 1798
THE FIND

"The Mansion of one of these 'Squires' was of plaister, or of red brick, striped with timber, called Callimancho work, large casemented Bow windows, a Porch with seats in it, and over it a Study; the eaves of the house were well inhabited by Martins, and the Court set round with Hollyhocks and clipt Yews. The Hall was provided with Flitches of bacon, and the Mantelpiece with Fowling

HARE-HUNTING, 1798
THE DEATH

pieces and Fishing rods of different dimensions, accompanied by the Broad Sword, Partisan, and Dagger, borne by his Ancestors in the Civil Wars; the vacant spaces were occupied by Stags' horns. In the window lay Baker's Chronicle, Fox's Book of Martyrs, Glanvil on Witches, Quincey's Dispensatory, Bracken's Farriery, and the Gentleman's Recreation. In this room at Christmas, round a glowing fire, he entertained his Tenants; here was told and heard exploits in Hunting, and who had been the best Sportsman of his time; and although the glass was in constant circulation, the traditionary tales of the village, respecting *Ghosts* and *Witches,* petrified them with fear. The best Parlour, which was never opened but on some particular occasion, was furnished with worked chairs and carpet, by some industrious Female of the Family, and the wainscot was decorated with portraits of his Ancestors, and Pictures of running Horses and Hunting pieces. Among the out-offices of the house, were a warm stable for his Horses, and a good Kennel for his Hounds; and near the gate was the horse-block, for the conveniency of mounting."

This is a pleasing picture of the old-time Squireen or Yeoman, a class even now not quite extinct. Here and there, in quieter parts of England and Ireland, one may yet come across a belated specimen of the little Squire or wealthier Yeoman, living in some quaint, old-fashioned house in which his forbears have dwelt before him for centuries. More probably than not he is a hare-hunter and takes his pleasure in the field, following with absorbing interest some old-fashioned pack of blue-mottled harriers, whose wonderful voices plainly denote their Southern hound ancestry. It is a thousand pities that these men have so nearly vanished from the countryside. But, as Macaulay notices, even in Charles II.'s time, the wealthy yeoman, possessing three or four hundred acres of his own land, was already vanishing from the soil, and being absorbed by the great territorial aristocracy.

Between the two characters here sketched - one of Charles I.'s, the other of George II. or George III.'s time - comes the type depicted by Addison with such loving and such astonishing fidelity in his portrait of Sir Roger de Coverley. It cannot be doubted that Sir Roger was drawn from the life, his original some country gentleman of Queen Anne's reign. Addison so admirably describes the hare -hunting of that period that I am tempted to reproduce some part of his letters on the worthy knight: [3] "Sir Roger, being at present too old for Foxhunting, to keep himself in action has disposed of his Beagles [4] and got a Pack of *Stop-Hounds.* What these want in speed, he endeavours to make amends for by the deepness of their Mouths and the Variety of their Notes, which are suited in such manner to each other, that the whole Cry makes up a compleat Consort. He is so nice in this particular, that a Gentleman having made him a present of a very fine Hound the other day, the Knight returned it by the servant with a great many expressions of civility; but desired him to tell his master, that the Dog he had sent was indeed a most excellent *Base,* but that at present he only wanted a *Counter Tenor.*....Sir Roger is so keen at this Sport that he has been out almost every day since I came down, and upon the Chaplain's offering to lend me his easie pad, I was prevail'd on Yesterday Morning to make one of the Company. I was extremely pleased, as we rid along, to observe the general Benevolence of all the Neighbourhood towards my friend. The Farmers' sons thought themselves happy if they could open a gate for the good old Knight as he passed by;

Which he generally requited with a Nod or a Smile, and a kind inquiry after their Fathers or Uncles.

"After we had rid about a mile from home, we came upon a large heath and the sportsmen began to beat. They had done so for some time, when, as I was at a little Distance from the rest of the Company, I saw a Hare pop out from a small Furze-brake, almost under my Horse's feet. I marked the way she took, which I endeavoured to make the Company sensible of by extending my arm; but to no purpose, till Sir Roger, who knows that none of my extraordinary motions are insignificant, rode up to me and asked *if Puss was gone that way?* Upon my answering Yes he immediately called in the Dogs, and put them upon the scent. As they were going off, I heard one of the Country Fellows muttering to his Companion, *That 'twas a wonder they had not lost all their Sport, for want of the silent Gentleman's crying* STOLE AWAY.

"This, with my Aversion to leaping Hedges, made me withdraw to a rising ground, from whence I could have the pleasure of the whole Chase, without the fatigue of keeping in with the Hounds. The Hare immediately threw them above a Mile behind her; but I was pleased to find that instead of running strait forward, or in Hunter's language, *Flying the Country,* as I was afraid she might have done, she wheel'd about, and described a sort of Circle round the Hill whereon I had taken my Station, in such manner as gave me a very distinct View of the Sport. I could see her first pass by, and the Dogs sometime afterwards unravelling the whole Track she had made, and following her through all her Doubles. I was at the same time delighted in observing that Deference which the rest of the Pack paid to each particular Hound, according to the Character he had acquired amongst them: If they were at a Fault, and an old Hound of good reputation opened but once, he was immediately followed by the whole Cry; while a raw Dog, or one who was a noted *Liar,* might have yelped his heart out without being taken notice of. [5]

"The Hare now, after having squatted two or three times, and been put up again as often, came still nearer to the Place, where she was at first started. The Dogs pursued her and these were followed by the jolly Knight, who rode upon a white Gelding, encompassed by his Tenants and Servants, and chearing his Hounds with all the Gaiety of Five and Twenty. One of the Sportsmen rode up and told me that he was sure the Chace was almost at an end, because the old Dogs, which had hitherto lain behind, now headed the Pack. The Fellow was in the right. Our Hare took a large Field just under us, followed by the full Cry *in View.* I must confess the brightness of the weather, the Chearfulness of everything around me, the *Chiding* of the Hounds, which was returned upon us in a double echo from the neighbouring Hills, with the Hallowing of the Sportsmen, and the Sounding of the Horn, lifted my spirits into a most lively Pleasure, which I freely indulged because I was sure it was *innocent.* If I was under any Concern, it was on the account of the poor Hare, that was now quite spent and almost within the Reach of her Enemies; when the Huntsman, getting forward, threw down his Pole before the Dogs. They were now within eight yards of that Game which they had been pursuing for almost as many Hours; yet on the Signal before mentioned they all made a sudden stand, and tho' they continued opening as much as before, durst not once attempt to pass beyond the Pole. At the same Time Sir Roger rode forward, and alighting took up the Hare in his Arms; which he soon after delivered to one of his Servants with an Order, if she could be kept alive to let her go in his great Orchard, where, it seems, he had several of these Prisoners of War, who live together in a very comfortable captivity....For my own part," concludes the *Spectator,* in this admirable account, "I intend to hunt twice a week during my stay with Sir Roger; and shall prescribe the moderate use of this Exercise to all my Country Friends, as the best kind of physick for mending a bad Constitution and preserving a good one."

It is extremely unlikely that many Queen Anne Squires, save the renowned Sir Roger de Coverley, preserved their hares at the finish of a long chase in the manner described by Addison. For years, I am bound to confess, I took the description of the jolly Knight's *Stop-Hounds* as a pleasing fiction, invented for the amusement of the readers of the *Spectator.* But research has convinced me long since that *Stop-Hounds* were really and truly employed by our ancestors. "The Southern Hounds," says Daniel, "were recommended for woodland and hilly countries, and used by those hunters who went on foot and hunted, as it was termed, *under the Pole,* by which is meant, that so exact was the discipline by which these Hounds were regulated, that in the hottest scent, if the hunting Pole were thrown before them, they stopped in an instant, and followed the Huntsman's heels in full cry, till he again permitted their going forward; this much lengthened the Chase, which sometimes lasted five or six hours." A strange method, truly!

Having presented portraits of hare -hunters from the reign of Charles I. to the middle of the eighteenth century, let me complete my gallery of old-time sportsmen by depicting an Essex squire named Saich, who flourished about the year 1800. "He was," says a writer in the *Sporting Magazine* for July 1827, "an old gentleman residing at Layer, in the country between Colchester and the Sea, on the Maldon side, who possessed and cultivated a considerable quantity of land and was much respected. He kept a pack of hounds, was a Nimrod by nature, and had a jovial soul, indulging in the spontaneous impulses of each without niggardly restraint. It was not the fashion in those days to organise your establishment in much refinement...My friend's harriers, as they were called, because they used to hunt the hares, were of a grotesque character, not definable as a whole by any rules of Beckford or Somervile. The deep-toned, blue-mottled, the dwarf foxhound, the true bred harrier, the diminutive beagle, all joined in the cry and helped to supply the pot. Being somewhat strangers to one another, discord prevailed having a butcher for one master, a baker for another, a farmer for a third, [6] spreading pretty well through the village. With such heterogeneous qualities, and not in *social* intercourse, with an impenetrable country to hunt over, whippers-in were indispensable, of which there was a plentiful supply, personated, I may say, by all the attendants, with immense long whips, and deep-sounding lungs not sparingly used.

"The huntsman was the owner, riding an old grizzled horse, rather lengthy both above and below the saddle, in a green coat, with flaps covering the boot-tops, and large yellow buttons, a scarlet waistcoat high in the throat and long in the waist, with a pair of pockets deep enough for a large tobacco box, or even for a leveret in a strait his breeches ribbed corduroys, short at the knee, and secured from rubbing over by a large pair of silver knee-buckles; boots allied to the *Jack* order, with tops somewhat short, and certainly *not white,* leaving a respectable space to shew the blue woollen stocking, and kept just over the calf by a pair of broad tanned straps across the knee. The spurs I forget, so they must be left. A bushy black wig, covered by a low crowned castor, with brims *a la Joliffe,* serving by their turn-up as *gutters for rain,* embraced a face oval and long, rouged in the nasal, and wide in the mouth, various in colour, having shades of red, blue and yellow; hands of Cyclops breed, too large for any Woodstock manufacturer, and never in genial warmth from the cuff of the coat; the whip long and heavy, always dangling by the side of the leg ready for action. The finishing embellishment must not be omitted, though not in place the whole person being kept in due order by a belt round the body, rather protuberant.

"He was a capital sportsman, and could almost hunt a hare himself; though old, his quick eye could discern the sitting victim through 'matted blade'; and though his helpmates were anything but as they should be, yet *who-hoop* generally closed the scene. He was early and late in the field, facing all weathers but frost, and with inexhaustible patience kept worrying on till dark. It was little matter where he left off, for the first signpost generally brought him and his friends to a stand, and the poor hounds, with a boy, got home as they could. He was always famous for especial care of the interior, and it was generally so contrived as to have a good repast prepared, particularly on the Saturday, the next day not calling for business. ... As he was late to begin, he was loth to leave off, and but few of his compeers could either go the pace or stay as long. The night worn away in smoke, mirth, and punch, he used to be left asleep, which no one dared disturb. The morn awoke and so did my friend, but yet no home for him; a good breakfast of beef steaks and malt wine composed any restlessness in his spirits, and kept him quiet till the dinner time came round. Boiled beef or roast, it was no matter which, with plum pudding for either, was too tempting to leave - and *aloo sus again!* Then a pipe to digest, and a bottle to wash down, brought on Hesper once more, and then it was either too dark, or too wet, or too cold, to move; so another night passed, and, strange to relate! such was the enchanting spell, that I have known this joyous buck, in his green costume, and all over mud, repeat this over and over again till the next hunting morning, the following Wednesday, with only a mop for the boots and a pump for the face not even a pillow for his head. A visit on the Monday of some of his companions excited fresh vigour, and gave a helping hand, with, occasionally, a choice brother spirit, to run the same gauntlet. This was called a *holiday.*

"His avocations at home were industrious and governed by intelligence he was an excellent farmer and worked hard, but always bearing in mind pipes, punch, and jollity for the evening."

A curious type this, one surely that might well figure in Mr. Cecil Aldin's gallery of ancient Georgian sportsmen! One night this curio and his old servant, Will, were shot out of a buggy on Tip-tree Heath. It was after a twelve hours' "dinner visit." So soon as they had recovered their senses and found no bones were broken, the old sportsman discovered that he had lost his wig. "'Will, where's my wig?' 'I does not know, but I'll see, sir.' Will made many a cast round the furze and at last struck the scent. '*Tantaro*, Master, here it is!' 'You lie, you rascal! it is not mine, by God! I won't take it: throw it away.' Will knew well his master's foible - whether from punch or by nature I cannot say (adds the narrator) - dead restiveness; therefore, with wits sharpened by good cheer, was not at a loss, and replied, 'I knew it, sir - it is not yours; and it is a d--d old thing; but you had better take it, for really, sir, wigs are very *scarce here,* and perhaps you *mant* get a better.' Temper soothed and head covered, chaise and daylight landed them safe."

There were certainly curious hunting folk in those days; they had wild spirits and could stand libations and feeding that would speedily destroy the sportsman of the present day. How they ate, for example! At a yeoman's dinner-table in 1825 - it was in Dorsetshire - there were served the following joints: 52 lb. of beef, 30 lb. of veal, a 27-lb. ham, six large plum puddings, and other etceteras. Truly a repast for giants!

Free living and too much conviviality told, however, in the end, even upon these hardened veterans. Somervile himself is a melancholy example in point. During the latter years of his life he became harassed by pecuniary troubles, "which in great part," says his biographer, "resulted from his love of dispensing hospitality on a scale entirely incommensurate with his means." Drink eventually got the better of him and brought him to his end. His favourite tipple was a kind of punch composed of rum, black currant jelly, and a little hot water, a mixture "excellent and healing," says his friend and neighbour, the poet Shenstone, "after a hard day's exercise, when taken moderately, but in Somervile's case an insinuating poison."

"Nimrod," in his second tour, tells some amusing anecdotes of one of these convivial souls of the eighteenth and early nineteenth centuries, a Cheshire squire, named Leech. "One of his bottle companions of the sacerdotal order asked him to go to church and hear him preach. He afterwards wished to know what he thought of his sermon. 'Why,' replied Mr. Leech, '*I like you better in bottle than in wood.*'" A smart repartee, truly!

It is clear that many of these squires of the eighteenth century drifted almost insensibly from hare-hunting to the pursuit of the fox. In the seventeenth century, as I have shown, the hare was regularly hunted with a pack of hounds, the fox not nearly so often, being more usually driven to earth by beagles and terriers, dug out and slain. In time the fox was promoted to a higher position in the scale of hunting, and the same hounds often pursued both hare and fox indifferently. In 1826 it is stated in the *Sporting Magazine* that Sir Watkin Wynn's harriers were then more like foxhounds, and drew for wild foxes as well as hunted bagmen. Bagmen, by the way, seem to have been much more common in those days than they are now. Like Sir Watkin Wynn's hounds now and for many years past one of the most noted packs of foxhounds in the kingdom - many other harrier packs, owned by hard-riding squires of the eighteenth century, were the forerunners, and often the nucleus, of the present well-ordered and well-managed foxhound establishments.

The present Monmouthshire Hounds are a case in point. Old Squire Lewis, of Llantillo, like many of his contemporaries, hunted, with the same pack of hounds, hare, fox, and otter. He did this down to the year 1835, in the country now demarcated as the Monmouthshire. In that year he relinquished hunting and presented his pack to Captain Stretton, who began thenceforth to hunt fox. Soon after this date the present Monmouthshire Hunt was formed. This, briefly, is the history of a great many packs of modern foxhounds, some of them provincial and comparatively unknown, some of them great and famous.

Many of the old school, however, held out decidedly against going after strange quarry, and stuck to the chase of the hare, which had given them and their forbears so many and such excellent hunts during long generations. Among these may be cited the amusing instance of an old Northumbrian master of harriers, who believed in hare and hare only, and loathed the sight of a fox. One day his hounds found and went away after one of these hated animals. The old gentleman was nearly frantic, his language most unparliamentary. "Stop 'em, you born idiot!" he yelled out to his whip, so soon as he could recover sufficient breath. "Stop 'em, you fule creature - *he's no fit to eat,* I tell you, stop 'em!"

From the beginning of the nineteenth century foxhunting began decidedly to assert its popularity. It was faster, it offered fiercer delights, straighter runs, more excitement. The rising school of fox-hunters, the men of the Regency, the bloods, the Toms and Jerries of that day, speedily began to assume an air of contempt and superiority towards harriers and the harrier-man, which for many years was maintained. The sport which had sufficed their fathers and grandfathers, and yet remoter ancestors, became unfashionable. "Currant Jelly" was invented as a term of reproach. And harriers and harehunting may be said to have remained unfashionable until a dozen or fifteen years since, when some decline in the extraordinary popularity of foxhunting, and other causes, of which I shall speak hereafter, led to that distinct revival of interest in a somewhat neglected sport, which now shows, year by year, signs of a vigour and vitality that would have been thought impossible during the heyday of fox-hunting fifty or sixty years ago.

[1] It is curious to remember how devoted to hunting are members of the Huntingdon family the present Earl and Lady Ileene Hastings to wit - in our own time.

[2] As a pendant to this picture of a sportsman of this period I give, in Appendix A, a curious poem on Hare-hunting, dated May 1660. It has some quaint political allusions, but was evidently written by a man who understood the chase of the hare.

[3] Spectator, No. 116, July 13, 1711.

[4] Here is a reference to fox-beagles, indicating, as I have said, that these little hounds were then still used for running foxes to earth, and thereafter killing them as vermin.

[5] This is excellent! Addison evidently knew much more about hounds and hunting than he would have his readers believe.

[6] Manifestly a trencher-fed pack, then common in rural England.

Chapter Three - The Hare and Its Ways

THE common brown English hare (*Lepus timidus*), which alone is hunted by harriers in this country, has a wide distribution, and was always found throughout the whole of Europe, except Northern Russia, Scandinavia, and Ireland. It was, however, to be met with in Denmark and East Finland. In Ireland the indigenous hare is the blue or mountain hare, sometimes called the varying hare (*Lepus variabilis*), similar to that found in the Highlands of Scotland, in Norway, Sweden, North Russia, and as far eastward as Japan. The English hare has, however, been long since introduced into Ireland, and is now common there. This hare is distinguished from others by its long ears and hind legs. A good average brown hare will weigh about 8lb., but examples are often shot scaling considerably more. The heaviest hare of which the writer has a note weighed 13lb., and another, shot on the Longwitten estate, near Morpeth, by Mr. R. Henderson in 1876, was stated in the *Field* of October 28 of that year to have weighed 13¼lb. The blue or mountain hare is a considerably smaller animal, and averages about 5½lb.; a heavy Scotch blue hare will, however, scale as much as 8¼lb., which weight has been several times recorded.

The outward form and appearance of our common brown hare are well known, but perhaps all readers may not be aware that the animal has imperfect collarbones, three pairs of premolar teeth in the upper jaw and two in the lower, five toes to the fore-limbs and four to the hinder pair. The thickly-brushed, hairy soles to the feet are well-known characteristics. These brushes serve two purposes: they protect the foot in those long chases during which the feet of a dog or hound are often badly cut and bruised; and they are used indefatigably for cleansing purposes. The hare is a beast scrupulously nice as to its person; it has no unpleasant scent; and it cleans itself with great perseverance. The hare's foot is not only, with the scut, a welcome trophy to the merry beagler after an exceptionally hard run, but has been used for many centuries by the fair sex, and especially by actresses and actors, for rouging the face. It is probably not known to every sportsman that in both hares and rabbits the insides of the cheeks, as well as the outer parts, are hairy. There are many instances of variation in colour in this animal. White examples are occasionally met with. In 1888 the Earl of Burford shot at Bestwood Park, Notts, a full-grown white hare with eyes of a pale blue. At Tilly four, Aberdeenshire, and in the Island of Mull, a large yellow variety, with hazel eyes, weighing about 10 lb., has been observed. A parti-coloured hare, says Mr. Harting, [1] was killed near Salisbury. "It was unusually white all over the face, and its hind-quarters were of a silvery-grey. Its pale colour could not be attributed to age, for it was a young animal, weighing about 5½ lbs." Mr. Holland Southerden, lately Master, and now Deputy Master, of the Hailsham Harriers, sends me a note of a curiously marked hare which, for a couple of seasons, was familiar with this pack. One side of her face was almost white, and she could be readily distinguished. She was, perhaps, the most clever, resourceful, and tricky animal ever hunted by these hounds, on several occasions getting the better of them in long runs. She usually bested them at a point where several roads cross, and where cottages and gardens exist. Her tactics were to double quietly about this locality, working about the gardens and roads, and she was repeatedly seen by the cottagers "creeping about in the cabbages and broccoli, and jumping about on the pavements, threading the boundary hedges, and then crossing over the roads very quickly." Her final exit was usually made in a certain wood, about a third of a mile away, abounding in rabbits. This clever hare came to an untimely end. She was shot by a farmer who was well acquainted with her history, but, meeting her with his gun one day, and seeing the wrong (*i.e.,* the brown) side of her face, he dropped her dead. On noticing her white cheek, he became aware of his misfortune he had on several occasions assisted in her pursuit with harriers and reported the sad occurrence to the master of the pack.

Albino hares are occasionally shot, and, more rarely, black hares have been met with. A black variety of the common English hare was killed in coursing at Enville, Lord Stamford's seat, in 1853, and other specimens have been met with here and there. Hares vary, of course, a good deal in colour, even in the same district. Only last winter, 1902-3, in drawing a small Sussex shaw with a pack of harriers, six hares were driven out by hounds. Of these three were peculiarly light-coloured, much more so than the generality of their kind in this district. These animals are very fecund, though not so much so as the extremely fertile rabbit. A male and female put together for a year, as an experiment, by a former Lord Ribblesdale, produced sixty-eight young ones. A pair of rabbits, enclosed under the same conditions, would have produced offspring to the number of three hundred. Still, the fecundity of the hare is so great that, given a reasonable amount of protection, especially in the breeding season, we should not have to lament their decline in so many districts. They couple at the age of twelve months, and, after a period of thirty days gestation, the mother produces usually from two to three, sometimes four, and even five, young ones. Under ordinary conditions the mother will produce two or three sets of young in the year usually between February and August, harvest time but Lord Ribblesdale's experiment indicates that, given absolute immunity from the many risks and cares of hare life, they can be much more fertile. The young are brought forth in the usual "form," or "seat," favoured by hares, and, unlike young rabbits, which, produced in burrows, are born naked and blind, are from parturition clothed with hair and have the eyes open. This, manifestly, is a development of nature suited to their more perilous position, exposed as they are to enemies in the open. The mother will occasionally treat them as a cat deals with her kittens, carrying them about in her mouth when danger threatens and she has to search for more secure quarters. It is usually stated, and with a certain amount of truth, that the brown hare, reared among hills and mountains, is stouter and gives better and longer runs than the lowland-bred hare. This is not an invariable rule. Hares bred on grass marsh, well dyked and drained, and not, therefore, too wet, are often extraordinarily stout. I have hunted for some seasons with the Hailsham Harriers, a foot pack, whose best hunting-grounds lie on Pevensey Marshes. The marsh hares of this district are extraordinarily stout and give wonderful runs, often exceeding an hour and not seldom two hours in duration. These are ig-inch harriers, and by no means to be accounted a slow pack; in fact, in addition to rare scenting powers, they have first-rate pace and fire. We occasionally hunt upland hares on the South Downs, hard by, with the same pack; and I am bound to say that, although they are good hares, we run into them at least as quickly as we do the hares of the neigh-bouring marshes.

The Ground Game Act has wrought in many districts infinite havoc among hares, and the stock of these animals is, as a whole, nothing like what it was before the introduction of that ill-judged and mischievous measure. The Hares Preservation Act of 1892 is, after all, of little protection. It enacts merely that hares shall not be sold or exposed for sale during March, April, May, June, and July. That does not provide against the killing of these unfor-tunates, and hares and leverets are slain in large numbers during these months. An Act ought to be passed giving absolute protection to hares be-tween the beginning of February and the end of July, and it ought to be the business of every follower of hare hunting, every courser, and every good sportsman, to see that such a Bill is without delay brought before the two Houses and made law. Combination only can ensure the proper protection of these unfortunate animals, which in many parts of the country are becoming almost unknown. I am bound to say that, in districts where they are decently protected, there is not the slightest difficulty in maintaining a good head of hares. In the Pevensey Marsh country, where farmers enjoy hare-hunting and coursing, we have too many of these animals, and I have seen no less than fourteen put up in the course of a single run.

Hares have many foes. In addition to coursers, hunters, shooting-men, poachers - and all poachers dearly love a hare - they have to run the gauntlet of foxes, weasels, and stoats. Weasels and stoats especially are deadly enemies, and young leverets, exposed in an open form, once they are discovered - and these bloodthirsty vermin are extraordinarily acute in hunting up their hiding-places - fall easy victims. The hare, however, manifestly from fear of these murderers, scarcely ever brings forth her young in a hedgerow, where stoats and weasels are so fond of hunting. The town poacher and his well-trained lurcher form an abiding danger to hares in localities where they are fairly plentiful, and many a good hare is destroyed by these vagrant and dangerous allies. Of late a new development in poaching has sprung up, and I know of an open district, where hares are plentiful, where poachers get at them in the following manner: These rascals cycle out with their dogs at night, make for certain places which they know are habitually favoured by hares, and, putting in their dogs, course and kill them. By this means they accomplish long distances, and can escape quickly with their plunder. However, even against these scoundrels, plans of protection can be devised, albeit with some trouble and difficulty.

Hares are excellent swimmers, and when pressed by hounds have no hesitation whatever in taking to water and crossing broad streams. They will swim long distances at times, and in the year 1898 an instance was recorded in the *Field* in which a hare had swum from the mainland to a small island in the lake at Waterville, County Kerry. This island is nearly three-quarters of a mile from shore. Personally, I am not surprised at this instance. I have watched hunted hares swimming rivers and streams many a time, and it is apparent that they progress with ease and fair rapidity. They are fine dyke jumpers, as from their conformation might be naturally supposed; they will either fly a ditch in their stride, or, if the banks are sloping, will run down to the margin, and leap over at a good bound. But they have no fear of water, and will plunge into a stream if hurried, or slip into it quietly if less hurried - preferably they do the latter - and make their way across. Only a few days before writing this chapter I saw a hare, hard pressed by the Bexhill Harriers, plunge souse into a marsh dyke, making as big a splash as a hound, and sending the water flying in all directions.

Scotch hares - the blue or mountain species - go to ground very frequently, but the brown hare seldom indeed resorts to this expedient, even when hunted. However, in dire straits she will do this, and I have on more than one occasion seen her hunted to ground in some earth at the root of an old tree, or other suitable place. Old sporting writers termed this "going to vault," an expression, I fancy, now never heard.

These animals are occasionally taken when young and kept in confinement. The three maintained by the poet Cowper, from about the year 1774, are well-known instances. "Puss, one of the trio," says Cowper, "grew presently familiar, would leap into my lap, raise himself upon his hinder feet, and bite the hair from my temples. He would suffer me to take him up and to carry him about in my arms, and has more than once fallen asleep upon my knee. He was ill three days, during which time I nursed him, kept him apart from his fellows (for, like many other wild animals, they persecute one of their own species that is sick), and by constant care, and trying him with a variety of herbs, restored him to perfect health. No creature could be more grateful than my patient after his recovery, a sentiment which he most significantly expressed by licking my hand, first the back of it, then the palm, then every finger separately, then between all the fingers, as if anxious to leave no part of it unsaluted; a ceremony which he never performed but once again on a similar occasion." By degrees Cowper habituated his pet to its liberty in the garden. "Puss" soon began to be impatient for the return of these excursions. "He would invite me to the garden by drumming upon my knee, and by a look of such expression as it was not possible to misinterpret. If this rhetoric did not immediately succeed, he would take the skirt of my coat between his teeth and pull it with all his force." This hare became, in fact, perfectly tamed, and was actually happier in human society than when shut up with his natural kinsfolk. "Tiney," another of Cowper's three pets, was of a totally different nature, and although, like his companion, nursed tenderly through an illness, was never anything but of a surly nature; if the poet took the liberty of stroking him, he would grunt, strike out with his fore feet, spring forward, and bite. "Bess," the third of this singular trio, was, says Cowper, "a hare of great humour and drollery; he had a courage and confidence that made him tame from the beginning." The poet always admitted the three hares into the parlour after supper, "when, the carpet affording their feet a firm hold, they would frisk and bound and play a thousand gambols, in which Bess, being remarkably strong and fearless, was always superior to the rest, and proved himself the Vestris of the party. One evening the cat, being in the room, had the hardihood to pat Bess upon the cheek, an indignity which he resented by drumming upon her back with such violence, that the cat was happy to escape from under his paws and hide herself."

Each of these hares had a distinct character of its own. "Their countenances," says Cowper, "were so expressive of that character that, when I looked only on the face of either, I immediately knew which it was. It is said that a shepherd, however numerous his flock, soon becomes so familiar with their features that he can, by that indication only, distinguish each from all the rest. ... I doubt not that the same discrimination in the cast of countenances would be discernible in hares, and am persuaded that, among a thousand of them, no two could be found exactly similar." These animals noted instantly the smallest alteration in their surroundings. "A small hole being burnt in the carpet, it was mended with a patch, and that patch in a moment underwent the strictest scrutiny." Any one with a knowledge of these animals is aware that their scenting powers are very highly developed. "They seem," adds the poet, "to be very much directed by the smell in the choice of their favourites; to some persons, though they saw them daily, they could never be reconciled, and would even scream when they attempted to touch them; but a miller coming in engaged their affections at once; his powdered coat had charms that were irresistible."

Hares, as Cowper intimates, have plenty of courage of their own. Of that I have no manner of doubt, although they are accounted by the vast majority of people among the most timid creatures in the world. They are also extremely pugnacious. A writer in the *Field* of February 8, 1902, signing his letter with the initials "V. T.," gives some very interesting details upon this subject:

"In August last a keeper brought me two leverets, only just able to feed themselves. They had been captured in a field of long clover, their mother being with them at the time. I put them into a low, wide tin bath, wired all round and over the top. They were at first terrified, and sat huddled together for the remainder of the day and night, refusing food of any sort. In the early hours of the morning I succeeded in feeding them with some warm milk and again later till, by degrees, they began to nibble clover. I tamed them by slow stages, till they would eat from my hand and let me nurse them. But as their fear of me gradually diminished, I was amazed to find how forcibly and persistently they were prepared to resent interference. They flew at me, bit and scratched me, making a most peculiar hissing sound, and so ferocious and hurtful were their attacks that I was forced to defend myself with a pair of thick gloves.

"Then followed a series of boxing matches, the assaults upon me frequently lasting several minutes, with periodical rests, when they would retreat to a corner, regain their wind, and attack me again more savagely than before. When completely beaten, they would let me stroke them and lick my hand as usual, and be friends again.

"One of these hares is now a most engaging animal, knows me perfectly, and will jump up on to my knee, climb up and kiss me when told, sit up and beg, jump through a hoop, and shake hands, always giving the right paw. It will also seek its food when I hide it, and does all in its power to show its affection for me. It lives in the house, is loose all day, and thoroughly enjoys a good roll on the rug, where it frequently lies stretched full length before the fire. It also plays with two retriever dogs, of whom it has no fear whatever, and often lies between them while asleep. I am sorry to say that the gardener let its companion escape one day during my absence.

"In the early part of last December I received two full-grown wild hares from Norfolk, and I was anxious to discover if it was possible to tame and train them. They sulked for a week, eating little, but I kept them near me, and by degrees tamed them, teaching them to feed from my hand, come to me when called, and sit quietly on my shoulder while I carried them about.

"Then, as with the others, when all fear of me had left them, the real trouble commenced; they flew at me, biting and scratching, and making that grunting and ' hissing ' sound already mentioned. Very slowly, almost despairingly so, we made friends; but, unfortunately, this friendship is not extended to others, who are treated with scant courtesy if they interfere with them. They know me very well, and will sniff my hand or my clothes most noticeably before allowing themselves to be touched. They possess keen intelligence and a dogged determination that I have not seen equalled in any other animal. They have a peculiar method of indicating irritation or fear; unlike rabbits, which stamp their hind feet in a similar predicament, they make a loud rasping or grating sound with their teeth, which is instantly received by the others as a signal of alarm."

As mad as a March hare has long since passed into a proverb. In reality, hares in March are no more mad than the rest of the world. They are merely engaged in a very serious and absorbing occupation, an occupation which renders them nervous and excitable and pugnacious beyond even their ordinary habits - to wit, the business of bringing up their families and defending their abiding-places against intruders. The courting season, also, naturally renders these curious animals fidgety, wild, pranksome, and quarrelsome. Their quarrels, which I have myself more than once witnessed, are most extraordinary affairs. Here is a description, given by a writer in *Country Life* of April 29, 1902, which affords a very singular insight into the habits of hares in springtime:

"From a cursory view of the fields at this season, one might imagine that hares migrate also, for now you scarcely see a couple where formerly they were dotted over the ground like mole-hills. The reason is, of course, that each pair of hares has withdrawn to the vicinity of some breeding cover, and the female are engaged in family cares. It is in defence of his hearth and home that the hare exhibits his most surprising ebullitions of ' March madness,' and the other day I witnessed a performance which would have brought down the house in a circus. We had put up one hare in a sloping meadow, and it went off up-hill like a steam-engine and skirted along the hedge at the top. Here, however, another hare, which had not seen us, and had reasons of his own for objecting to the stranger's presence, dashed out upon the fugitive and bowled him over. The latter quickly picked himself up and knocked over his assailant in turn, and then leisurely continued his flight. The other hare, however, was furious, and dashed after him, causing the fugitive to turn and await the onset.

"Several times they met with a bang, and at last grappled, each standing bolt upright on his hind toes and trying to pull the other down. They were so evenly matched, however, that they slowly revolved like a pair of old-fashioned waltzers, their long, thin hind legs giving them the quaintest human aspect. For fully three minutes they thus danced together on the green, but I shall never know which was really the better hare. I was accompanied by two human boys, who stood it as long as they could, cramming pocket-handkerchiefs into their mouths and writhing in agony of suppressed mirth. But the longer the combat lasted the funnier it seemed to grow, and at last, with a splurt, the boys broke into roars of laughter, and the hares bolted in panic and in opposite directions. It is not often that wild creatures thus fight in earnest, and when they do it is almost always, as in this case, under a mis-apprehension. The object of the assailant was to drive the intruder back, and he did not know that this was rendered impossible by our presence; so, where one had to go on, and the other was determined that he should not, a fight was inevitable."

The eyes of hares are large and prominent, and so placed that they can see well on either side and even behind them. When chased, their attentions are naturally directed chiefly towards their pursuers clamouring in the rear. A pack of foxhounds were, many years ago, hunting at Terling, in Essex, and some hares as well as foxes were disturbed in cover. Running headlong down one of the rides, a hare met a terrier which had joined in the pursuit, and was also going at great speed. The two animals met in mid career, and the shock was so great that both lay apparently dead. The dog eventually recovered, but not so the hare, whose skull was found to be completely shattered.

Cowper has some very interesting observations on the food of his tame hares, which seem to be well worth reproducing. He says:

"I take it to be a general opinion that they graze, but it is an erroneous one, at least grass is not their staple; they seem rather to use it medicinally, soon quitting it for leaves of almost any kind. Sowthistle, dandelion, and lettuce are their favourite vegetables, especially the last. I discovered by accident that fine white sand is in great estimation with them; I suppose as a digestive. It happened that I was cleaning a bird-cage when the hares were with me; I placed a pot filled with such sand upon the floor, which, being at once directed to by strong instinct, they devoured voraciously; since that time I have generally taken care to see them well supplied with it. They account green corn a delicacy, both blade and stalk, but the ear they seldom eat; straw of any kind, especially wheat-straw, is another of their dainties; they will feed greedily upon oats, but if furnished with clean straw never want them; it serves them also for a bed, and if shaken up daily will be kept sweet and dry for a considerable time. They do not, indeed, require aromatic herbs, but will eat a small quantity of them with relish, and are particularly fond of the plant called musk; they seem to resemble sheep in this that, if their pasture be too succulent, they are very subject to the rot; to prevent which, I always make bread their principal nourishment, and, filling a pan with it, cut in small squares, placed it every evening in their chambers, for they feed only at evening and in the night; during the winter, when vegetables were not to be got, I mingled this mess of bread with shreds of carrot, adding to it the rind of apples cut extremely thin; for, though they are fond of the paring, the apple itself disgusts them. These, however, not being a sufficient substitute for the juice of summer herbs, they must at this time be supplied with water, but so placed that they cannot overset it into their beds. I must not omit that occasionally they are much pleased with twigs of hawthorn, and of common briar, eating even the very wood when it is of considerable thickness."

In a state of nature hares are extremely fond, in addition to some of the foods described by Cowper, of pinks, parsley, and birch. They have a great weakness for clover, and will go far to feed upon it; they devour the bark and wood of many young trees, and are, therefore, by no means desirable neighbours of a rising plantation. They are said, however, to have an antipathy to

35

alder and lime.

In the daytime hares seldom leave their forms. Towards evening they begin to move, and at this time often frisk and play about in a most amusing manner. Evening, in fact, is as much the playtime of the hare as it is of the cat. They travel about and feed during night time, and at early morning return to their forms again. In doing this their instinct prompts them to take extraordinary precautions, weaving a maze of tracks, returning upon their foil, and often making a series of leaps, the final one landing the hare in her seat. A hare, presumably from fear of discovery, does not use the same form for long together. In the autumn these animals are often to be found in roots, especially turnips, stubble, and long grass, where they lie extraordinarily close. They will sit, too, in copses, woods, gorse, withy beds, and plantations. In marsh country, especially where the marshes are, as in the Pevensey district, not too wet, hares will be found lying out all winter. Towards November they quit the coverts and are found more frequently on ploughs and fallows. They are not fond of windy situations, and are said to be able to foretell changes of weather and to seat themselves accordingly. The hare must truly be a hardy beast to lie out as she does, exposed to the weather, in the depth of winter, sometimes amid heavy snow.

Hare-finding is an extraordinarily difficult business, and a man must be lynx-eyed indeed to be able to note a hare quickly in her form. Some men seem to possess this faculty by instinct, and are invaluable when hounds are drawing for their game. As a rule, there are but two or three men in each Hunt, sometimes fewer, who have the gift of hare-finding. Constant practice may help, of course; but the novice, unless he is naturally fond of the country and country pursuits, and has the faculty of observation, will find his education in this respect a difficult one. In looking over ploughs, he should walk slowly, keeping his eye constantly searching the soil, and not trying to cover too much ground at once. A dozen yards is quite enough for the eye to range over, and many a man overlooks and passes a hare lying within a few feet of him. As a friend once remarked to me, "walking a hare up is not finding her." The hare found in her form - and she will usually lie close, unless she catches the searcher's eye, in which case she will probably start off - the finder will cry out, "See ho!" or, better still, hold up his hat. The accomplished hare-finder never, if he can possibly help it, lets his eye meet the hare's. He just moves on quietly for a few paces, or stands looking the other way, and by holding up his hat, or by his voice, lets the huntsman know that he has found.

It has been said that hares seldom live much beyond seven years. This, I think, is not always the case. Hares, of course, run many risks, and their lives are not what insurance companies would call good ones. But that they are capable, in the ordinary course of nature, of living to as much as twelve or fourteen years is certain. Of Cowper's hares, which, although protected from the assaults of enemies, could hardly be said to lead natural lives, one died at maturity, from being placed in a damp box; another lived to the age of nine years; while the third, "Puss," survived to the respectable antiquity of twelve years all but one month.

The tricks and devices by which a hare attempts to throw off her pursuers are infinitely varied, and add an extraordinary zest and interest to the chase. In the case of one hare that a sportsman watched, "as soon as the hounds were heard," says an old writer, "though at the distance of nearly a mile, she rose from her form, swam across a rivulet, then lay down among the bushes on the other side, and by this means evaded the scent of the hounds. When a hare has been chased for a considerable length of time, she will sometimes push another from its seat and lie down there herself. When hard pressed, she will mingle with a flock of sheep, run up an old wall and conceal herself among the grass on the top of it, or cross a river several times at small distances." These are, with the exception of the wall-trick, of which I have never had ocular demonstration, familiar expedients in the pursuit of a hare. I believe that hares do, on occasion, run walls for the purpose of evading their pursuers; they will spring on to hedges and, it is said, even gorse, for the same purpose. In fact, they are so clever and so resourceful that they will do almost anything. The mazes they weave in foiling their own line are perfectly astounding. Jack hares, travelling after the turn of the year on errands of love-making, will sometimes give excellent and straightaway runs. Jacks are said to be stouter and better stayers than the does, and there is probably truth in this assertion. An old writer has remarked that the hare runs against the wind. The truth is that, unlike the fox, which almost always takes down wind as soon as he can manage it, the hare will run in any direction, and takes little or no account of the direction in which the wind is blowing. Hares nearly always return to the country in which their form lies, and, if they escape, may be found seated there the following day. How often has one seen, after a good hunt, the hare killed within a field or two, sometimes even in the very fallow or plough, or grass pasture, from which she was put up! The direction in which she first leans is most usually that which she will subsequently follow, and when a check happens the huntsman, if he understands his business, will usually cast that way. The ringing tactics of the hare are, of course, one chief reason why sport with harriers can be conveniently enjoyed on foot. A good runner need never be very far away from hounds, and even ladies and people of middle age, especially if the chase is in fairly open country, can see a good deal of the fun. "After a rainy night in a woody country," says Daniel, "neither buck nor doe will keep the cover, owing to the drops of wet hanging to the spray; they therefore run the highways, or stony lanes, for, as the scent naturally lies strong, they hold the roads which take the least, not that a hare judges upon *what soil* the scent lies weakest; [2] it is her ears that chiefly direct her, for, the hounds being oftener at fault on the hard paths than the turf, she finds herself not so closely pressed, and is not so much alarmed with the continual cry of the dogs at her heels. The louder the cry the more she is terrified, and flies the swifter, the certain effect of which is a heart broken sooner, than with a pack equal in number and goodness, but who spend their tongues less free." There is much sense in much of this, especially in the latter remark. I believe in plenty of hound music with harriers; not only are the deep voices of the old-fashioned harrier blood delightful to hear, but the hare is perpetually alarmed by them, and a good cry serves indubitably, as Daniel remarks, towards hastening that end and object of the chase, towards which huntsmen and hounds are striving so indefatigably.

Dry coverts, particularly those frequented by rabbits, are naturally sought by the hare upon every possible occasion, especially if she is hard pressed. Fallen leaves help very considerably to assist her flight and baffle the noses even of keen-scented hounds. Hares always run better and show more sport in open country than in a district much enclosed, where woods and coverts are abundant. Their rings are larger and bolder in the former, and hounds can there get at them more rapidly and push them with greater certainty. Beckford, who hunted hare before he kept foxhounds, notices this fact. "In enclosures," he says, "and when there is much cover, the circle is for the most part so small that it is a constant puzzle to the hounds. They have a Gordian knot in that case ever to unloose; and though it may afford matter of speculation to the philosopher, it is always contrary to the wishes of the sportsman: such was the country that I hunted for many years."

When a hare takes to the road, as she often does, there is no time at which hunting becomes more difficult. Very few hounds are good road-hunters, and even in these the trait is seldom developed until after some two or three seasons of hunting. A good road-hunter is a perfect treasure, and it is very interesting to note how the rest of the pack fly to the voice of such a one when he hits off the line. The best road-hunter I ever remember was "Captain," an old hound with a wonderful nose, belonging to the Hailsham pack. Hares will sometimes run road for an incredibly long distance, and I well remember this staunch old fellow leading the pack unerringly for a full mile or more. On quitting the road a hare will, as likely as not, make a huge bound, which often succeeds in putting the hounds at fault. This ought always to be remembered by the huntsman. When scent fails, as it often does upon a road or path which a hare has traversed, the science of "pricking" comes in. The men who can prick a hare by its "spoor," or footprints, are even greater rarities than good road-hounds. In Beckford's time this practice seems to have been regarded with disfavour, and one old-fashioned sporting author of the eighteenth century speaks of it with contempt. He calls it "foul sporting," and as unfair as "the vile practice of hallooing hounds off *a scent* to lay them on after *a view*." He adds, "equally unfair and to be condemned is the suffering the pricks of the hare's footing to be smoothed when she runs the foil: for altho' it is admitted that by such pricking and discovering her steps no Hare can escape, yet it is an unmanly mode of assisting Hounds, which no Huntsman, who is a *Sportsman,* will ever be guilty of himself, or condescend to make use of when done by others."

This hatred of pricking is quite unintelligible to the modern hare-hunter, and at the present day the practice is considered perfectly legitimate. Personally, I cannot see why it should ever have been thought otherwise. Many a hare that would otherwise have escaped the pack has been handled, thanks only to the skilful pricking of some expert in that nice and most difficult business. It is an invaluable gift, especially with foot harriers and beagles, and every huntsman and whip - one might almost say every good hare-hunter - ought to try and cultivate it.

I have said that hares will take readily to fresh water; instances where they will swim out to sea are of much rarer occurrence. In the season of 1900-1, however, in a run with the Hailsham Harriers, a foot pack which sees a good deal of its hunting in the vicinity of the English Channel, the hare, being hard pressed, took to the sea and was killed actually in salt water. I find such another instance in Daniel. "In October 1792 a hare, after a chase of sixteen miles by the Seaford Hounds, took to the sea near Cuckmere, in Sussex, and swam a quarter of a mile from shore before she was overtaken." The Bexhill Harriers have also in recent years killed hares which had taken to the sea. Mr. P. H. Trew, Master of this pack, tells me that it has happened several times since he has had these hounds. On one occasion they ran a hare into the sea at Galley Hill, near Bexhill, and a hound named Manager swam out some fifty or sixty yards and brought her back, laying her at the feet of the whip, who was the only one up at the moment. On another occasion a coastguard went out in his boat and brought the hunted hare in from the sea. These, and another case mentioned in the chapter on Basset hounds, are the only instances of the kind with which I am acquainted, and all, save one, curiously enough, happened on the coast of Sussex.

The good brown hare has always had a great attraction for the Briton, rich or poor, whether he pursues it with hound or shot-gun, or, if he be a poacher, with lurcher or the deadly wire. A curious instance of this attraction happened in one of the battles of the Peninsular War - Sabugal. A rifleman, named Flinn, took aim at a Frenchman and was in the very act of pulling trigger. At that moment a hare sprang from her form just in front of him. The shot was too tempting, and Flinn swung his aim from the French soldier and shot the hare. After the action, one of his officers reproached him for having thus wasted his cartridge. "Sure, your Honour," said the ready Irishman, "we can kill a Frenchman anny day, but it isn't always that I can bag a hare for your supper." During the Peninsular War Sir Harry Smith and other officers not only kept greyhounds and coursed hares, but even managed to get together some harriers, and hunted them when they had leisure and opportunity.

In concluding this chapter on hares, I do not think I can do better than quote some words of Beckford's on the pursuit of this animal - words which I think ought to be pondered by every harrier-man. "I hope you will agree with me, that it is a fault in a pack of harriers to go too fast; for a hare is a little timorous animal that we cannot help feeling some compassion for, at the very time when we are pursuing her destruction: we should give scope to all her little tricks, not kill her foully and over-matched. Instinct instructs her to make a good defence when not unfairly treated; and I will venture to say that, as far as her own safety is concerned, she has more cunning than the fox, and makes many shifts to save her life far beyond all his artifice."

[1] "The Encyclopedia of Sport."
[2] Here I join issue with this writer. I have no doubt whatever that the unerring instinct, or reasoning power, of the hare prompts her to choose cold ploughs and greasy fallows with never-failing resource, and with the sole object of baffling her foes.

From a photograph by Edwin Kelley, Newton Abbot
THE HALDON (MR. BARON D. WEBSTER'S)
OLD ENGLISH HARRIERS

Chapter Four - The Old-Time Harehound

I HAVE already shown that, in the very early days of the English Chase, fox-hunting and foxhounds, as we now recognise them, were unknown. Modern fox-hunting, in fact, only began to be evolved towards the middle of the eighteenth century. The harrier of the eighteenth century, the descendants of which are now known to us as "Pure Harriers," was in like manner not evolved much, if at all, before the reign of George I. or George II. Up to the end of the seventeenth century the hare was hunted by more or less slow, old-fashioned, deep-voiced hounds known as Southern or Northern hounds or by the Talbot, which latter, in the opinion of some authorities, was near akin to the bloodhound of the present day. The bloodhound is, in fact, the surviving representative of the massive hunting hounds with which our ancestors pursued stag and hare. The Talbot, Bloodhound, and Southern hound were, in point of fact, of much the same ancestry and possessed of the same characteristics. The Talbot is described by some as a pied hound, by others as white, while the bloodhound has, so long, at all events, as it has been known to modern folk, been invariably black and tan, the tan colouring being considerably in the ascendant. The colour of the Southern hound has been much debated, some asserting that it was originally black and tan, while others maintain that blue mottle was the true Southern hound colour. Personally, after a good deal of research, I am inclined to think that the old Southern hound ran in many colours, black and tan, red, the varied colouration which we now attribute to foxhounds, blue mottle, badger pie, hare pie, pure white, and even slate colour. In Devon and Sussex, which seem to have been always strongholds of the Southern hound blood, blue mottle is still a very noticeable colour in some of the best of the old harrier stock, which owe their ancestry largely to the Southern hound strain. Yet, even in far-away days, the fancies of different owners led them at times to cling to a particular colour and a particular strain. Mr. Baron Webster, Master of the Haldon Harriers, which hunt between Torquay, Paignton, and Exeter, tells me that Mr. Webber's harrier pack, the predecessors of the present Silverton Harriers, which for many years hunted in this country, consisted entirely of hounds of a slate-grey colour, or of the exact colour of a hare. They were a very beautiful pack, level, and of extremely ancient blood. Mr. Webster himself has two or three hounds of this breed, which are hare-pied or slate-grey, and he is endeavouring to re-establish the ancient strain.

These hounds, the Southern and the Talbot, whatever their colour, were big, well-boned hounds, with long falling ears, drooping eyes, deep, thick, hanging flews (lips), an absolute dewlap, and a most wonderful voice, deep, mellow, and, as some writer has said, possessing "the true cathedral note." They were the Southern hound especially heavy and slow, but with the most wonderful scenting powers; the chase they followed gave them such absolute enjoyment that they would, as I have already shown, actually stop upon the trail and, lifting up their big, heavy heads, give vent to their ecstasy in notes which could be heard for some miles over the countryside. This type of hound is almost perfectly illustrated by Shakespeare in "The Midsummer Night's Dream." He makes Theseus say:

"My hounds are bred out of the Spartan kind,
So flu'd, so sanded; and their Heads are hung
With Ears that sweep away the Morning Dew.
Crook-knee' d and dew-lap' d like Thessalian Bulls;
Slow in Pursuit, but matched in Mouths like Bells
Each under each; a Cry more tunable
Was never hallow' d to, nor chear'd with Horn."

The Southern hound stood probably about 26 in. in height, and it is a fact that, until a hundred and fifty years ago, or even less, there were still country squires hunting hare with hounds of this size. These big, lumbering, low-scented hounds had various defects, which may still be traced in old-fashioned harrier-blood, and to which fox-hunters, with some reason, have always testified strong dislike. They were throaty, sometimes bowed in the fore-legs, slack-loined, occasionally splay-footed, and with poor thighs, lacking in muscle. Against these their wonderful patience and scenting powers have to be set off, as well as that grand music which still renders a good pack of Old English Harriers - descendants of the Southern hound - a real delight to listen to on a winter's day. Nimrod, who was one of the rapid sportsmen of the first quarter of the nineteenth century, when everything had to be fast and "slap-up," led the fashion in that contempt for hare-hunting which so long flourished among these gentry. He refers to the "old psalm-singing harrier," and manifestly inculcated, whenever and wherever possible, the doctrine that the modern harrier ought to be of pure foxhound blood. Even at the present time the mischief done by Nimrod and men of his school has not by any means entirely vanished. The late Earl of Suffolk and Berkshire, who speaks up warmly for the harrier in the Badminton Library volume on Hunting, tells an amusing story of the courtly sneer of the late Mr. George Lane Fox, the famous Master of the Bramham Moor Foxhounds, when asked his opinion on hare-hunting. The Squire of Bramham was one of the old school - Nimrod's school - and his reply was: "I have always understood it to be a most scientific amusement." As Lord Suffolk well says: "There is many a true word *spoke sarcastic.*"

The Northern hound, whose ancestral headquarters seem to have been chiefly in that sporting county, Yorkshire, differed widely from his Southern cousin. He is described by Markham, who flourished in the time of Elizabeth and even earlier, as having "a head more slender, with a longer nose, ears and flews more shallow, back broad, belly gaunt, joints long, tail small, and his general form more slender and greyhound like. But the virtues of these Yorkshire hounds," continues Markham, "I can praise no further than for scent and swiftness, for with respect to mouth, they have only a little shrill sweetness but no depth of tone or music." It is from the Northern hound, beyond doubt, I think, that the modern foxhound has been largely evolved.

Upon this subject of hound voice Sir John Heathcoat Amory sends me an interesting note. Sir John, in addition to maintaining a pack of staghounds for hunting the now superabundant wild red deer of Exmoor, has had for many years (since 1859) a pack of old English harriers. These are very light-coloured hounds, the original stock of which came from a pack maintained by Mr. Froude, a North Devon hunting parson, who flourished in the early part of the last century. "Parson Froude's hounds were bred," says Sir John Amory, "from the same Southern hounds that formerly were used for stag-hunting, and report says that Froude crossed them with a celebrated pointer, and in this way reduced their size. I have always endeavoured," continues Sir

John, "to keep to the original breed, and above all never to allow foxhound blood to creep in. I find two faults with foxhounds, when used for hare-hunting; one is that they are not sufficiently patient to hunt a cold scent and puzzle out the foil, and the other is that the sharp voice of the foxhound does not suit the soft, mellow tone inherited from the Southern hound."

The North-country fox-beagle, referred to by Beckford as suitable for crossing with the Southern hound to produce good harriers, must evidently have been in existence long before modern harriers were dreamed of, and when I say modern harriers, I mean the hare hounds used by Beckford and the more advanced squires of the eighteenth century, who preferred a somewhat quicker, livelier hunt to the long, dragging, six hours' chase of the Southern hound.

Daniel, quoting from an earlier author, mentions that "the Hounds used for hare-hunting are the deep-tongued, thick-lipped, broad and long-hung Southern Hounds. The fleet, sharp nosed Dog, ears narrow, deep-chested, with thin shoulders, shewing a quarter cross of the foxhound. The rough, wirehaired Hound, thick quartered, well hung, and not too much flesh on his shoulders. The rough and smooth Beagle. Each of these sorts have their excellencies, nor can one be with justice commended as superior to the other: it is according to the varying inclination of Sportsmen that a preference is to be established. He that delights in a six hours' chase, and to be up with the Dogs all the time, should breed from the Southern Hound first mentioned, or from that heavy sort which Gentlemen use in the Weald of Sussex; their cry is a good and deep base music, and considering how dirty the country is, the diversion they afford for those who are on foot for a day together, renders them in high estimation; they generally pack well from their quality of speed, and at the least Default, every nose is upon the ground in an instant to recover the scent. In an open country, where there is good riding, the second sort is to be preferred; their tongues are harmonious, and at the same time they go so fast as to prevent the Hare from playing many tricks before them; they seldom allow her time to loiter and make much work; she must run and continue her foiling or change her ground; if the latter, she is soon killed, for fresh ground, especially on Turf, is, in some degree, one continued view. It is difficult, however, to procure a pack of fast Hounds that run evenly together; some are usually found to tail, and their exertions to keep up to the leading Hounds make them of little use, farther than enlarging the cry, unless when the scent is over-ran, then Hounds thrown out or tailed often come up and hit off the fault.

"It is very common for the fleetest Hound to be the greatest favourite, but let a Hound be ever so good in his own nature, his excellence is obscured in that pack which is too slow for him. At most times there is work enough for every Hound in the field, and each ought to bear a part; but this it is impossible for the heavy Hounds to do, if run out of wind by the disproportionate speed of a leading Hound; for it is not sufficient for Hounds to run up, which a good Hound will labour hard for, but they should be able to do so with ease,

43

with retention of breath and spirits, and with their tongues at command; it can never be expected that any scent can be well followed by Hounds that do not carry *a good head.* It is too frequent a practice in numerous kennels to keep some for their music, others for their Beauty, who at best are silly and trifling, without nose or sagacity: this is wrong, for it is a certain maxim that every dog which does no good, serves only to foil the ground and confound the scent, by scampering before or interrupting their betters in the most difficult points. *Five* couple of trusty Hounds will do more execution than *thirty* where half of them are eager and head-strong."

These observations seem to me so just, and so much informed with the modern spirit of hunting, that I have thought them worth reproducing. Their author is far less well known than Beckford, who followed him, but he is, as regards hare-hunting, with which only he deals, at least as well worth reading.

"The third sort" - (the "rough, wire-haired Hound") he continues, "are scarce, and an entire kennel of them seldom seen; they are of the Northern breed, and by many esteemed for the chase of the Otter and Marten, and in some places are encouraged for that of the Fox; but they are bad to breed from, being subject to produce thick, heavy shouldered dogs, unfit for the chase. [1] Beagles, rough or smooth, have their admirers; their tongues are musical, and they go faster than the Southern Hounds, but toil much. They run so close to the ground, as to enjoy the scent better than taller dogs, especially when the atmosphere lies low. In an enclosed country they do best, as they are good at trailing or default, and for hedgerows; but they require a clever Huntsman, for out of eighty couple in the field during a winter's Sport the author observed not four couple that could be depended on.

"Smooth-haired Beagles," he adds, "are commonly deep hung, thick lipped, with large nostrils, but often so soft and bad quartered as to be shoulder-shook and crippled the first season they hunt; crooked legs, like the Bath turn-spit, are frequently seen among them; after two hours running many of them are disabled, and the Huntsman may proceed to hunt the Hare himself, for he will never receive any assistance from the greater part of them, their form and shape sufficiently denote them not designed for hard exercise."

This author, who wrote in 1750, must surely have come across some infamously bad beagles. At the present day, if he could return to those hunting-grounds in which he enjoyed his sport, he would find, among the fifty packs of foot-beagles now hunting in the United Kingdom - chiefly in England - a very different sort of animal from that which he describes. Much more attention is, however, now paid to the breeding and hunting of these little hounds than was the case a hundred and sixty years ago. And yet even the eighteenth-century beagle could kill a fox very handsomely. In 1822, at the sale of the furniture and effects of the Earl of Aboyne, at Orton Hall, near Peterborough, there was to be seen a large painted board, which had once been decorated with a stuffed fox's head. On this board was the following quaint inscription: "February 16th, 1756. This fox was hunted by twenty-three cou-

44

ples and a half of beagles, the highest measured no more than sixteen inches, and, after a sharp run of three hours and upwards, killed him. After this chase Mr. John Bevis' horse was obliged to be blooded in the field, and with much difficulty supported to Peterboro' by two men.

'Oft have I run before the swiftest hound,
But this small cry gave me the mortal wound.'"

This must have been a gallant little pack of beagles, truly enough; even the best of those of the present day could show no finer a performance.

Notwithstanding the fact that in many parts of England, at least as late as, probably later than, the middle of the eighteenth century, country gentlemen still kept for hare-hunting the old cumbrous Southern hound but too often out at elbows, crooked-legged, slack-loined, badly coupled, and splay-footed, yet possessing always that wonderful nose of his and that grand voice other and more progressive sportsmen were continually striving for a smarter, quicker, and more up-to-date hound. Somervile's picture of a good hound is worth recalling. The points are all excellent, even at the present day:

"See there with count' nance blithe,
And with a courtly grin, the fawning hound
Salutes thee cow' ring, his wide op'ning nose
Upward he curls, and his large sloe-black eyes
Melt in soft blandishments and humble joy;
His glossy skin, or yellow-pied, or blue,
In lights or shades by Nature's pencil drawn,
Reflects the various tints; his ears and legs,
Fleckt here and there, in gay enamel' d pride,
Rival the speckled pard; his rush-grown tail
O'er his broad back bends in an ample arch;
On shoulders clean, upright and firm he stands;
His round cat-foot, straight hams, and wide-spread thighs,
And his low-dropping chest, confess his speed,
His strength, his wind, or on the steepy hill,
Or far extended plain; in ev'ry part
So well proportion'd, that the nicer skill
Of Phidias himself can't blame thy choice."

A beautiful portrait indeed! The Warwickshire squire exhorts his reader not to prefer the large hound, which gets hung up and tugs painfully in every thorny brake; nor patronise pigmy hounds which swim in every furrow and are speedily moiled in the clogging clay, but to choose hounds of middle size, active and strong. For otter he preferred the old-fashioned, deep-voiced, deep-flewed hounds, with pendant ears, thick, round head, strong, heavy, and slow, but sure. Of these he seems to have preferred "the bold Talbot kind, as white as Alpine snows."

The eighteenth-century squires, then, who began to require a somewhat less tedious chase than that of the Southern hound, bethought themselves of crossing this hound with the sharp and active fox beagle, and from that blend undoubtedly sprang the old-fashioned English harrier of the last hundred and fifty years, the animal which we now call "pure harrier." All hounds known in Britain are more or less blended or manufactured varieties. This is, of course, perfectly natural, for the reason that during all ages mankind has been constantly aiming at altering and improving his stock, whether it be sheep, cattle, horses, or dogs. Of the races of hound left to us at the present day, probably the oldest and least changed is the rough-coated, noble-looking otter-hound. With this I should place the bloodhound. Next comes the beagle, which, although altered a good deal in many packs from the type of three or four hundred years ago, is nevertheless of very ancient ancestry. This is especially so in the West of England. The foxhound and harrier, as we now know them, are, as I have said, manufactured races; the foxhound especially, magnificent animal though it is, being a most skilful blend of various hunting hounds, selected with the greatest care during innumerable generations, and uniting in its frame qualities unsur-passed for the particular chase in which it is em-ployed.

HAILSHAM PACK

PEPPER, A SOUTHERN HARRIER

SCARTEEN BEAGLE, TIPPERARY

Some of our existing har-rier packs can boast a more than respectable antiquity. Sir John Heathcoat Amory's are, as I have said, descended from Parson Froude's pack, which were hunted by that sporting divine early in the last century, and were mainly of Southern hound blood. Sir John Heathcoat Amory's pack are now all white, or badger-pied, and are described by the owner as having no touch of foxhound blood. The Penistone, a Yorkshire pack, trace their descent so far back as 1260, when Sir Elias de Midhope was Master. The Wilsons of Bromhead Hall are stated to have mastered the pack during the fourteenth, seventeenth and eighteenth centuries. The Wortleys of Wortley Hall, the Riches of Bullhouse Hall, and the Fentons of Underbank Hall seem also to have been connected with these hounds during far-distant generations. The last Wortleys who have acted as Master were the Hon. Charles Stuart Wortley, from 1829 to 1843, and Mr. J. W. Taylor Wortley, from 1875 to 1876. There is a tradition that Robin Hood and his men hunted with this pack. That may be reasonably doubted. The bold Robin Hood had, I imagine, his own methods for killing a deer when he wanted one. The hounds are of old English breed. The Brookside were established in the eighteenth century, and were originally of Southern hound breed. The Cotley are another eighteenth-century pack, formed in 1793 by Mr. T. Deane, grandfather of the present Master. The Craven Harriers, hunting in North-west Yorkshire, trace their formation far back into the eighteenth century. The Holcombe, in Lancashire, are believed to have been kennelled for close on two hundred years, and the hounds are still described as "Old English Harriers." The Lyme Harriers, long maintained by the Legh family at Lyme Park, Cheshire, were believed to be one of the most ancient packs in the kingdom. Lord Newton, of Lyme Park, was the last Master; but the pack was, unfortunately, given up a season or two ago. The hounds were "Old Southern black and tan," twenty-three inches in height. Mr. Netherton's harriers, hunting near Dartmouth, are stated to have been established in the fifteenth century and have always been in the hands of this family. They are pure harriers of the old-fashioned type, and said not to have been crossed in any way. The Pendle Forest, Lancashire, is another old pack, dating from 1770 or earlier. They are cross-bred with foxhounds, but some of the old Lancashire hound blood is still in evidence. The Ross Harriers (Herefordshire) date from 1820, while the Rossendale, another Lancashire pack, boast a much longer pedigree, and have been in existence some centuries. Until about seventy years ago they were trencher-fed.

All those accustomed to hunting know what "trencher-fed" means. But there may be readers who do not. In the old days all packs of hounds were not confined in kennels, but were allowed to roam about the Master's premises, being fed with broken victuals, or picking up their food irregularly from trenchers, dishes and so forth. In many instances a number of people maintained hounds together, each keeping a hound, and appearing with it or sending it to the pack on hunting-days. These again were trencher-fed. Here and there in Ireland trencher-fed harriers still exist; these are the so-called "Kerry beagles," which are kept by village folk and come to the horn for Sunday hunts. In England, at least two packs of foxhounds, the Goathland and the Farndale, hunting in a wild moorland district of the North Riding of Yorkshire, are trencher-fed. And in England also the Holmfirth, Henley, and Meltham Harriers, which have hunted near Huddersfield since 1800, as well as the Glaisdale, another Yorkshire pack, hunting in the North Riding, are still trencher-fed. I fancy there are one or two other such packs still in existence.

Another pack with a long history is the Stannington, which hunts in Lord FitzWilliam's country, in the neighbourhood of Sheffield. The Tanat-Side, a Shropshire pack, have a quite respectable antiquity, their own records going back to 1828, and those of their predecessors dating beyond 1754.

It may be not inappropriate to wind up this chapter on harriers of the remote past with some ancient hound names. Here is a short "Catalogue of some general Names of Hounds and Beagles," dating back to the reign of Charles II. Some of these names may seem a little curious at the present time:

Beauty	Jewel	Royal
Blueman	Jocky	Rapper
Bowman	Joler (Jowler)	Russler (Rustler)
Bouncer	Jolly boy	Spanker
Captain	Jupiter	Soundwell
Countess	Juno	Stately
Caesar	Keeper	Troler
Dido	Lively	Thunder
Driver	Lady	Thisbe
Drunkard	Lilly	Truman
Drummer	Lillups	Truelove
Damosel	Madam	Tickler
Darling	Merry-boy	Tattler
Duchess	Musick	Tulip
Dancer	Nancy	Venus
Daphne	Plunder	Wanton
Fuddle	Rockwood	Wonder
Gallant	Ringwood	Yonker
Hector	Rover	
Juggler	Ranter	

For other lists of hound names see also Appendix B.

[1] The otter-hound of the present day is supposed by some to be the truest modern representative of the Southern hound. It is clear that otter-hounds were also bred in the North, and some of that strain no doubt remains to us.

Chapter Five - Modern Harriers

THE revulsion of feeling against the old Southern hound and its methods which, as I have shown, had already taken place by the middle of the eighteenth century, rapidly gained strength, so much so that by the end of the first quarter of the nineteenth century not only were a large number of Masters using a strong cross of foxhound blood, but others were hunting the hare with pure foxhounds. From the sporting literature of that time and long after one might have gathered that there was scarcely any pure harrier blood left hunting in England at all. If "Nimrod" and his followers could have had their way, it is certainly pretty evident that by this time the dwarf foxhound, pure and simple, would have composed the harrier packs of England, to the exclusion of almost every other kind of hound. The "cathedral note and the table-cloth ear," typical of the Southern hound, were completely out of date, or said to be so, and sharp, quick scurries of twenty minutes and half an hour were being not only recommended but practised. A Sussex pack of that time killed six hares in a morning, and the huntsman is described by a rightly indignant onlooker as "trying to mob his seventh hare!" Mr. Yeatman, a gentleman hunting near Sherborne, was famous in those days for his harriers, and his pack consisted of eighteen or twenty couples of about three-parts-bred foxhounds, averaging nineteen inches. In 1832 these hounds killed one hundred and nine hares out of one hundred and sixteen hunted, which is undoubtedly an extraordinary feat in fact, much too extraordinary for fair harehunting. In 1826, "Nimrod," in one of his famous tours, printed in the *Sporting Magazine,* speaks of Sir William Wake's harriers, hunting near Northampton. These he describes as "hare-hunting foxhounds." Sir William Wake, it may be noted, had then been a Master of harriers nearly forty years. The foxhound-harrier evidently maintained its vogue pretty consistently among the most forward school of harrier-men for a long period. In 1855 appeared "Stonehenge's" excellent volume of "British Rural Sports." I quote what he says concerning the harrier of that time: "The harrier is now a crossed animal, bred in all sorts of ways, and varying from twenty-one inches down to fifteen or sixteen. In looks more like the foxhound than the beagle, he has some remnants of his old breed in the longer ears, wider head, and stouter body which he possesses. He should, however, have a most delicate nose, even more so than the beagle; for as his increased size carries him faster over the ground, so he is more likely to overrun the scent and foil it so that he cannot recover it. Some of these hounds, however, have a wonderful power of carrying a scent at full speed, and will race into a hare in such a time as to finish her up almost as soon as found; this, however, spoils sport in great measure, as, by their speed, they prevent all those artifices on the part of the hare which give zest to this otherwise slow amusement. For this reason it is that harriers appear to have as good noses as beagles, though they really have not; for by depriving the hare of scope to double back, by pressing so closely upon her scent, they give themselves so much less to do and have only to work out a forward scent. Many huntsmen of harriers now cast forward as if hunting a fox, and with reason too, for, as the hare *cannot* double back, she tries all her wiles in a forward or side direction - hence the alteration in the principles called for by the alteration in the speed of hounds. It is, however," adds "Stonehenge," "in my opinion, an alteration for the worse."

This description, by one of the foremost writers on sport of his generation, seems to me to sum up admirably some of the objections to the foxhound-harrier which were perceived fifty years ago by a fair-minded and far-seeing sportsman. Beckford, seventy years before "Stonehenge," thus wrote, had vigorously expressed his ideas on the same subject. "I have," he says, "also seen a hare hunted by high-bred fox hounds: yet I confess to you it gave me not the least idea of what hare-hunting ought to be."

Happily for hare-hunting, the men who thus set the fashion at the early part of last century and attempted to transform a pursuit differing in all its characteristics essentially from fox-hunting into the vain semblance of that sport, although they made much noise in the world, were not so successful in effecting their purpose as many people seem to have imagined. There remained in quiet country places, remote from railways, and therefore little heard of, a large number of sportsmen who preferred to stick to hare-hunting proper, and were not carried after strange gods. By this I do not mean to say that they preferred the obsolete chase of the old Southern hound. That had become a thing of the past, and the brisker style of hare-hunting, as advocated by Beckford, was recognised as the proper way to hunt hare, even by old-fashioned squires.

Devonshire, especially, remained the stronghold of good old English harrier blood - the fruit of the union of Southern hound and beagle, recommended by Beckford; and Devonshire is to this day the country in which, if you want to pick up old-fashioned harriers, little if at all crossed with the foxhound, you can still do so. Devonshire, eighty years ago, seems to have been regarded as rich in hare-hunting, but of no account for sport with the fox. In 1826 "Nimrod" says of it, "Devonshire has some things to recommend it - fish and venison for little or nothing, and leverets ten pence per head."

But, besides Devonshire, other parts of the country cherished also what may be called pure harrier blood. In Wales, parts of Yorkshire, Cumberland, Westmoreland, and Lancashire an old-fashioned breed of hound was kept on foot for hare-hunting, and to-day, in various packs in these localities, you may yet see strong traces of this blood, even now little contaminated by the foxhound infusion.

Within the last twenty years, and especially within the last dozen, there has been a remarkable revival of interest in the old harrier blood, and indeed in hare hunting generally; and there is now, I think, little fear that the old English harrier, with his wonderful scenting powers, his grand voice, his natural and inherited aptitude for hare-hunting, is ever likely to disappear or be driven out by the foxhound pure and simple. There are at the present time three schools of harrier-men in existence:

1. The admirers of the pure harrier, or what may be *called* the pure harrier.

2. The Kennel Stud-book harrier-men, by which may be understood the admirers of a harrier showing strong foxhound cross.

3. Those who prefer to hunt with the dwarf foxhound.

All three schools have, naturally, many things to urge in favour of their own views of hare-hunting and harehounds. With these matters I propose to deal a little later in this chapter. For the purpose of illustrating as far as possible the relative strength and numbers of these schools, I have made a rough summary from the list of packs of English and Welsh harriers, to be found in "Baily's Hunting Directory." It runs thus:

Stud-book Harriers	38 Packs.
"Pure" and "Old English" Harriers	35 "
Cross-bred Hounds	14 "
Dwarf Foxhounds	10 "
Mixed Harriers and Foxhounds	8 "

In addition to these I have a note of three packs which are simply described as "Harriers," and which I have, therefore, not allocated to any of the above.

From this it will be seen that, although "Stud-book Harriers" head the list, "Pure" and "Old English" harriers run them pretty close. Stud-book harriers consist, of course, largely of hounds which show strong traces of the foxhound; in many instances, in fact, the average stud-book harrier is almost overpoweringly foxhound in type. Still, he is not a pure foxhound, and the harrier leaven left within him gives him a better nose for his work than the foxhound, and steadies somewhat those instincts for driving and flashing over the line which characterise the pure foxhound when hunting hare. Again, stud-book harriers are not necessarily all of overpowering foxhound blood. The fact that Sir John Amory's pack, which are pure harriers, almost untainted, I believe, by any admixture of foxhound blood, were admitted into the Stud-book, is convincing proof that the foxhound strain alone is not a qualification for entry. So much the better for harriers and hare-hunting. On the other hand, it is not absolutely certain that packs entered as "Pure Harriers" or "Old English Harriers" are completely uncontaminated by foxhound strain. It is impossible to assert this with conviction, and the fact that during the progress of generations different hounds have been introduced for breeding purposes, even among old-established packs, renders it possible that a distant strain of the foxhound may have been unwittingly blended with the old harrier blood. Here and there, I grant, you may find packs so carefully guarded that they really do represent at the present day practically the blend first devised by our ancestors for providing a good harrier I mean the blend of Southern hound and beagle advocated by Peter Beckford himself. But among a good many of the "pure harrier" packs there is, I am convinced, a slight tinge of the foxhound. In such infinitesimal quantity this is productive of no harm but rather of good.

In some cases I believe that the incessant effort by admirers of the old stock to perpetuate their favourite strain must necessarily react with unfortunate results. In-and-in breeding is always to be discouraged, and the lack of fresh blood must tell. This, I believe, has a good deal to do with the bad points so often instanced as characteristics of old harrier blood I mean slack loins, bad feet, poor thighs, and so forth. I am told that the old Bexhill pack of harriers, maintained by the Brook family for the best part of a century, had become practically ruined by in-breeding. They were largely of Southern hound blood, black and tan, with a wonderful cry. On the death of Mr. A. J. Brook, it was apparent that fresh blood was needed, and Lord De La Warr introduced a bloodhound strain. There was a good deal of prejudice against this variation, but, after all, the bloodhound and Southern hound were much of the same type and ancestry, and some remedy had to be found. The present hounds are certainly a really good hare-hunting pack, and probably kill more hares and more speedily than did their predecessors.

"Cross-bred Harriers" number fourteen in my list. Nearly all harriers are now more or less cross-bred, but these would probably partake much more of the foxhound than of the old harrier. "Mixed packs," numbering eight, indicate, in the majority of cases, that the Master has been unable to get together the requisite number of harrier or of dwarf foxhound couples - whichever sort he has a preference for - and therefore runs a mixed pack, some harriers, some foxhounds, until he can suit himself. In starting a new pack of harriers there is always a good deal of difficulty in getting together what one wants. Sometimes a pack may be bought outright, in which case a good deal of trouble is saved. On the whole, it is no bad thing to begin with a scratch pack, got together, as one can best manage it, by drafts and purchases from different kennels. It is a good education, and the Master, who is probably his own huntsman, begins in time to breed a pack that meets his own fancy.

I have shown, then, by this list that the foxhound has by no means yet ousted the pure harrier from the scene of his triumphs. Nor, now that real harrier blood is again beginning to be appreciated at something like its real worth, is this ever likely to be the case. The fact is, there is in these islands plenty of room for the supporters of all three modes of hunting - i.e., with pure harrier, Stud-book harrier, and dwarf foxhound.

Personally, I do not believe in hunting hare with foxhound pure and simple, not even if the hound be reduced in size to twenty or twenty-one inches. The foxhound is, in my view, too fast for hare-hunting, and has too much fling and fire and too little patience for this form of chase. He has, too, been trained for generations to the pursuit of the fox, and there is a great deal to be said for long usage and hereditary instinct in hunting. A hare hunted with foxhounds has, in my humble opinion, not a fair chance for her life, as she has when hunted by harriers; she is overmatched, driven to trust to speed alone, too often outpaced altogether, and is run down usually in far less time than ought to be the case. She has no opportunity of displaying all those wonderful tricks and expedients which render a hare-hunt, to the man who really enjoys this form of sport, so interesting and delightful a pastime. After all, if a sharp gallop is the great desideratum sought for, the horseman can gain his ends in a drag or a fox-hunt, without wishing to burst up an unfortunate hare in a scamper of twenty minutes. Pace, pure and simple, is not the great desideratum in hare-hunting; nor do I think, as a matter of fact, that it is even in fox-hunting. I am one of those who believe that too much has been sacrificed to pace with fox-hunting packs, and that sport would be better, even with foxhounds, if there were displayed by its votaries a little less desire for galloping and a little more interest in the actual science of hunting the fox.

As between the pure harrier-man and the supporter of the cross-bred or Stud-book harrier there is no illimitable void of opinion or of practice. The Stud-book harrier is, of course, a faster animal than the old English harrier, and kills his hares with less deliberation. Here and there, no doubt, packs of Stud-book harriers are to be found which favour the foxhound strain unduly and are rather too much for their quarry. But in most packs of what are called harriers there still remains sufficient of the old Southern hound and beagle blood - far away though it may be - to ensure that the hare shall not be done to death without some reasonable chance for her life. In fact, in what is called the harrier, even if it be a Stud-book harrier, showing very strong indications of foxhound blood, there remains some faint trace of that low-scenting and deliberation which made the pursuit of the hare what it ought to be.

From a photograph by R. B. Lodge, Enfield

HAILSHAM HARRIERS

WATCHMAN AND FARMER

ROCHDALE HARRIERS

RATTLER

COL. ROBERTSON AIKMAN'S HARRIERS

RUTLAND

(*Winning Stallion Hound, Peterboro' 1899*)

As regards pure harriers, or old English harriers, or what are called Southern harriers, these packs have, within the last fifty or sixty years, been so much improved in pace that they are not, after all, so far behind the Stud-book harrier type as might be supposed. Imperceptibly, no doubt, even among these the foxhound blend has crept in and the pace thereby been improved. Runs with such packs are not, therefore, anything like the long and tedious business that hare-hunting used to be in the days of our great-great-grandfathers. A pure harrier pack of good stamp may at the present day be trusted to run into its hare in from forty minutes to an hour and a half, according to the stoutness of the hare itself and the state of the country. Personally, I think a *good* hare-hunt ought not to occupy much less than an hour. I have seen hares killed by a nearly pure-bred pack of nineteen inch harriers in five-and-twenty minutes, when scent has been extraordinarily good and the hare, perhaps, only an average one; and I have seen with the same pack magnificent runs lasting from two to three hours, in which hunting was most enjoyable from beginning to end.

The modern harrier, as even the unsophisticated reader may have already gathered, is an animal, then, running in various shapes and sizes. He runs also in a variety of colours. The majority of harrier packs are hunted on horseback, and average from eighteen to twenty-one inches. The Pendle Forest, a foxhound cross, reach as much as twenty-two and a half inches, while the Scarteen Beagles, a very old-fashioned Irish pack of black-and-tans (Kerry Beagles), are twenty-three-inch hounds. Among the harriers of least stature among English packs are Lady Gifford's, hunting near Chichester, which average seventeen inches; the Glanyrafon, an eighteen-inch Montgomeryshire pack; Mr. Lethbridge's Stud-book harriers of eighteen inches, hunting in Cornwall; Mr. Lloyd-Price's, a pure harrier, eighteen-inch pack, hunting in Carmarthenshire; Mr. Mill's (Dorsetshire), seventeen to eighteen-inch; the Mostyn and Talacre, North Wales, seventeen-and-a-half to eighteen-inch; the Plas Machynlleth, North Wales, a cross-bred eighteen-inch pack; Mr. Sperling's, eighteen-inch pure harriers, South Devon; the Stockton, seventeen-and-a-half-inch Stud-book harriers; the Tre thill, seventeen-inch pure harriers, Cornwall; and the Windermere, eighteen-inch, described as "harriers." The smallest harriers of which I can find record are Mr. Frank Wood's, hunting from Newton-le-Willows, Lancashire. These are also described as "harriers," and their height as no more than sixteen inches, which is no greater a stature than that of a fair number of beagles.

To my mind the ideal height for harriers is from eighteen to nineteen inches. Twenty inches should be an outside measurement, and the pack will be all the better for hare-hunting, in my humble opinion, if the Master from the beginning rigorously makes up his mind to draft hounds over that standard. Twenty-one inches is too big for a good harrier; and for a perfect pack, which every Master after all tries to attain to, although few, indeed, have the luck to reach the summit of their desires, it is desirable rather to have hounds averaging under twenty inches. For several seasons I have hunted with a pack of nineteen-inch harriers of old English blood, much of it Southern hound. I find these harriers fast enough and clever enough - their noses are good enough for anything - to account for their hares in masterly fashion.

Having dealt with the question of height, let us now, in looking at the modern harrier, consider his colour, shape, and other qualities. With a view of assisting the reader in this respect, I have included among the illustrations reproductions of a number of hound photographs, which, I believe, as demonstrating various types, will be found not uninteresting. A good hound, it has been said over and over again, can never be of a bad colour. The majority of packs nowadays show on the whole much more of what we know as foxhound colour than any other. But in many packs, especially in the West and South of England and in Wales, may be found a good deal of the blue-mottle or blue-pied colouring, which, in the opinion of many good judges, present and past, is the true harrier type. By breeding and careful mating and selection it is quite possible, within a comparatively brief period, to re-make, as it were, and re-shape a pack of hounds. I have watched very closely for some years the improvement of a pack of harriers in the South of England. Originally these were of Southern hound strain, a good deal crossed with other blood. Seven or eight years ago three or four good blue-mottle bitches were procured from Devon and Sussex. They were, obviously, strongly of Southern hound strain, with long ears, old-fashioned heads, and grand voices. These were judiciously mated with some of the best hounds - for work as well as for looks - in the pack; and at the present time these harriers have a very handsome appearance, a large proportion of them showing strong traces of the blue-mottle blood. Such a blend, judiciously strengthened by just a faint foxhound cross - obtained through harrier blood - for the purpose of adding speed and correcting faults in shape often noticeable in pure harrier blood, gives, in my judgment, an almost perfect pack of hounds for hunting hare. This is what has been arrived at in the pack I have in my mind, the Hailsham, hunting about Pevensey Marshes and the surrounding district. They average nineteen inches, have plenty of pace, and wonderful noses; and their grand Southern hound voices afford magnificent music over the wide countryside.

As to other colours, hare-pie, badger-pie, lemon-pie, and even slate-grey or white may be occasionally met with, especially in the West of England. Hounds of these colours are usually of good old stock and are seldom bad ones. Old English red, as it is called, is also a famous hound colour in the West, although now not often met with. The rare black-and-tan is another good colour, usually associated with deep mellow voices, antique heads, and great scenting powers. Hounds of these old-fashioned colours, when they can be procured, unless drafted for any real fault, are valuable auxiliaries in the formation of a real harrier pack.

Having had due regard to height and colour, the novice, in attempting the building up of a pack, must, of course, be guided to a considerable extent by certain hard-and-fast axioms well recognised among hunting men. Good looks and true shape are always to be considered, yet they are not to be placed before everything else. Many a splendid-looking hound is a skirter, or a babbler, or runs mute, or has a poor constitution, or some other fault which renders him worthless, an encumbrance which should be drafted quickly from the pack, or destroyed altogether. And, on the contrary, many an odd-looking hound is a first-rate performer. I remember well an old hound named Captain in the pack I speak of, the Hailsham. He was throaty, not well shaped, and had a poor head; yet as a worker he was unsurpassed, his nose was unfailing, and as a road-hunter I never saw his equal. Mated with the blue-mottle bitches I have spoken of, his stock have done remarkably well, and are now a source of strength to the pack. It is not wise, therefore, to pick your hounds by looks alone. Where you get a good-looking hound, well-shaped, and with good shoulders and feet, and a good performer in the field to boot, by all means stick to that hound. Straight shoulders, splay feet, throatiness, weak thighs, and slack loins are, I know, abominations to hound-men, and, whenever possible, should be avoided. But, on the other hand, if you have a right good working hound with but one of these faults - especially if you are getting together a pack and have the usual difficulties always present in such a case - don't draft him in too great a hurry. You may look farther and find yourself worse served. Always avoid hounds of weak constitution, and never breed from them. False hounds, mute hounds, babblers, and skirters should never be tolerated in a pack; they contaminate others, especially young hounds, with their own vices, and, above all, they should never be bred from.

As regards points, Beckford's description of a good hound is still worth quoting and remembering. "There are certain points," he says, "in the shape of a hound which ought always to be attended to by a sportsman, for if he be not of a perfect symmetry, he will neither run fast, nor bear much work; he has much to undergo, and should have strength proportioned to it. Let his legs be as straight as arrows; his feet round, and not too large; his shoulders back; his breast rather wide than narrow; his chest deep; his back broad; his head small; his neck thin; his tail thick and bushy; if he carry it well, so much the better. Such hounds as are out at the elbows, and such as are weak from the knee to the foot should never be taken into the pack." Beckford qualifies partially what he says on the subject of a hound's head. "I find," he says, "that I have mentioned a small head, as one of the necessary requisites of a hound, but you will understand it as relative to *beauty only;* for, as to goodness, I believe large-headed hounds are in no wise inferior. The colour I think of little moment; and am of opinion with our friend, Foote, respecting his negro friend, that a good hound, like a good candidate, cannot be of a bad colour." Beckford's observations on the points of a hound still leave little to be desired, and will probably remain a standard authority.

It is most desirable to have your pack closely approximating one another in size, if not always in colour. Nothing is more unsightly or more unsuitable than a pack of all sorts of sizes. You want a pack that will, in truth, pack well together, and not follow one another in a long unsightly string. For this reason it is desirable, as far as can be managed conveniently, to breed or select hounds not only of a similar size, but approximating pretty closely in speed. It is fatal to a pack to have one or more hounds much faster than the rest. It strings out the rest, and those that cannot go the pace of the leader become annoyed, breathless, and jealous, and get their heads up. Quite recently I saw a pack of first-rate harriers, to which a new hound had been lately added. This hound was far too fast for the rest, and as soon as a hare was found, went right away, leaving behind it the unsightly spectacle of the pack strung out into an attenuated line. While this and another hound remained, the hunting of that pack was almost completely spoilt.

I have shown that practically three types of harrier - or rather hare-hunting hound - are now to be met with: the true harrier, the Stud-book harrier, and the dwarf foxhound, all having their admirers and all hunting well in their own fashion. The fashion of the pure foxhound is, as I have indicated, not that generally acceptable to the genuine hare-hunter, and I believe that if all hare-hunting men could be polled, a considerable majority would be found in favour of the methods of the true harrier, that is, the true harrier modernised. No one, of course, could put up with the tedium of the old Southern hound style of hunting. It is a real pleasure to find that there are still so many packs of harriers hunting in England, which can show so much of the old stamp of hare hound. I believe, in spite of much adverse opinion, that the admirers of real harriers, as opposed to foxhound blood, are by no means diminishing, and I am certain that much more interest is now taken in this hound than was the case thirty or even a score of years ago. This being the case, it seems to me a pity that the foxhound type should still be permitted to have its way so much at shows of the present day. It is certain - and I believe even most Stud-book harrier-men will agree with me - that the complete elimination of old harrier blood would be a great disaster for hare-hunting. Yet the methods of judging at the present day still tend in that direction. A Master of a fine old-fashioned pack of harriers quite recently wrote to me as follows: "Only last year, at a big Show, one of the judges went to my huntsman, after hounds left the ring, and said he was sorry he could not give us first prize, as we ought to have it, and that he wished there were more harriers like ours; but he was told to judge on foxhound lines, and so, of course, had to do so." At Peterborough, the Studbook harrier, which is to all intents and purposes a dwarf foxhound, with a faint tinge of harrier, has it practically all his own way, and the real harrier, still, as I have shown, very largely represented among English packs, seldom has a look in. This is, of course, largely the fault of the various Masters of this stamp of hound, who will not take the trouble to send up representatives from their packs. The question of distance and expense has, doubtless, a good deal to do with the matter.

There ought to be, in my opinion, a class for the pure harrier, and I believe that such an innovation would be in time very largely justified and would lead to the vast improvement of many old harrier packs. It cannot in justice be denied that the so-called "pure" harrier ought to be represented at what purports to be a harrier show. [1] These observations are made without the least reflection on the supporters of the Stud-book harrier, who have, undoubtedly, done much to improve the make and shape and style of a particular stamp of hound. Here let me interpose some remarks of Colonel Robertson Aikman's from the Stud-book harrier point of view, which, I think, in fairness should be quoted here. His opinion, as a well-known Master of harriers, and one of the most noted hound-breeders in the kingdom, is worth stating.

"The Association of Masters of Harriers and Beagles," he writes, "instituted on March 25, 1891, has, without doubt, done an immensity of good. It has brought Masters together, and those who have taken advantage of this have seen other countries, packs, kennels, servants, and many things which have led to improvements. It is also the means of settling, when appealed to, any differences or disputes referred to it. The Peterborough Show and Stud-book have done incalculable good in improving the breed of harrier. The chief good in a hound show is to be able to see all the best dog-hounds together. This is a great advantage to the careful breeder. It has a good effect in smaller ways, such as the way hounds are turned out, a good lesson to Hunt servants, and even to their own personal appearance. I have noticed a marked change in these respects since the show was originated.

"I was on the original committee appointed by the Association in 1891 to investigate and report as to what a harrier should be. The committee found there were perhaps twelve or fifteen different kinds of hounds hunting the hare, more than half the owners calling their hounds pure harriers, [2] though quite diverse in type, such as the Brookside, Sir John Amory's, the Southern, the blue-mottled Northern, the Welsh, the Shotesham, the Duke of Hamilton's. If any one type had been selected there would have been few to adopt it, so the committee recommended that all hounds, however bred - foxhound, the many types of pure harrier, and the many different types of crossbreeds - should be admitted to the Stud-book, and then the book be closed, leaving the future to develop a type. This recommendation was unanimously agreed to, and the results have proved good, a greater similarity of type existing now, and the improvement in make and shape being very marked."

There are, of course, many things to be urged from both points of view in the case of the harrier. A good sportsman, Mr. C. Garnett, secretary of a well-known pack of harriers - the Holcombe - in Lancashire, has well contrasted, in a letter to me, the merits and demerits of pure and Stud-book harriers. The old-fashioned harrier, as he points out, "excels on a bad-scenting day; he will never go a yard without scent and is a particularly good road hunter. He also has most lovely music, which, in a hilly country, is very useful. He can go a good pace, but, as each hound likes to own the scent himself, they do not pack so nicely when running hard. Stud-book harriers get away quicker, and are, I think, easier to turn, and, when scent is good, are better to ride to, as they push a hare more, and consequently you get straighter runs. To my mind their great fault is that they have too much drive, and at a check flash a field or so over the line, whereas, in nine cases out of ten, the hare has doubled back. They (Stud-book harriers) are easier to breed with good legs and feet, and are, I think, much smarter hounds; but in a hilly, rough country, I feel sure you would get far better sport with the old type; while in a good country, with large fields, the Stud-book harrier is to be preferred, as he gets away from the horsemen and does not dwell so much on the line."

This seems to me an excellent and pithy summing-up of the two schools of modern English harriers.

Mr. J. S. Gibbons, Master of the Boddington Harriers, one of the most experienced hare-hunters in the kingdom, has been good enough to send me his views on the modern harrier. As one of the founders and supporters of the Harrier and Beagle Stud-book, and of the harrier classes at Peterborough Hound Show, his views are not only entitled to the greatest respect, but are certain to be of interest to all harrier men, and I have with great pleasure here reproduced them.

"To write on the various merits of the different descriptions of hounds used to hunt the hare," says Mr. Gibbons, "is no very easy task; for there are few sporting subjects on which so few men can be found to agree. It is not very easy to say why this should be, for Masters of foxhounds have long ago decided on the type of hound they wish to hunt the fox with, which is, practically, identically the same in all hunting countries, with the exception of the wilder parts of Wales, where a rougher description of hound is still to some extent used. The rough Welsh hound, however, makes no headway outside this particular district, probably because this class of hound cannot be bred to the levelness of pace which is necessary to make hounds pack together when going at top speed; which quality is a *sine qua non* in any country where hounds can be ridden up to in the modern style. But I am straying from my subject, that of the different sorts of harriers. I think that perhaps the main reason of the existence of the very different types of hounds lies in early education and custom. The man who was entered with the light-coloured hounds of the West country, which have a character all their own, does not forsake his first love; the same with the man of Lancashire, who swears by the large, blue-mottled, deep-toned hounds used in that country; while the man who began his hare-hunting with a pack of small, smart foxhound bitches will be equally sure that he is right in his choice. Now, in a country where it is not possible to ride continuously close to hounds, there is no doubt that a great deal of cry is a necessity, and the fact of hounds being not very level in pace does not so much matter; for this reason hounds of the rougher and more old-fashioned description may do their work very well, and it may be that they are really better suited to that sort of country. But when the work has to be done in a rideable country, especially over grass which carries a good scent, you cannot afford to have tailing hounds; the pace of the leading hounds must be the pace of all the pack, or you may have horses and hounds all mixed up together; the only way to acquire this levelness of pace is to breed hounds with as good shoulders, backs and loins, legs and feet, as you can; and these qualities, with the exception, perhaps, of the backs and loins, are what the old-fashioned harriers were, and are, sadly deficient in; but then, their Masters did not want them to go fast.

"Well, to get these qualities we must go to the foxhound - for there is nowhere else to get them from - the modern foxhound being certainly the most perfectly shaped animal, for combining the use of nose and legs, in all the canine world, which indeed is not to be wondered at, considering the accumulated experience that has produced him. Nor do I think that by making use of this experience we lose so much hunting power as some people suppose. The Southern and other older sorts of harriers appear to puzzle out a bad scent better, it is true; but I fancy that their success is more apparent than real; they make more fuss and noise about it, but I have often seen a foxhound or two working in a pack of regular harriers, and have generally noticed that the foxhound held its own well with the rest of them, even on the cold scent that the others are supposed to be superior in coping with. But while advocating a strong cross of foxhound blood, I would by no means lose that of the harrier altogether; keep it as much as you can; the hereditary instinct of hare-hunting must be worth something. My own ideal pack of harriers, suitable, be it understood, for a country fit to ride to hounds in, would be composed of hounds as near twenty inches as I could get them, as perfectly shaped as possible, which means as much like a foxhound as can be, but a little lighter in build, to show their harrier ancestry. Keeping down the size is the great trouble; you are constantly finding your nicest puppies too big for you, and the temptation to keep them is great.

"Some people may think that even the size I name is too large; but I find that, if you want your hounds to get away from horses, twenty inches is none too big, and, at the end of the day, if you have a long journey home, hounds of that size will come cheerfully along with their sterns up, at a good pace, when smaller ones tire and make the miles much longer than they need be. Personally, I began with eighteen-inch hounds, which were then my ideal; now my pack runs up to twenty-one inches, which suits me well; but I should like them better still if they were one inch smaller. However, I have been twenty years breeding them to what they are, and if I had twenty years more they might be no nearer my ideal than they are now, nay, perhaps further off; for it is much harder to keep a pack at a certain pitch than to get it there. In conclusion, my ideas, I know, will not be acceptable to all who may read this; but I will offer one piece of advice without hesitation, and that is, to make up your mind as to what type of hound you want, and go at it as hard as you can. You will not find a lifetime too long in which to breed a pack of hounds exactly to your ideal."

The case for the Stud-book harrier could hardly be more effectually stated than it is here by Mr. Gibbons. The conclusion of the whole matter must be that for different countries different types are required. There must be "give and take" in these things, and so long as the old English harrier is not swamped by foxhound blood, no one - not even the keenest supporter of the ancient type - can have much reason to complain. After all, England is wide enough to accommodate the partisans of every type of hound.

[1] Colonel Robertson Aikman reminds me that there were special classes for the old English harrier, which were only discontinued for the reason that the class did not receive support - only two packs ever showing. The experiment might surely be tried again in future years.
[2] In a note upon this point Colonel Aikman says: "I take exception to the division of harriers into 'Stud-book' and 'Pure Harrier.' Let it be *Stud-book* and *Non-Stud book* Harrier."

Chapter Six - Modern Hare-Hunting

THE conduct of a modern hare-hunt differs, as I have shown, a great deal from the style of our forefathers. It is brisker, smarter, and less dragging. Instead of rising in the dark and following up the trail of a hare which had been afoot during the night, until she was traced to her form and thence put up, the hare-hunter at the present day prefers, very wisely, to reserve his energies for a considerably later hour. The sportsman of 1780 had but two, or at most three, posts a week, even if he lived within a hundred miles of London, and those in remoter districts fared much worse. None of them had the pleasure of a glance at a morning paper or the convenience of opening their letters before starting for the chase. The modern sportsman gets his breakfast comfortably, has time for a look at papers and correspondence, is in the saddle by ten o'clock, or later, and is in good time for the meet at eleven o'clock.

Having got to the formation of a pack of hounds, it is desirable, for the benefit of the uninitiated, to indicate briefly something of the procedure of hounds in the field. The strength of the pack depends, of course, on the number of hunting-days. This, again, somewhat depends upon the depth of the purse of the owner of the pack or the amount of subscriptions forthcoming, if it be a subscription pack. A two-day-a-week pack can, with economy, be comfortably kept going with from fifteen to eighteen couple of hounds. Some Masters manage to hunt two days a week with ten or twelve couples, but this is running the thing rather fine. However, it is accomplished, and fair sport provided, to my certain knowledge. For three days a week, from twenty to twenty-five couples of hounds are desirable. Some Masters maintain even more. The Dunston, hunting near Norwich, muster thirty-two and a half couples; and Mr. Henry Hawkins' pack, hunting in Northamptonshire, are of similar strength; while Mr. Quare, hunting in Essex, maintained during the season 1901-2 no less than thirty-five couples of hounds. But this is doing it *en prince,* and as with most harrier packs economy has to be carefully considered, from twenty to twenty-five couples of hounds may be considered ample even for a three-day-a-week country. The Hailsham, a Sussex pack, which turn out regularly three days a week, and are real hard workers, and kill usually some sixty hares in a season, number twenty couples. These hounds are always in splendid condition, and can afford to give even an occasional seventh day in a fortnight. The Biggleswade, Mr. George Races', put in three days a week with but twelve couples; and the Glanyrafon, a Welsh pack, hunt three days also with but eleven and a half couples. These are rare instances, however, and few people would care to undertake hunting three days a week with less than eighteen or twenty couples twenty-two or twenty-five couples is a more comfortable number. It should be always borne in mind that bitches are more likely to get out of order than dogs, and where the pack contains many bitches, therefore, a larger number of hounds is required.

Hounds should be at the meet punctual to time. At the meeting-place some packs are shut up in a stable, but the majority are kept in the open, as with foxhounds, until the word is given and a move made. It happens not seldom that a farmer or shepherd is well aware of a hare seated, and can take the field straight to her form. That saves a good deal of trouble, and the hunt quickly begins. But, more often, the hare has to be found, and this, in country where these animals are scarce, is occasionally a very tedious process. Personally, I have never had the misfortune to hunt in a country where hares were scarce; but one can sympathise with those who suffer from this drawback, and can understand their betaking themselves to deer, fox, and even baser substitutes - of which more anon. Where the pack is hunted on foot, hares are, I think, more easily found than with a mounted pack.

Good hare-finders are, as I have shown, scarce commodities, and the pack that owns one among its followers has a treasure indeed. How many a rousing hunt do I not owe to a certain hare-finder of my acquaintance! How often have I not seen his square hat go up quietly, and the hare put gently from her seat, so that she should have a fair start from the on-coming hounds! Beckford had a prejudice against hare-finders which, I confess, I do not share. He maintained that they made hounds idle as well as wild. "Mine," he says, "knew the men as well as I did myself; could see them almost as far and would run full cry to meet them." It would, of course, be unwise to let them get into such a habit as Beckford indicates; but in my experience this is not often likely to happen, and I am bound to say I have seldom known hounds spoilt in this manner. In Beckford's time hare-finders seem to have been well paid for their pains, and at the present day, where hares are scarce, it is just and politic to encourage native talent among shepherds, labourers, and the like, by rewards now and again.

But hare-finders - even the best of them - are not always certain of picking up a hare quickly, and in any case it is right and necessary that hounds should be taught to scatter well, so soon as the signal is given, and they are thrown off, and hunt out their quarry for themselves. Hounds that show keenness in this respect are most valuable, especially in a country where hares are scarce. Beckford has well said that hare-finders are of great use in one respect: they hinder the hounds from chopping hares, a calamity so fatal to good sport. Some huntsmen - and some hounds also - have a knack of chopping hares, and a very unfortunate knack it is. Usually these are Hunt servants, who are getting careless and lazy, or who are too much occupied in running up a big score of kills. They are by all means to be discouraged.

It has often been debated whether, when a hare is found, she should be put off her seat quietly, before hounds can get a view, or whether the finder should wait until hounds can see her start from her form. It is maintained by many that a view makes hounds wild and gets their heads up. Personally, I see no harm in the view. It must inevitably happen when hounds, as they so frequently do, find their own hare. I believe that it heartens and fires the pack, and is effectual in giving the hare a sound fright, and so inducing her to fly from her nearer haunts and give a real good run. After all, the view, stirring as it is, is not for long, and hounds are brought to their noses at the first hedge.

A view Holloa or two, as the hare jumps up and hounds go off at score, does no great harm. But it cannot be too much insisted that in hare-hunting silence is golden. Why is it that every one who sees a hare, unless, happily, he is an old stager, and understands his business, must instantly start holloaing? The Master of a foot-pack with which I am well acquainted prints always at the head of his postcards and lists of meets: "Horsemen are objected to. Make no gaps, always close and fasten gates after passing through, and never holloa when the hounds are running." This last rule is the first axiom of hare-hunting, yet it is the most frequently broken. How many and many a hare has been lost by this annoying practice! Nine times out of ten, especially in a country where hares are plentiful,

From a photograph by R. B. Lodge, Enfield
ALDENHAM HARRIERS
DRAWING THE COMMON

From a photograph by R. B. Lodge, Enfield
ALDENHAM HARRIERS
AFTER THE KILL

the hare seen by the too excitable onlooker who starts yelling is not the hunted hare; and if she is the hunted hare, hounds are almost surely on her line. A holloa is only justified when the person who has viewed the hare understands his business, sees that hounds have checked or lost, and knows that the *hunted* hare has passed him. And still better than a holloa is the practice of holding up a hat, or even a handkerchief. Holloaing gets hounds' heads up and tends to make them wild and unsteady, almost more than any other practice, and it cannot be too severely discountenanced.

Having found their hare, away go the pack in pursuit, with a grand burst of music. The hare may run, contrary to the habit of the fox, as likely up wind as down. She will almost certainly travel in a circle, more or less wide, according to the way she is pushed, or her own natural stoutness. A travelling jack hare, out of his country, may, and very likely will, run straight; and in dense fog a hare, jack or doe, will occasionally lose its bearings and afford a fine tailon-end chase. A hare that has been thoroughly scared, either by a narrow escape from the ravening pack as they put her up, or from the yells or near presence of foot people, will in like manner sometimes go straight away and give a rousing good hunt. The best run I ever saw with harriers happened in this way. We found a hare near the sea. She ran through a number of people - it was near a village, and there were a good many out and much holloaing - and she sustained such a fright that she took straight away over a splendid line of country and was killed seven miles away in a direct line, hounds having traversed not less than fourteen miles of country.

When scent is first-rate, hounds hunt themselves, and little assistance is needed; and it should always be remembered with harriers, especially with the tender-nosed, old-fashioned harrier, that hounds understand much more of the great business of their lives than does the human hunter, clever though he may think himself. An old Irish huntsman once said to a noble lord, who was making various suggestions at a check: "Me Lard, the most ignorant hound in the pack knows a great deal more about hunting than you or me." A very just rebuke.

Most harrier packs are hunted by the Master, and the Master has, naturally, great responsibilities as well as great power. Even if he employs a professional huntsman, every Master of harriers should have a fair working knowledge of the sport he pursues. It is humiliating, as well as unbusinesslike, to be entirely at the mercy of your Hunt servant; and it is always far better for the man himself and for the sport of all that the Master should be conversant with what is going forward, and be able to give a sound opinion when required. He is, of course, always anxious to show sport, but he will, if he understands the science of hare-hunting rightly, leave as much as possible to the intelligence of the pack, and will only attempt to assist them when they are obviously at an *impasse.* The Master - *qua* Master - requires and, it must be admitted, fairly often possesses many necessary qualifications. He should, first of all, know his hounds well, and for this it is evident that, during their long summer vacation, he must have familiarised them with his person. He should be firm yet courteous, remembering always that strong language is in no wise necessary for the conduct of hunting. Bad language is always to be deprecated, and its employment is a fashion in hunting which, in my humble opinion, needs reform. Much of the strong language used in the field is entirely unnecessary and unwarranted. However, in this respect, Masters of harriers are nothing like such transgressors of good manners as are their brethren of foxhounds. They have, it must be admitted, far smaller and less troublesome fields to keep in order, and in other ways their burdens are more easily to be borne. In the chapter on "Hunt Servants," I deal at some length with the duties of huntsman, but reference must necessarily be made here and there in this chapter also as to the methods of handling hounds when running.

So soon as hounds run, it will be the duty of the field - and the Master or huntsman will ensure that this duty is performed - to see to it that the pack shall have plenty of room to carry on their operations. Hounds hate being pressed, and harriers, it may be noted, are more nervous in this respect than are foxhounds. They are more timid, and more easily put out, and, once their heads are up, they are more difficult to get to their work again. The field should ride wide of the line, and not directly in the wake of the hounds, a custom which is by no means too often observed, even among hunting folk who ought to be considered experienced. In rough, and especially in hilly country, hounds, when scent is good, can usually take care of themselves, but in more level, open country, especially where some of the field are inclined to ride hard, it is another matter, and hounds are not always allowed the law and the space that is necessary to them.

When a check comes, as is certain to be the case, it is especially necessary that hounds should have plenty of room; and here, again, it is most important that silence should be observed as much as possible. Loud talking gets their heads up and disturbs them. A good pack of harriers will spread out and cast eagerly for themselves, and they should be allowed plenty of time in the process. It is always to be remembered that in hare-hunting there is not the violent necessity for haste that there is in the pursuit of the fox. The hare is always above ground, and, sooner or later, you are bound to come up with her, while your fox may be progressing at his best pace, all the time you are at a check, for some open earth, where he can get snugly to ground. I have heard of a pack of foot harriers, hunted by an old-fashioned huntsman, where the latter was accustomed to climb on to a gate when his beauties checked. This is carrying the thing to extremes, and one by no means advises such deliberation. But give your hounds plenty of time, and don't be afraid of trusting them. It may happen that, having tried all round, the hounds may turn back on the line and appear to be hunting heel. Even in such a case it is by no means absolutely certain that they are hunting heel. A hare has so many dodges, and slips back often so unaccountably, that some knowing old hound may be in the right. This is one of those junctures when the judgment of the huntsman must be relied upon. It is a difficult point, and the huntsman himself, in such a case, is guided by various surrounding circumstances. There may, for instance, be a holloa back, and if the huntsman is convinced that the holloa is a good one - that is, one worth listening to - he will let the pack go, though they may seem to be running heel. Hounds, in fact, should not be whipped off unless the huntsman is absolutely certain they *are* running heel.

But we will suppose that hounds have really come to a fault, have tried in various directions, and cannot make good the line. The huntsman's turn now comes. In the earlier part of the chase, a hare that is fresh is more likely to be forward than back. I am aware that some huntsmen believe in casting back for a hare; personally, I do not agree with that theory, until it is proved that the hare has not gone on. The huntsman should hold his hounds forward. In Beckford's words, which are applied in this case to a pack of harriers: "It is an almost invariable rule in all hunting to make the head good." The hounds, then, are encouraged to cast quietly forward in the direction in which the hare was trending, taking care to get their heads up as little as possible. If this fails, a circular cast should be made. This may again fail. Then there remains the chance that the hare may have squatted somewhere near at hand, and close search should be made before giving up and trying for a fresh hare.

Where a hare has been hard pressed, and hounds come to a check, the chances are that she is down somewhere, or that she has doubled back on her old line; when hard put to it, she will resort to all sorts of tricks; she may even have run a hedge or a wall for a little way. She has a favourite dodge of leaping on one side and squatting in a ditch, especially after having run a road for some little way. The experienced huntsman has to remember all these and a score of other possibilities, and use his judgment accordingly. He can often tell by the demeanour of some knowing old hound, poking about mysteriously, what is likely to have been the hare's ruse on this particular occasion. It ought always to be remembered that, while a fox will almost invariably cross a road straight away and make across the next field, a hare will almost as invariably run the road for some little distance. Occasionally, as I have mentioned in the chapter on "The Hare and its Ways," these animals will run road for an incredible distance. Here comes the turn of that jewel of the pack, the good road-hunter. If scent is so poor that even the best road-hunters can make nothing of it, then the expertness of the human tracker can be utilised. I have seen a hare "pricked" for an extraordinary distance along a road, the line presently recovered by hounds, and the quarry handsomely killed, after what would have seemed to many a hopeless difficulty.

Woodlands, especially big woodlands, are a source of much trouble to the hare-hunter. A big woodland is almost certain to hold rabbits, and your hounds, once involved in its recesses, may run riot for half an hour or more before you can get them off. Again, the pack may happen on the line of a fox, and there is the devil to pay. Many harrier packs hunt their country by the courtesy of Masters of foxhounds, and, to put it mildly, the least their Master can do is to keep them from hunting the quarry that does not belong to them. The woodland may not have been shot, and pheasant-preservers are not likely to be amiably disposed if the pack is disturbing the coverts in all directions. A large woodland, then, is for many reasons to be avoided as much as possible, and hounds extricated from its depths as soon as may be. I have known harriers on several occasions to hunt a hare right through a big woodland and kill her at last; and I have also known the same pack hunt a wood, under various distractions, for something like half an hour, and, by patience and good luck, succeed in forcing out a dodging hare and killing her fairly in the open. But, on the other hand, how many, many times can one not remember the delay and confusion, riot and disappointment, of the same woodland! On the whole, where large coverts are concerned, I think, with the mercantile man, that it is better to cut one's loss quickly and get away in search of a fresh hare.

Small patches of wood, withy beds, of which, by the way, hares are extremely fond, and odd patches of covert, are much more readily dealt with. Where a hare runs into a covert of this sort, it is by no means to be taken for granted that the first hare ejected by hounds, or even the second or third, is necessarily the hunted one. The covert ought to be, and usually is, carefully watched by a whip or some of the field, who can tell the hunted hare when they see it. Only a month or so ago I saw harriers run a hare into a small withy bed, little more than a couple of acres in extent. The hare slipped round the covert, and actually entered it, as it were, on the very heels of the pack, as they were making their circuit. Two hares were one after the other pushed out, some foot people on a hill just above (up which each hare made its way) meanwhile yelling and holloaing vociferously. Both these hares were absolutely fresh and unstained. The pack went out after the second one, and ran her hard for several minutes. Luckily the Master, who was also huntsman, and was in covert, was informed that the hunted hare had not yet been ejected. He went away quickly after hounds, and with some difficulty got them off and brought them down again. Again they plunged into the covert. This time the hunted hare, which had been very cannily lying close, in expectation, no doubt, that she would be overlooked, was driven out and a first-rate run ensued. Hares, as has already been pointed out, take freely to water, and where the hare has been well pressed and the scent leads to the bank of a stream or small river, the assumption is that she has gone over. Before crossing, a hare will often carefully foil her line so as to confuse the puzzle yet more. I have watched a hare come to the bank of a broad stream, sit up for a second or two, with one ear cocked, and then, for a minute or so, busy herself in weaving a perfect labyrinth of foil, before crossing. She then ran down the bank, slipped quietly into the stream, swam across, and pursued her way. Where the stream runs swiftly, she may be carried fifty or a hundred yards down, and this ought to be borne in mind in picking up the line on the farther bank.

Sheep are among the most fruitful sources of checks in hare-hunting, as in the pursuit of the fox. After hounds have made their own cast, and have failed, and the huntsman has taken them in hand without success, the neighbouring hedges and other likely places should be tried. Not impossibly the hare may have squatted in the middle of the very field in which the check occurred, confident in the knowledge which she undoubtedly possesses, that the sheep stain may finally baffle her pursuers. This field ought, therefore, to be carefully searched, and if there are any roots adjacent, these also should be thoroughly tried. It is astonishing how closely a hare will squat, especially if she has been hard run. Mr. Southerden, late Master of the Hailsham Harriers, tells me of a remarkable incident witnessed by him many years ago with this Hunt. A hare that had been hard run for some hours was lost, and, do what they could, neither hounds, Master, nor field could account for her. Close to the side of a road was a rough piece of ploughed land, which was carefully but unsuccessfully drawn. Thereupon a short consultation was held. While this was going on, a farmer suddenly cried out that one of the hounds had its foot on the hare. This was literally and actually the case. The animal, startled by the cry raised, leaped from under the noses of hounds and men and made off. She was so tired, however, that she was run into in the same field. The hound treading upon her was, curiously enough, at least as frightened as the hare herself, and howled and ran off as the hare jumped up.

The knowledge that a hare is sinking, and will be soon pulled down, seems intuitive to most seasoned hounds and not a few experienced sportsmen. Towards the end of a hard run the huntsman observes that some of the older hounds, which have hitherto allowed the younger and more excitable of the pack to make play, begin to work to the front; these hounds are aware that the hare is sinking, and are quietly taking their places for the final scene. The scent of a tired hare often begins to fail a good deal towards the last of a run. I have even heard experts declare that a failing hare leaves no scent behind her, except that from the very tips of her feet as they touch the earth. A huntsman needs to be especially keen and especially careful towards the end of the chase, when the beaten hare, finding that she cannot outstrip her pursuers by speed alone, is twisting, doubling, and playing every conceivable prank and device in her well-stocked repertory, with the object of throwing off the pursuit. It is these wonderful devices, this extraordinary fertility of resource, which, to my mind, add so great an interest to the chase of this animal.

The death is the least pleasant part of the whole business. One can see a fox die unmoved. He is a ruffian and a robber, and he meets the ruffian's doom boldly and becomingly, turning at the last moment to confront the leading hounds with bared teeth, and the grin of death and defiance upon his face. But with the hare it is widely different. The run is enthralling enough; the death one is glad to get over as speedily as possible. The end is sudden enough, and the sufferings of the hunted hare last but a second or two. Occasionally, especially with foot-packs, it may happen that hounds have run clean away from their field; in such a case the hare, when run into, is speedily devoured, and the huntsman finds but a rag or two of skin when he reaches the scene. In the ordinary way, the huntsman, or a whip, or one of the field will be there, and the dead hare is rescued from the jaws of the pack. The huntsman, after sounding his horn and giving vent to inspiring "Who-whoops," heard far over the fields, now proceeds, either personally or by his deputy, the whipper-in, to the obsequies. Taking out his knife, he makes an incision in the hare's stomach, withdraws the entrails, and gives them to the pack. It is the custom to encourage young or timid hounds by smearing them with some of the blood. This is calculated to promote keenness; it is an ancient form, and there is certainly no harm in it.

As for the dead hare, if she has been hunted hard for an hour or two, her corpse is by this time so stiff that you may hold her out by her hind legs, straight and rigid, almost, as a piece of board. It is the custom of hare-hunting, in most countries, and a very excellent custom too, that the dead hare should be handed over to the farmer upon whose land she was first found. Every farmer likes a hare for his dinner, jagged or roast, and the practice cementing, as it does, friendliness between the field and the man who is good enough and keen enough to provide the sport is always to be encouraged. Some huntsmen like to take the ears of the hare to nail up at the kennels as trophies and evidences of their prowess. The scut is usually required for some one of the field, especially if a lady or a school-boy happens to be present. And occasionally, after an exceptionally good run, a pad is begged for some budding Nimrod, or even by some veteran, who likes to have a memento of a rousing chase. These are, however, more often the incidents of a run with foot-harriers or beagles than of a hunt in which the field is mounted.

After killing a hare it is desirable, if hunting in enclosed country, to make a move for a fresh hare at some little distance. There are two good reasons for this: one, that there is a better chance of a run in fresh country that has not been much foiled by the hunted hare and her pursuers; the other reason is that an adjournment to another farm lessens the possibility of riding over the same fences over and over again. Farmers are wonderfully forbearing and wonderfully generous, but it is unfair to subject their fences to the wear and tear of more than one hunt in the day if it can be avoided. These remarks do not, of course, apply with the same force to foot hunting, in the course of which fences suffer very little.

When a hare has been apparently completely lost, and every possible method of picking her up again has been tried, there is always one remaining chance, that she may have slipped back unperceived to the place from which she was first put up. I saw a good instance of this with the Hailsham Harriers on the last day of the season of 1901-2. We had a first-rate marsh run of an hour and a half, going at a great pace. Then scent failed somewhat, and the hare presently slipped us in the middle of the marsh. We tried all ways without success, and ultimately got on a fresh hare. The huntsman had an idea that our hare had made her way back to her old ground, and we presently whipped off. Again, hounds picked up a fresh hare, and so hard did they go that it was impossible to get them off. We ran over a little eminence of the marsh near where we had first found, and here, by great good luck, we came upon the hare we had so lately hunted. Getting hounds off the fresh hare, by a stroke of fortune, they were clapped on to the right line, and in a few minutes our original quarry, stiff and leg-weary, was run into and killed.

Fresh hares are an evil that many countries in these days would be glad to be blessed with. In the district in which I see a good deal of hunting, we have at times rather too much of this plethora, especially in our marsh country. I have seen in the course of a single run no fewer than fourteen hares put up. This sounds like fiction, but it is plain fact. Constant changing of hares is very trying indeed to the pack; and it is occasionally a matter of some difficulty to get blood, although hounds may be running hard all day. Still, even this difficulty can be surmounted, with care, judgment, and a little good fortune, and although now and again a disappointing day is scored, these are very few and far between. Where hares are too thick on the ground, the aid of coursers or shooting-men may be called in. In moderation, coursing is no great drawback to hare-hunting. I have seen the two sports flourish side by side in the same country, and many people aver that, where hares are coursed occasionally, they give better runs than is otherwise the case.

Scent is a subject which has exercised the minds of hunting-men for untold generations. All writers upon the chase have devoted more or less time and trouble to the elucidation of its mysteries; yet none have succeeded. Scent still remains, and will probably always remain, one of the most vexatious of all problems, a thing baffling, unaccountable, inscrutable. Countries vary very much, of course, in their scent-carrying capacity; the changes of soil may be noted frequently in the course of a single run. Temperature has, of course, much to do with the matter, as has the constitution, and even the sex, of the animal hunted. For instance, many old hunters are agreed that a doe, and especially a doe in young, affords a good deal less scent than a buck hare. Storms are against good scenting, and a sunshiny, melting morning, after a night's sharp hoar frost is, perhaps, the most fatal of all for good hunting. Northerly or easterly winds used popularly to be supposed to be extremely bad for scent, and indeed they are so, perhaps, rather more often than not. Yet, as most sportsmen know, there are days of easterly and northerly wind when hounds run like wildfire. Shortly before Christmas 1902, I hunted on Pevensey Marshes, which were white with a powdering of snow, in a freezing north-easterly wind. It was one of the bitterest of hunting days I ever remember in a long experience of fox and hare-hunting. Yet on this day we enjoyed a magnificent run of two hours and ten minutes, with excellent scenting, and wound up with a kill. I should mention that we changed twice during the course of this run. I was out with a foot-pack, and there were many dykes to get over, and hounds, huntsman, and some of the field, who had got wet, went home with a not inconsiderable coating of ice about them. The southerly wind and cloudy sky, so often sung, are by no means the unerring heralds of a good scenting day. In a fine, warm mist, with driving rain, I have noticed that scent will often lie magnificently; while, *per contra,* in thick, white, still fog I have occasionally experienced very poor sport. There are a few rare and wonderful days those days which Beckford rightly calls *jours des dames* - when every one can with safety predict scent and a good hunt. But, as a general rule, it is of little use prophesying on this subject, for the reason that, over and over again, the best and wisest of sportsmen find themselves but false prophets. I am one of those who do believe that when hounds roll much and betray indifference scent is very rarely good. This I take to be one of the surest signs that may be relied upon, a sign one hates to see, hoping against hope that hounds for once may be mistaken; yet they seldom are in this particular demonstration.

In countries where hares are scarce, it may be necessary to offer rewards to farmers, especially where holdings are small, for the finding of the game desired on their land. Bailiffs, shepherds, keepers, and others who have a voice or control in the maintenance of game, are, of course, worth looking after. Hare-hunting has, in this respect, its amenities, its duties, and its diplomacy, in like manner with foxhunting. Masters of foxhounds, who hunt the same country, and by whose courtesy hare-hunting often exists, are always to be thought of. Owners of coverts, who are often extremely liberal in preserving hares, deserve, and should receive, due consideration and thanks. In the case of farmers, more is effected by diplomacy and civility than in any other way. A hunt dinner is an excellent institution, and the practice of puppy walking and an annual prize-day and luncheon are also found to work very successfully. Puppy walking is, however, necessarily somewhat less often practised than in the case of fox-hunting. Without the farmer, hare-hunting, like fox-hunting, could not exist for a twelvemonth. It is a real pleasure, then, to find this good old English sport more popular among farmers than it has been any time this century past, that is, taking an average of countries throughout the length and breadth of England. Of the reasons for this revival of hare-hunting popularity I shall treat in another chapter.

Chapter Seven - A Glance at English Packs - Northumberland to Oxfordshire

THERE are at the present time hunting hare in different parts of England and Wales no fewer than one hundred and fourteen packs of harriers. Beagles and basset hounds, of which I shall treat in later chapters, number in the United Kingdom some fifty packs. In Ireland about thirty-one packs of harriers are maintained. Scotland is neither a good fox-hunting nor a good hare hunting country, and but three packs of harriers are put into the field by sportsmen north of the Tweed. These figures, added together, give the formidable total of one hundred and ninety-eight packs of hounds hunting hare in Great Britain and Ireland, or, deducting the trifle of three Scottish packs, one hundred and ninety-five packs in England, Wales, and Ireland. The Isle of Man supports a pack of its own, which, however, is, in the usual way, credited to the account of England. These figures are surprising. When one remembers how often hare-hunting has been declared to be in its dotage, and how frequently it has been predicted that hares would shortly be extinct, one has, obviously, some matter for reflection. In the year 1879 there were hunting hare in the United Kingdom no more than one hundred and sixty packs of harriers and beagles; so that, so far from the popularity of hare hunting having diminished, it is pretty certain that in the last four and twenty years the followers of the timid hare have spread abroad and flourished. There are at the present moment more packs of hounds following hare than there ever were before at any time during the history of the chase in Britain.

There seem to me to be two chief reasons why hare hunting has maintained and even augmented its ancient vogue. The first of these is that it is popular among the farmers. Many a sport-loving yeoman and tenant-farmer has been compelled reluctantly to give up fox-hunting, for the plain reason that he cannot afford it. Many a man, whose father, in the good days of agriculture, kept a hunter or two and went out regularly twice or thrice a week, now watches foxhounds from afar off; he gives them the run of his land and takes down wire fencing; but for himself he can afford fox-hunting no longer and, with a sigh, he leaves the sport to other and richer, but assuredly not worthier, folk. But with harriers it is different. The farmer, riding out on his rough nag or pony, which would be useless for fox-hunting, is enabled by the very nature of the chase, the ringing tactics of the hare, to see a good deal of the sport, and he goes home refreshed and heartened. It costs him nothing, fields rule small, little damage is done to his fences and crops, and more often than not he gets a good hare for his dinner. As for the beagle packs, they are always welcome. They are hunted on foot, and, again, no damage whatever is done to the farmer's property.

Hare hunting varies considerably in the style and nature of the sport shown, in the numbers of the pack and the turn-out of the staff, and in various other respects, in different localities. In some places you will find the general equipment and turn-out very much resembling that of a good pack of foxhounds; in another - probably a rough hill country - you may see, perchance, seven or eight couple of hounds, most probably of old-fashioned type, taking the field, under the command of a huntsman - some frosty-faced veteran - on foot, of course, whose faded green coat and general rusticity tell of hunt funds none too plentiful and of methods that were familiar in the hill country long before even John Peel himself waked the echoes with his cheery voice.

An analysis which I have made of the various harrier packs in different parts of England seems to me worth putting before the reader. Here, briefly, are the results: [1]

Devonshire is the foremost county in England as regards the number of packs it puts into the field. Fourteen packs of harriers are supported by the famous Western shire. Kent maintains ten packs; Yorkshire ten; Somerset nine; Lancashire eight; Sussex eight; Norfolk, Suffolk, Gloucestershire, and Cornwall three each. Other counties follow in twos and ones. Wales is, as befits a rough, wild country, strong in hare-hunting, and puts into the field eleven packs.

It will, I think, be not uninteresting to pass from north to south of England, glancing at the various harrier packs and their countries *en route*. Let us begin with Cumberland and Westmoreland, homes of lakes and mountains, of grand scenery, and of the sturdy yeomen-farmers of the dales. The Aspatria, a pack dating from 1870, hunts a country between Wedholme Flow in the North and Maryport in the South, and from Binsey Hill on the East to Silloth on the West. Of this, 70 per cent, is pasture, the rest plough, woodland, and moor. Eleven couples of cross-bred harriers are kennelled; the pack is a subscription one, and capping is not practised. In Cumberland also hunt the Brampton Harriers, which are kennelled near Carlisle, and have a history of some fifty years. Ten couples of pure harriers form the pack. The country consists for the most part of grass and moorland, and the hearty fell farmers are keen followers of the first-rate sport provided. In Westmoreland the Windermere pack, owned by Mr. Bruce Logan, with kennels at Ambleside, hunt some of the most beautiful country in the kingdom. It consists chiefly of moorland and lies partly in Westmoreland, partly in North Lancashire. Hounds number seventeen couples and hunt three days a week.

In Northumberland we find but one pack existing. This is Mr. Allgood's, which, maintained at Alnwick, consists of sixteen couples of eighteen-inch cross-bred hounds. They hunt a country of grass and moorland, part of it within the limits of the Tynedale, Percy, and Border foxhounds. In Durham are to be found two packs, the Darlington and Mr. Meysey Thompson's. The Darlington is a subscription foot-pack, consisting of twelve couples of seventeen-inch harriers, which are described as "pure." They hunt in South Durham, chiefly in plough country, varied as to about a third of its area by grass. Mr. Meysey Thompson, hunting from Rokeby, Barnard Castle, kennels eighteen couples of harriers, which go out two days a week. These are described as "pure harriers and black and tans," which seems to indicate that the pack is one of the old-fashioned sort.

We now come to Lancashire, the home of a very old type of English hound, the descendants of which may here and there be seen among harrier packs. The Aspull Harriers, maintained by Mr. Carlton Cross, of Crooke Hall, Chorley, number twenty-five couples. They are modern Stud-book harriers, of twenty- and twenty-one-inch standard, and hunt an area of about seventeen miles by twelve, consisting chiefly of pasture. A subscription is guaranteed by the Aspull Hunt Club, and strangers are capped 5s. *per diem.* The country is a very nice one to ride, with plenty of flying fences; it carries a good scent, and sport is excellent. There is some wire, but arrangements are made for taking it down yearly. Wire, by the way, although always objectionable, is not quite so great a curse in a harrier country as in a fox-hunting one. It is always interesting to have a Master's ideas on his own and other people's hounds. Mr. Cross tells me that he likes a harrier cross a long way back. He has a good deal of Belvoir blood in his pack. He tries to maintain a slight harrier strain, as he thinks it gives hounds business and perseverance, when a sinking hare is foiling her ground and dodging. Mr. Cross, however, holds an opinion, heretical, of course, to most pure harrier men, that a foxhound has just as good a nose as a harrier. And as to pace, he asserts that, for a race, with a hare in view, a harrier goes quite as fast as, or faster than, a foxhound. I am afraid I, for one, scarcely share either of these two opinions. Mr. Cross tells me that he bought about ten years ago a bitch which was "about a quarter either bloodhound, or the old black and tan Talbot." He bred from her and has the strain now and finds it very valuable for nose and hunting when crossed with quick-driving hounds. It is by experiments such as these, undoubtedly, that packs of hounds are improved and shaped. The Aspull have been distinguished at Peterborough Hound Show in recent years.

The Holcombe, which hunt near Bolton, number twenty couples of twenty-two-inch Old English harriers (sometimes called the old Lancashire hound), and are believed to be one of the most ancient packs in the kingdom. Tradition asserts that James I., after resting at Houghton Tower, on his way to York, hunted one day with the Holcombe, and was so pleased with the sport that he granted to these hounds the right to hunt three days a year for ever in the township of Quarlton, which was part of the Royal Manor of Tottington. The country consists of rough land bordering the moors, with stone walls, and grazing land with a small proportion of plough. There are a fair amount of posts and rails, and the hunt, to keep down wire, supply rails to the farmers in May, for mending gaps. There is a good stock of hares, which is scarcely

COL. ROBERTSON AIKMAN'S HARRIERS, LANARKSHIRE

HOLCOMBE HARRIERS, LANCASHIRE
ON THE MOORS

to be wondered at, when one remembers that a reward of 5s. for each hare killed is paid to the farmer on whose land she was first started. This fine old-fashioned pack has a rather curious custom. Some of the Northern packs, which hunt a good deal in hill country, have the kennel huntsman out on foot as well as a mounted huntsman. The Holcombe kennel huntsman, as well as a whip, is a pedestrian, and his attire, when hunting, consists of cord breeches, cord leggings, buttoned down the side, a cut-away red coat, and a tall hat. He carries a horn, shaped like a coach horn; it measures three feet in length, and has been in the possession of the hunt for two hundred years. Quaint though the get-up, the results are very satisfactory. Lancashire moorland hares are proverbially stout, and the Holcombe show capital sport. The Kirkham is another Lancashire pack twenty-one-inch Stud-book harriers this time hunting a country consisting almost entirely of pasture. They have been established since 1834, and have long been mastered by members of the Birley family. The Pendle Forest I have already said something about. They are a very old pack, dating from 1770, and consist of twenty couples of twenty-one-inch hounds, a cross of the foxhound and the old Lancashire hound. They are admitted to the Harrier Stud-book; they hunt from Clitheroe over parts of north-east Lancashire, and the country known as Craven, in the West Riding of Yorkshire. No foxhounds hunt this country, and the Pendle Forest pack hunt deer one day a week after Christmas.

Other Lancashire packs are the Rochdale, the Rossendale, both hunting a pasture and moorland country, Mr. Frank Wood's, hunting from Newton-le-Willows, and the Vale of Lune. The Rochdale are a particularly nice pack of hounds, showing a good deal of the real old-fashioned harrier type; they consist of eighteen couples of twenty-one-inch harriers, hunting three days a week, and kennelled at Cronkeyshaw, a mile from Rochdale. I am enabled to give a portrait of one of these hounds, Rattler, who is as good at work as he is to look at. Captain C. R. N. Beswicke-Royds is the present Master of these hounds, the Deputy-master being Mr. J. T. Pilling. The pack is hunted by the Master, or Deputy master. Mr. Pilling has been good enough to send me some interesting notes upon this pack. He tells me that the country hunted over is of a rough, hilly description, the land being chiefly enclosed within substantial stone walls, which, fortunately for the hares, are amply provided with what are locally called "smeuse" holes, which serve the double purpose of assisting drainage, and are so constructed as to allow the hare to run through; and especially at a find, or when hard pressed, they give the hare an enormous advantage over hounds, the latter being compelled to jump or scramble over.

The hounds were, up to 1879, carefully bred from the old original strain, great care being taken, when crossing with neighbouring packs, to keep to the fixed type. In 1879, however, dumb madness broke out, and the entire pack had to be destroyed, with the exception of a few puppies then out at walk. These carried the old blood on, some of their descendants being in the kennels at the present time. The best of these are the stock of Dulcimer, a most indefatigable worker, and in his day one of the best hounds that ever hunted.

Rattler, whose picture is shown, is a direct descendant of this hound. At the time of their misfortune, the hunt were able to secure a few hounds of their own blood from neighbouring packs, notably a hound named Brutus, whose stock has proved wonderfully good.

Owing to the roughness of the country and the difficulty of procuring pure harriers suitable for it (the majority being deficient in the important points of legs and feet), of late years a foxhound cross has been resorted to; fresh blood has been imported from time to time, Mr. Vaughan Pryse's, Mr. Quare's, the Pendle Forest, the Holcombe, and the Aspull being requisitioned. In 1896-97, when the pack won the Edgeworth Cup, in keen competition with neighbouring hunts, these hounds killed no less than one hundred and thirty-three hares. This is a record with this pack, which usually kill about a hundred hares in a season. The Rochdale, like many other Northern packs, have a very interesting history of their own. The Rossendale, another pack with a long history behind them, are kennelled at Newchurch-in-Rossendale, where they have been established these sixty or seventy years past, and hunt from thence three days a week. They number eighteen couples of twenty-one-inch Stud-book harriers, and hunt over a wide moorland and pasture country, varied by stone walls. The Vale of Lune, mastered by Colonel W. H. Foster, M.P., are kennelled at Hornby. They are a first-rate pack of Stud-book harriers, numbering twenty couples, and great pains have been taken in their breeding. In 1899, Rakish, a beautiful hound, took the Champion Cup at Peterborough for bitches between sixteen and nineteen inches. The Vale of Lune lies in some of the most beautiful parts of Lancashire, Westmoreland, and Yorkshire; but there is a good deal of wire, the country is cramped, and a horse is needed that can jump timber, stone walls, and water.

Yorkshire has, from time immemorial, been famous as a sporting county, and in Yorkshire, naturally, one finds harriers well represented. Here are the Colne Valley, the Craven, Glaisdale, Hallam and Eccleshall, Holmfirth, Penistone, Rockwood, Sheffield, Stannington, and Stockton the last-named a foot-pack. The Colne Valley - ten couples of pure harriers - hunt pasture and moorland in about equal parts. The Craven, an old pack whose records reach back far into the eighteenth century, hunt a wide district in north-west Yorkshire, in a country untouched by foxhounds. They are twenty-one-inch Stud-book harriers, chiefly of foxhound blood, number twenty-seven couples, and hunt three days a week. Mr. Amcotts Wilson is Master. The Glaisdale, hunting in the Cleveland country (foxhound), number ten couples and go out two days a week. They are, as I have previously stated, a trencher-fed pack, somewhat of a curiosity in these days. The Glaisdale, by the way, are a harrier and beagle cross, and run from seventeen to nineteen inches. The Hallam and Eccleshall are a Sheffield pack. The Holmfirth are another trencher-fed pack - twelve couples of pure harriers - established so far back as 1800, hunting near Huddersfield. The Penistone and their singularly ancient history I have already touched upon. The present pack consists of ten couples of pure harriers, or "Old English hounds," standing from twenty-two to twenty-four inches. They hunt low-ground, grass country until December 10, after which they betake themselves to the grouse moors west of Penistone, where they enjoy first-rate sport. The Rockwood, nineteen couples of twenty-one-inch harriers and foxhounds, find their sport in the West Riding, partly within the borders of the Badsworth Hunt; while two other Sheffield packs - the Sheffield and the Stannington - are quartered within or near the town of Cutlery. The Stockton, a foot-pack, numbering thirteen couples of seventeen and a half-inch Studbook harriers, hunt a rough country, parts of it cold clay, near Stockton-on-Tees. This pack started with beagles and was transformed into harriers in 1892.

Coming down to Derbyshire, one is somewhat surprised to find hare-hunting so little pursued in a country where foxhounds are not too much known, and where many wild districts might be supposed to lend themselves to fine sport with harriers or beagles. I do not find that a single pack of beagles exists in this beautiful county, while of harriers the High Peak are the only pack which have their head-quarters in Derbyshire. The Dove Valley Harriers, it is true, hunt partly in Derbyshire, but their kennels and head-quarters are at Mayfield, in Staffordshire. [2] This last-named pack numbers twenty couples of twenty-one-inch foxhounds, and hunts three days a week. Their country is a very beautiful one, grass for the most part, with moorland here and there, and plenty of stone walls.

In the High Peak we find one of the best countries and the most brilliant packs in the kingdom. Hunting in the fine, upland district round about Bakewell and Buxton, these harriers have the advantage of pursuing their hares over old pasture, which affords excellent scenting. There is practically no wire. This is a stone-wall country, the walls being built of limestone, loose, wide, and of a fair height. I have had the pleasure of seeing hare-hunting in the High Peak country, and I am bound to say the sport shown is very excellent indeed. A good and clever hunter is needed, and as enclosures, where they exist, are small, and walls frequent, the amount of jumping is very considerable. I have seen more and better fencing in a hunt with these harriers than in many a good run with the Pytchley or Grafton hounds. Colonel Robertson Aikman, who has mastered and hunted the High Peak Harriers since 1901, has a great reputation. For many years he hunted hare in Scotland, and for a season or two performed the difficult feat of mastering a pack of foxhounds as well as a pack of harriers. His harriers have been long famous. He breeds the Stud-book type, showing much foxhound blood, and his hounds have invariably been most successful and most persistent prize-takers at Peterborough. In 1901, for example, he took no less than six prizes, including the Champion Cup for dog-hounds between nineteen and twenty-one inches. Colonel Aikman's pack consists of twenty-two and a half couples of twenty to twenty-one-inch Stud-book harriers, hunting two days a week.

The High Peak harriers have been many years established - since 1848 - but until 1901 were practically dwarf foxhounds. Mr. Nesfield, of Castle Hill, who mastered these foxhounds from 1860 to 1892, and showed great sport, was agent to the Duke of Rutland, and was able in consequence to make use of a good deal of Belvoir blood. In 1901 Colonel Robertson Aikman brought with him his own pack from Lanarkshire. I quote a few remarks which Colonel Aikman has sent me on his new territory. "The High Peak country is in many respects ideal. It has probably more sound grass and less wire than any country in the British Isles. The absence of towns, or even villages, or much sign of life, makes it a happy hunting ground. Its scenting qualities are somewhat mysterious. The grand old turf looks like carrying a scent at all times, but in 1901-1902 it was woefully disappointing the whole season through. [3] The following season scent was the reverse, with scarcely a very bad scenting day up till February 1. The absorption of moisture by the limestone may explain absence of scent in dry weather. Some of the country is rough, and to those who hunt to ride it may be monotonous to jump nothing but stone walls, which are seldom small, often formidable, and cut a horse badly if he makes a mistake. On the whole, I doubt it there are many or any better countries for hare-hunting."

At one time another pack existed in this part of Derbyshire, known locally as the "Chapel Harriers," which were real old-fashioned harriers, trencher-fed, kept at Chapel-en-le-Frith, Dove Holes, and the villages round. These hounds are described to me by an old inhabitant, who remembers them well as a lad, as of all colours and sizes, blue-pied, brown-pied, black and tan, yellow, and white. In 1845, or thereabouts, they were hunted on foot by a working man, named Green, a strong, wiry fellow, who, in his grey coat and brass buttons, looked a typical moorland huntsman. In his absence another working man, known as "Owd Jim Noble," used to carry the horn. "Owd Jim" was a most enthusiastic huntsman, and his holloa was to be heard far away across the country-side.

The Isle of Man Harriers are a comparatively new introduction, having been established so recently as 1893 by Mr. Leigh Goldie Taubman, who remained Master till 1899. They hunt all over the island, going out twice a week. The pack consists of fourteen couples of seventeen-inch modern harriers, and is kennelled at The Nunnery.

Returning to the mainland, and proceeding further south, we come to Cheshire, where the Wirral, with kennels at Hooton, are to be found. This pack consists of twenty-nine couples of pure harriers, ranging from nineteen to twenty inches, entered in the harrier Stud-book. They hunt the whole of the Wirral peninsula lying between the rivers Dee and Mersey and their estuaries. This is a fine grass tract, with a good deal of wire in the northern part of the country. These harriers succeeded Sir Thomas Stanley's foxhounds, and the country has been hunted by them since 1868.

Between Lancashire and Yorkshire and the south and west of England, if we except Norfolk, we find packs of harriers rather few and far between. It is, by the way, a curious circumstance that no pack of harriers is to be found hunting in Lincolnshire, if I except the occasional incursions of the Marquis of Exeter's pack from Stamford. This is a reproach, which, in so excellent a sporting country, ought surely to be removed.

In Nottinghamshire the Clumber, owned by the Duchess of Newcastle, show good sport, chiefly within the borders of the country hunted by Lord Galway's and the Rufford foxhounds. They number eighteen couples of Stud-book harriers, ranging from nineteen and a half to twenty and a half inches. The Duchess of Newcastle, who hunts her own hounds, started the pack in 1895, recruiting it by drafts from the Brookside, Aspull, Mr. Greswolde Williams', and the Eamont kennels. Shropshire is represented by the Tanatside, a very old established pack, hunting from Oswestry, partly in their own county, partly in Montgomeryshire. The hounds, under the new Master, Mr. W.L.

Thursby, will consist of some twenty-three couples of twenty-one-inch cross-bred harriers - the late Foremark pack - and hunt two days a week. Wire is a trouble in this, as in many other parts, and apparently is on the increase.

Turning towards the borders of Wales, we find Herefordshire supporting only one pack of harriers, the Ross, whose history dates back at least as far as 1820. Fifteen couples of twenty-inch mixed hounds compose the pack, which is kennelled at Goodrich, near Kerne Bridge, on the Great Western Railway. Most of the Ross country consists of light plough.

Worcestershire is well represented by the Bentley Harriers, owned by Mrs. Cheape - known throughout the country-side as "The Squire" - of Bentley Manor, near Redditch. This lady is both Master and huntsman of her pack, which is maintained entirely at her own expense, no subscription being taken or "capping" practised. The pack, established in 1892, consists of twenty-two and a half couples of nineteen-inch pure harriers, which are entered in the Harrier and Beagle Stud-book; it hunts five days a fortnight over a wide country in Worcestershire, Warwickshire, Gloucestershire, and, occasionally, in the Old Berkshire country, by invitation.

Warwickshire, the home of fox-hunting, save for the incursions of the Bentley pack, is guiltless of hare hunting. In Leicestershire was found till this year the Foremark, with kennels at Foremark Hall. This was a strong pack, hunting a nice country, part plough, part pasture, in Leicestershire and Derbyshire. It ought to be resuscitated.

Northamptonshire, considering that it is so great a stronghold of fox-hunting, is fairly well represented. The Marquis of Exeter maintains at Burghley House, Stamford, a nice pack of nineteen couples of Stud-book harriers (eighteen- and nineteen-inch), hunting two days a week in this shire as well as in Rutland, and a piece of Lincolnshire. In the very heart of the Pytchley and Grafton countries, famous in the fox-hunting world for so many generations, we find Mr. Henry Hawkins hunting a first-rate pack of harriers from Everdon Hall, near Daventry. As a youngster I saw a good deal of fox-hunting in this part of England, but I never, in those days, heard of a pack of harriers anywhere within hail. It is a pleasure to find hare-hunting now so firmly established in this fine country. Mr. Hawkins bought his pack of harriers from Mr. John Horsey, who had hunted from Dallington, near Northampton, since 1888. The hounds, which are Stud-book harriers, are exceptionally good ones, taking in 1900 three prizes at Peterborough Show. They consist of thirty-two and a half couples, the present standard being nineteen inches. Formerly they were seventeen and a half- to eighteen-inch harriers, and one is sorry to note the rise in standard which too often seems inevitable among breeders of harehounds at the present day. I am afraid foxhound blood has much to answer for. This tendency to increase the size of harriers is one which is growing, and which ought to be repressed. Harriers as big as foxhounds are an anomaly, and are, into the bargain, quite unnecessary. Hare-hunters do not require to course their hares, but to kill them by fair and downright hunting. However, if Mr. Hawkins maintains his harriers at nineteen inches he is quite within reasonable limits, for a mounted pack. Mr. Hawkins tells me that by the kindness of the landowners and farmers he has been enabled to increase his area of sport very considerably. "Situated in the heart of one of the most favourite fox-hunting shires of England, one might, perhaps," he remarks, "have anticipated some reluctance on the part of the farmers to welcome an additional pack of hounds on their land; and it speaks volumes for the sporting spirit innate in the Northamptonshire yeoman, when one is able to announce quite a different sentiment as prevailing on all sides." Few harrier packs can claim to be more fortunate than Mr. Hawkins's. He has a splendid and diversified country. He uses the hound-van and railway very frequently, and wherever there are hares to hunt he is glad to take his pack. The flat pastures on the

From a photograph by Elliott & Fry, 55 Baker Street, W.

MR. H. HAWKINS' HARRIERS

Rugby side of the Pytchley country, the wooded slopes of Cottesbrook, and the wilder tracts round Northampton, where plough is more abundant, are often visited. Mr. Hawkins gets some of his best sport, he tells me, in the fine vale along the borderland of Northamptonshire and Warwickshire, through which runs the famous Braunston Brook. Hereabouts hares are wonderfully stout, surpassing in strength and endurance their fellows in the other regions round about. Braunston, Staverton, and Flecknoe are parishes all well known to fox-hunting fame, and in these localities it is a pleasure to find Mr. Hawkins and his harriers obtaining first-rate sport.

Cambridgeshire supports a pack of harriers the "Cambridgeshire" - consisting of twelve couples of dwarf foxhounds, ranging from nineteen to twenty-one inches, with head-quarters at Cambridge. Mr. Hugh Cheape masters and hunts them. Formerly run by farmers in the vicinity, these harriers are now hunted by some member of the University. Their country is chiefly plough, and lies within the limits of the Cambridgeshire, and Newmarket and Thurlow foxhounds. The North Bucks, with kennels at Bletchley, hunt in Northamptonshire, Bucks and Bedfordshire, chiefly in the territories of the Whaddon Chase, Grafton, Oakley, South Oxfordshire, and Hertfordshire Hunts. The country is mainly grass. The pack consists of eighteen couples of nineteen-inch harriers, mastered and hunted by Mr. W. F. Fuller.

Norfolk supports three packs of harriers, of which the Downham hunt a light plough country in the neighbourhood of Downham Market. Fifteen couples of twenty-inch pure harriers, entered in the harrier Stud-book, compose the pack. They hunt two days a week. The Dunston, kennelled near Norwich, and owned and mastered by Mr. Geoffrey Buxton, of Dunston Hall, hunt over a country, chiefly composed of plough, in South Norfolk. They are undisturbed by foxhounds and have very little wire. The pack consists of twenty-eight couples of nineteen- to twenty-inch Stud-book harriers. The Melton Constable were formerly owned by Lord Hastings, who gave them up a season or two back. They are now mastered by Mr. H. Gibson, who hunts two days a week from Melton Constable, in North Norfolk. The pack consists of twenty couples of twenty-inch Stud-book harriers.

Suffolk puts into the field three packs, the Hamilton, the Henham, and the East Suffolk. Of these the Hamilton, owned for many years by the late Duke of Hamilton, are now mastered by Mr. Carnaby Forster, with Mr. Sidney Heywood as Field Master and huntsman. They hunt from their old kennels at Easton, in the eastern part of the county, and number twenty couples of twenty- to twenty-one-inch pure harriers, entered in the Stud-book. The Henham, mastered and hunted since 1888 by the Earl of Stradbroke, hunt over a wide area in Suffolk and Norfolk, untouched by foxhounds. This country is chiefly plough, with about one-fourth pasture. The kennels are at Henham Hall, near Southwold. The pack number twenty-three couples of nineteen-inch pure harriers (Stud-book), which hunt two days a week. The East Suffolk are a new pack, enrolled this season, with kennels at Melton, near Woodbridge. They are mastered by Mr. R. E. Walford and consist of nineteen-inch hounds.

In Bedfordshire are to be found two packs. The Biggleswade, a small pack of twelve couples of Studbook harriers (nineteen to twenty inches), has been owned and mastered by Mr. George Race, of Road Farm, Biggleswade, since the year 1840. Mr. Race must be almost the oldest - I believe he is *the* oldest - Master of harriers in the United Kingdom. His father, Mr. John Race, well known as "Thistle Whipper" of the old "Sporting Magazine," kept harriers before him, and the pack was in the family before that gentleman's time. These harriers hunt in Hertfordshire and Cambridgeshire as well as in Bedfordshire; the country consists chiefly of plough, but as a set off there is very little wire. Mr. Carpenter's harriers, kennelled at Bedford, hunt in that county and in part of Bucks. Fourteen couples of nineteen-inch Stud-book harriers compose the pack, which has been in the hands of the present Master his own huntsman since 1884. Oxfordshire supplied, until the end of last season, 1902-03, a single pack of harriers, that of Mr. Mason, otherwise known as the Eynsham Hall, kennelled for many years near Witney. These consisted of twenty-four couples of seventeen-inch, pure harriers (Stud-book), hunting for the most part over arable country, varied by some pasture, in the Heythrop territory. I believe these hounds are being given up. In the interests of sport it may be devoutly hoped that the country will be carried on by a new Master.

[1] I have to acknowledge my indebtedness in these chapters to Baily's "Hunting Directory," the *Field* Hound List, and to many masters of harriers who have supplied me with information.
[2] The Foremark Harriers hunted, until recently, partly in South Derbyshire, but have now been given up.
[3] The season of 1901-1902 was, incontestably, one of the worst scenting seasons, if not the very worst, during the last score of years.

Chapter Eight - A Glance at English Packs (continued) - The South and West of England

GLOUCESTER furnishes one of the best packs in the kingdom, the Boddington Harriers, maintained by Mr. J. S. Gibbons at Boddington Manor, near Cheltenham. Mr. Gibbons has long been a Master of harriers, having hunted a pack in Worcestershire before he established the present pack in 1883. No one has taken more interest in the breeding of harriers than Mr. Gibbons, and the fact that his hounds have been prize-takers at Peterborough attests the excellence of his kennel. He maintains twenty couples of Studbook harriers, which now reach twenty inches. The Boddington is a good country, lying in the Vale of Severn, partly in Gloucestershire, partly in Worcestershire; it runs from Tewkesbury and Gloucester as far as the Cotswolds and Brendon Hill. The Vale carries mostly pasture, but there is here and there heavy plough. On the hills, the going consists a good deal of light plough. The country is well stocked with hares, and sport is very good. Wire exists, but is well marked where it has not been taken down. For nine years Mr. Gibbons hunted thrice a week, but he has now returned to his earlier practice of two days. The Longford harriers, established in 1840, hunt a good grass country in the neighbourhood of Gloucester. They are a subscription pack, belonging to the farmers of this district, with kennels at Longford. They number twenty-three couples of twenty-inch harriers, mostly entered in the harrier and beagle Stud-book. Mr. J. G. Blagrave, last season joint Master with the late Mr. O. E. Part, hunts them. The Clifton foot harriers, sixteen couples of sixteen and a half-inch Stud-book harriers, carry on operations in no less than four counties, to wit, Gloucester, Somerset, Wilts, and Monmouth, chiefly in the territories of the Duke of Beaufort's, Lord Fitzhardinge's, and Mr. Curre's foxhounds. The kennels are at Yatton, in Somerset, and the pack hunts two days a week.

We now come to the home counties. Hertfordshire boasts but a single pack of harriers, the Aldenham, which, however, is a very good one. Seventeen and a half couples of twenty and a half-inch Stud-book harriers, kennelled at Chiswell Green, near St. Albans, hunt a country chiefly composed of plough. The late Mr. L. E. Rickards, who mastered this pack from 1885 to 1890, took a very keen interest in the improvement of the modern harrier, and to him in great part is to be attributed the foundation of the Harrier and Beagle Stud-book, and the harrier classes at Peterborough Hound Show. Mr. H. S. Bailey, the present Master, who owns the pack, is also his own huntsman. The Aldenham have been at different times very successful at Peterborough. Essex is by no means strong at the present time in hare-hunting, yet its solitary pack, Mr. Quare's, is distinguished as one of the best and most successful in the country. Hunting chiefly in the territory of the Essex foxhounds, this pack is numerically the largest in the kingdom, mustering as many as thirty-five couples of pure harriers, crossed with foxhound blood. They are duly entered in the harrier Stud-book. As regards quality, this is quite one of the first-rate packs, considered from the point of view of the powers that be, presiding over the harrier classes at Peterborough Hound Show, where Mr. Quare's are distinguished and repeated prize-takers. From about 1830 to 1892 the late

Mr. Vigne, a fine sportsman of the old school, was at the head of this pack, and showed good sport in the country about Epping Forest, where, by the way, these hounds have still permission to hunt. [1]

ALDENHAM HARRIERS

MEET AT NO MAN'S LAND, NEAR ST. ALBANS

Kent, with ten packs, is well to the fore, proving incontestably that hare-hunting can flourish at no great distance from London. The Ashford Valley, hunting a good country, twenty miles wide by twelve miles north and south, muster twenty couples of twenty-inch hounds part of them entered in the Stud-book consisting of a cross between Southern hound and dwarf foxhound. Wire, as in many other countries, is, unfortunately, a growing trouble. The Blean, nineteen couples of pure harriers, kennelled at Bleanwood, near Canterbury, hunt a varied country

MEET OF BEXHILL HARRIERS

towards the sea, consisting of grass marshes, ordinary pasture, plough, hop gardens, and woodland. This is a comparatively new pack of harriers, which has developed from beagles, which, in turn, had as predecessors, from 1853 to 1883, a pack kept by the neighbouring farmers. The Fordcombe, with kennels near Tunbridge Wells, are a small pack of nineteen-inch, pure harriers, numbering ten or eleven couples and hunting a beautiful and varied country, partly in Kent, partly in Sussex. The Foxbush, hunting about Sevenoaks, Tonbridge, Hadlow, and Penshurst, is quite one of the first-rate modern packs. Mr. C. Middleton Kemp, of Foxbush, near Tonbridge, has mastered and hunted these hounds since 1883. They were first started as a foot-pack, and although one or two privileged mounted folk may occasionally be seen out, this pack has been hunted on foot down to the present time. Sixteen couples of eighteen to nineteen-inch Stud-book harriers are kennelled at Foxbush. They are quite a first-rate type of the modern harrier, have been frequently successful at Peterborough, and show capital sport. Mr. Kemp, himself the Editor of the Harrier and Beagle Stud-book, is an enthusiast in hare-hunting. He, unfortunately, gave up hounds after the season of 1902-3, and will, needless to say, be much missed from a country which he has hunted so successfully during so long a period. The West Kent, with kennels at St. Mary Cray, muster fifteen couples of twenty-inch dwarf foxhounds. Their territory lies within the limits of the West Kent and Old Surrey foxhounds, where, unfortunately, a good deal of wire is to be found troubling .all classes of hunting-men. Mr. Mercer's pack, hunting from Rodmersham, near Sittingbourne, have a nice country between Faversham and Rainham. They number twenty couples of twenty-inch Stud-book harriers. The Romney Marsh, twenty and a half couples of mixed foxhound and Stud-book harrier bitches, ranging from twenty to twenty-one inches, have a fine territory of their own, consisting chiefly of maritime marsh pasture. The kennels are at Brookland, and the late Master, Mr. Thomas Bayden, hunted his own hounds. [2] The Thanet and West Street harriers are two neighbouring packs, also hunting near the sea. Both, curiously enough, consist of twenty-one-inch dwarf foxhound bitches. Lord Decies masters and hunts the Thanet; while Mr. J. E. Allen is Master, and Mr. A. Ffrench Blake the huntsman, of the West Street pack, which until 1902 had been hunted for some seasons by the Earl of Guilford. Both are pleasant countries, somewhat troubled, however, by wire. The Sandhurst is a fine old-fashioned looking pack of genuine Southern harriers, fifteen couples in number, and ranging in standard from nineteen to twenty inches. Hunting the Weald of Kent they are kennelled at Boxhurst Farm, Sandhurst. Mr. James Farley, of Forge House, Ticehurst, is Master and huntsman. The country is a fair one, little troubled by wire, and comprising pasture, plough, and woodland in about equal proportions.

Surrey is by no means strong in harriers, the only pack hunting in that goodly county being the Ripley and Knaphill, with kennels at Worplesdon, near Guildford. Mr. Echlin, the Master, hunts his own hounds, and is assisted by his wife, who whips to him, with the aid of a kennel huntsman. The pack consists of seventeen couples of twenty-one-inch dwarf foxhounds, which hunt a country consisting in great part of rough, heathy common-land. The Ripley and Knaphill are a pack with a history, having been first established so far back as the end of the eighteenth century by the Rev. Onslow, in whose family they were maintained till about thirty years ago.

Sussex, with eight packs, has fully its fair share of hare-hunting; still, in this wide county, there is plenty of room for at least another half-dozen packs. In the most easterly part of the county a foot-pack, the Guestling foot-harriers, are to be found hunting. They show, I believe, very good sport. The Bexhill I have already said something about. Hunting a most pleasant country, partly the good grass marshes of Pevensey Level, partly undulating land, consisting of grass, plough, and woodland, they are well stocked with hares and show excellent sport. The pack, consisting of seventeen and a half couples of twenty-one-inch black and tan hounds, is a blend of the old Southern harrier with a strain of bloodhound and perhaps the least trace of foxhound, They have a very fine deep cry, first-rate noses - as, indeed, they ought to have - and plenty of pace. These qualities ensure that they shall be successful harriers; they are well handled, and kill a large number of hares each season. Mr. P. H. Trew, the present Master, tells me that in the late Mr. Brook's time, when the pack were all Southern harriers, these hounds hunted very well so long as they were left alone. If, however, a whip was cracked, they would sneak away and were of little or no use for an hour or two. Former writers speak of the timidity of the old-fashioned harrier, and, where the ancient blood remains pure, it is, I think, incontestable that harriers can stand 'much less whip than foxhounds. This is a point worth remembering by budding Masters of harrier packs. Adjacent neighbours of the Bexhill are the Hailsham foot-harriers, which hunt the western half of Pevensey Marshes and a large area of country round Hailsham, including the South Downs above Eastbourne. These hounds, numbering twenty couples of nineteen-inch harriers, are bred largely from Southern hound blood, with some faint trace of the modern harrier cross. They are a typical, old-fashioned, English harrier pack, having a grand cry, first-rate noses, and plenty of pace. Kennelled at Hailsham, they are the property of Mr. Holland Southerden, who was for some years Master of the pack, and at present lends his aid as Deputy-master. Mr. Alexander Campbell, the present Master, hunts them himself, assisted by a kennel huntsman and whip. The pack dates back to 1823, when Mr. R. King-Sampson, of Hailsham, first hunted both hare and fox. Mr. Algernon Pitcher afterwards had them, and hunted hare only. To him succeeded the late Mr. Robert Overy, a yeoman-farmer of Hailsham, who hunted them many years. In Mr. Overy's time the pack consisted chiefly of large Southern harriers, standing as much as twenty-two to twenty-four inches in height. Mr. Overy relinquished hunting some ten years ago, when Mr. Southerden assumed the Mastership, built new kennels, and with much care and judgment re-modelled the pack upon its present lines. Some of the best sport in Sussex is provided by these hounds, which hunt three days a week. It is a real pleasure to hunt in this Hailsham country, which is full of hares, and where never a hunting-day passes without good sport. The Brighton harriers have been an institution for some generations. At present they are mastered by Major H. V. Welch, who is his own huntsman. These hounds consist of twenty couples of twenty-inch Stud-book harriers. They are fast, show good sport, and upon the open Downs account for a large number of hares. Brighton and its neighbourhood also supports a pack of foot harriers, the Sussex County, which

From a photograph by G. E. Swain, Bexhill

THE BEXHILL HARRIERS

hunt two days a week. The Brookside, next-door neighbours to the Brighton harriers, hunted an area of about ten square miles of country in the vicinity of Rottingdean, where they were kennelled. This country is partly down, partly arable land, and is unvexed by wire. For many years this excellent pack had been in the possession of the Beard family, the last Master, Mr. Steyning Beard, having controlled them since 1870. Resigning at the end of 1901-2, Mr. Beard was succeeded by Mr. E. Helme, who hunted the pack himself. [3] These hounds consisted of twenty-five couples of twenty-one-inch cross-bred harriers (entered in the harrier Studbook), which showed capital sport. The Iping harriers, hunting a beautiful country about Midhurst, formerly hunted over by the defunct Goodwood foxhounds, consist of eighteen and a half couples of twenty-one-inch pure foxhounds. They were established in 1893, and are owned by Sir Edward Hamilton, of Iping House, whose son, Mr. E. A. W. Hamilton, acts as Master.

Proceeding along the South Coast we come, just before the Hampshire border, to Lady Gifford's harriers, which hunt from Old Park, Chichester. Lady Gifford is one of the few ladies who hunt as well as master their own hounds. First getting together a pack of harriers in Northumberland in 1894, she migrated South in 1897, and took up her present quarters. Her pack consists of twenty-three and a half couples of seventeen-inch harriers, which, in the varied country about Chichester, afford excellent sport. Hunting is a tradition in the Gifford family. An old Lord Gifford is said to have been the original of Lord Scamperdale in "Sponge's Sporting Tour." A brother of the present Lord Gifford hunted the Berkeley hounds a few years since; and the Hon. Maurice Gifford, despite the loss of an arm in the Matabele war, is a devoted foxhunter.

Crossing into Hampshire, we reach the country of the Chilworth and Stoneham harriers, with kennels at Chilworth, near Romsey. These hounds muster twenty-five couples of twenty-one- to twenty-two-inch dwarf foxhounds. They hunt a good country within the borders of the Hursley, Hambledon, and H.H. foxhounds. Master Bob Podmore has for the last two seasons (1901-3) been the nominal head of a pack of harriers in the Vine country, of which his father, Mr. E. B. Podmore, was Master. Mr. Podmore himself hunted both packs of hounds. Master Podmore is, I suppose, the only schoolboy in England filling the high office of Master of Harriers. His pack numbers twelve couples of twenty-and-a-half-inch hounds. The kennels were at Overt on, near Basingstoke. As Mr. E. B. Podmore has migrated from the Vine to the Cotswold, it is to be supposed that his son's harriers will no longer hunt in Hampshire. The Isle of Wight shows one harrier establishment - "The Isle of Wight," a private pack, maintained at his own expense by Mr. F. T. Mew, of Newport, with kennels at White waits Wootton Common. The pack consists of fifteen couples of harriers, bred mainly from the Taunton Vale, Seavington, and Mr. Chorley's strains. They hunt two days a week over a varied country, consisting of plough, grass, moor, and downland. It is not very unusual for a hare to run the seashore.

Dorsetshire has, apparently, no single pack of harriers of its own, surely a strange phenomenon! Here, in a sporting country, with plenty of rough, wild land in places, one would have thought a pack or two of hare hounds would have been an absolute necessity of existence!

Berkshire is another county in the South of England which is, though it assuredly ought not to be, innocent of the merry harrier. This used not to be a reproach to Berkshire, and one hopes that hare hunting may, ere long, reappear in the royal county. Passing to Wiltshire, one finds only one pack of harriers hunting in this large county. This is the Netheravon, consisting of twelve couples of eighteen-inch pure harriers - entered in the Stud-book - kennelled at Netheravon, near Salisbury. This is a private pack, owned and hunted by Mr. A. E. Hussey, who established it in 1899. The Netheravon hunt over the country of the Tedworth foxhounds, consisting of about half pasture, the remainder plough, with a very small percentage of woodland. It is a pleasing fact to record that there is no wire in this excellent territory.

We now come to the two great Western counties; I mean Somerset and Devon, which may be looked upon, with Kent and Sussex, as the chief strongholds of harriers and hare-hunting south of the Trent. Somerset, with nine packs, does very well, though the old English harrier is not so much in evidence there as it used to be. The Bath and County pack, with kennels at Claverton, muster twenty-one couples of Stud-book harriers (twenty-inch), hunting two days a week. They hunt a very nice country, two-thirds of it grass, the remainder plough, in a district lying east of Bath, in Somersetshire, Gloucestershire, and Wiltshire, most of it within the limits of the Duke of Beaufort's territory. The Cotley is a fine, old-fashioned pack of pure English harriers, which have been in the families of Deane and Eames for more than a hundred years. Mr. Edward Eames, of Broad Oak, near Chard, is the present Master and huntsman. His pack numbers seventeen and a half couples of twenty-one-inch hounds, which hunt two days a week. Their territory lies in Somerset, Devon, and Dorsetshire; it consists of rough, strongly-banked, hilly country, with a good deal of downland. Wire is increasing. No foxhounds own this country, and the Cotley hunt both hare and fox. Hares, one is sorry to find, are decreasing, while foxes are on the increase. Upon the oft-debated point whether it is a good or a bad thing for harriers to hunt fox occasionally I shall touch in the chapter on "Hound Management." Mr. Eames tells me his is a fair scenting country. Among other notes of interest, to which I shall refer in later chapters, he says: "For hunting a hare there is nothing like a pure harrier; where you hunt both hare and fox, an occasional dash of foxhound blood is desirable, to give the pack stamina. My lot are the old English harrier; they are hard to beat for nose, and they can go a good pace. I have a very slight strain of foxhound in some of them now, as we find foxes getting more plentiful and hares decreasing; our hill foxes take a lot of killing, and you must have strong hounds to do it." It would be a pity so it seems to a harrier-man if this good, old hare-hunting pack, with its record of well over a century, should be gradually transformed into a foxhound establishment. I am a keen admirer of fox-hunting, and enjoy the sport as much as any man; but with one hundred and sixty-six packs, we are surely well enough stocked with foxhounds in England at the present day.

The Minehead, a West Somerset pack, with kennels at Minehead, consists of fifteen couples of twenty-inch cross-bred harriers, and takes the field two days a week under the mastership of Mr. L. E. Bligh, who carries the horn. They hunt over a mixed country, chiefly in the territories of the Devon and Somerset staghounds and the West Somerset and Exmoor foxhounds. Mr. Holt Needham's, with kennels at Galhampton, near Bath, number twenty-two couples of eighteen and a half -inch harriers, mostly pure-bred. They hunt a country of about fourteen square miles in East Somerset, almost entirely consisting of pasture, with but 5 per cent, plough. The Quarme hunt over a large area in Somerset and North Devon, in a fine wild district, consisting mainly of pasture and moorland, uncontaminated by wire. This country lies within the borders of the Devon and Somerset staghounds and the West Somerset, Exmoor, and Dulverton foxhounds. The kennels are at Exford, the nearest station being Dulverton, twelve miles distant. Few packs of hounds are more remote from a station than this, at all events in England. The pack consists of sixteen couples of eighteen and a half-inch pure harriers, which are entered in the harrier and beagle Stud-book. Mr. Morland Greig, the present Master, himself carries the horn, and has done since 1900, in which year the hounds were presented to him by the late Mr. W. L. Chorley, who had maintained them at Quarme for forty years. Mr. Chorley himself bought the hounds at the sale of the effects of the late Captain Evered, of Stone Lodge, Exton, Somerset. The Seavington has a large area of country in Somerset and Dorset, over which it hunts two days a week. The pack consists of fourteen and a half couples of twenty-inch pure harriers and cross-bred hounds, and is kennelled at Seavington, near Ilminster. The country is an excellent one, chiefly in the Blackmore Vale, Cattistock, and Taunton Vale foxhound region, with flying fences and wide ditches. The Stainton Drew, a pasture country in North Somerset, with some moorland on the Mendips, is hunted two days a week by a mixed pack of twenty-one and a half-inch foxhounds and harriers, seventeen couples strong. The Taunton Vale have a nice country of mixed pasture and plough, which they hunt two days a week. Eighteen couples of twenty-inch harriers compose the pack. The Weston harriers hunt a big country to themselves, untouched by foxhounds and scarcely vexed even by wire. The pack consists of twenty couples of twenty-inch pure harriers, kennelled at Springfield, Worle. The Wells Subscription harriers complete the list of Somersetshire packs. These harriers consist of eighteen couples of twenty to twenty-one inch pure harriers and foxhounds, kennelled at Coxley, near Wells. They hunt, two days a week, a mixed country, over an area of ten miles round the ancient town of Wells, the greater part of it pasture land, half of it on the Mendips, where stone walls are plentiful. Like the Cotley, these harriers hunt fox as well as hare. The pack is mastered by Mr. L. B. Beauchamp, who hunts them himself and receives a subscription.

Wherever you turn in beautiful Devon, with its fourteen packs of harriers, its ancient traditions of hare hunting, and its kennels of pure English hare hounds, showing, so many of them, strong traces of the old Southern hound blood, you are almost certain to find excellent sport. I am not able to devote a fourth part of the space I should like to Devon and its harriers, but a brief summary may give the reader some idea of the wealth of this county in old English harriers and first-rate hare-hunting. I have already mentioned Sir John Heathcoat Amory's pack in North Devon. These, which undoubtedly show some of the purest blood in England, consist of seventeen and a half couples of twenty and a half-inch pure harriers - all white or badger-pied - with kennels at Collipriest, Tiverton, and hunt a big country, 50 per cent. pasture, 35 per cent. plough, and 15 per cent. moorland. Mr. Carew hunts the pack two days a week, and Mr. Ludovic Heathcoat Amory whips to him. The farmers are very fond of hunting and preserve plenty of hares, which are very stout and afford first-rate sport. The Ashburton, fifteen couples of nineteen and a half-inch pure harriers, possess a sporting country in South Devon, the bulk of it moorland, with big stone walls and banks, the remainder pasture, plough, and woodland. Mr. Wilson Ranson, the Master, hunts the pack, which is kennelled at Rew, near Ashburton, and goes out twice a week. The Axe Vale country lies in East Devon, and extends just over the edge of Dorset. The pack consists of thirteen couples of harriers (twenty-one-inch), which, mastered by Mr. J. I. Scarborough, are hunted two days a week. These harriers now hunt fox as well as hare, and, during the season 1902-3, had killed, down to the end of February, seven brace of the former quarry. The Barnstaple and North Devon, mastered and hunted by Captain Paterson, assisted by Mr. Clarke, show good sport twice a week, over a wild, rough country, much of it moorland, with a good deal of pasture. Hares are stout and plentiful, and an occasional wild red deer, which has wandered from Exmoor, affords at times a right good hunt. The pack consists of twelve couples of cross-bred hounds (twenty-one-inch), kennelled at Sowden, near Barnstaple. The Culm Vale are a pack of foot-harriers, kennelled at Craddock, Cullompton, North-east Devon. They number fourteen couples of seventeen-inch pure harriers (entered in the harrier Stud-book), and take the field under the Master, Mr. C. Chester-Master, who hunts them himself, on Wednesdays, with an occasional by-day. Their country lies partly in Devon, partly in Somerset, in territory for the most part hunted by the Tiverton and East Devon foxhounds. The pack was established so recently as 1900. The Dart Vale comprise twenty couples of twenty-one-inch pure harriers, mastered by Mr. Leigh Densham, who hunts the pack himself. The kennels are at Staverton, four miles from Totnes. The Dart Vale country lies chiefly within the territories of the Dartmoor and Mid Devon foxhounds, in which, happily for all parties, wire is non-existent. The Furlong harriers have a big country, twelve miles wide by twenty miles north and south. Half of this is moorland, the remainder grass and plough. The pack consists of ten couples of nineteen-inch pure harriers, kennelled at Furlong, near Chagford. These harriers have a long history, having been maintained by the Bragg family, which till lately owned them, for many generations. In 1878 Mr. G. A. Bragg, of Forder, Moreton Hampstead, had the misfortune to lose his pack by dumb madness, after which he got together a pack of foxhounds which he hunted for ten or eleven seasons. In 1892 his nephew, Mr. William Bragg, returned from India, settled at Furlong, where the family have been established three hundred years, and started a fresh pack of harriers, naming it after the family place. [4] The Haldon comprises a large and a good country in South Devon, measuring about twenty miles by ten, which runs from the coast between Torquay and Paignton to the River Kenn and ranges up to within three and a half miles of Exeter. Teignmouth, Dawlish, Bovey, Chudleigh, and Newton are within this area, which is hunted over by the South Devon and Mid Devon packs of foxhounds. Formerly known as the Chudleigh, the pack was moved to Kingsteignton and called the Haldon. In 1897 Mr. Baron D. Webster, the present Master, bought the pack and now hunts from kennels at Oakford Lawn, Kingsteignton, Newton Abbot. The hounds consist of fifteen couples of twenty-one-inch pure harriers, mostly old English red or hare-pied, of which I have already made some mention. Few packs are believed to be more free from foxhound strain, or from any appearance of it. Mr. Webster hunts two days a week; his country consists of pasture and plough in equal proportions, with stretches of moorland ("The Haldons"), now somewhat invaded by barbed wire, and some heavy woodland at Ugbrook, Milber, Luscombe, and elsewhere.

The Modbury, consisting of eighteen couples of twenty-inch pure harriers, with kennels at Modbury, Ivybridge, hunt a big country, twenty miles square in the territory of the Dartmoor foxhounds. They have been established some fifty years, the present Master, Mr. W. Gage-Hodge, hunting the pack two days a week, with an occasional bye-day. Pasture, plough, and moorland are all found within the limits of the Hunt, and little wire exists. Mr. Netherton's is yet another South Devon pack, hunting a country about twelve miles square, between the Dart and Avon, south of Totnes. One-third of the area lies on Dartmoor, elsewhere there is a good deal of plough, with a small proportion of grass, and a fair amount of woodland. These hounds, which consist of fourteen couples of pure harriers (twenty-one-inch), have a very ancient history, having been in the hands of the Netherton family, it is said, since the fifteenth century. Mr. L. R. Netherton, of Bowden House, Stoke Fleming, Dartmouth, has mastered the pack since 1868 and acts as his own huntsman. It is a pleasure to record that there is no wire in the Netherton country.

The Silverton harriers are another old-fashioned Devonshire pack, which were established as far back as the end of the eighteenth century. Mr. T. Webber had them for many years - 1863-1895 - and in his time they were of that slate-grey and hare colouring, which I have already mentioned elsewhere. The pack now consists of sixteen and a half couples of twenty-inch pure harriers, which hunt two days a week over a fine grass country round Bradninch, where the kennels are situate. The East Devon foxhounds hunt over the portion of the county lying east of the river Culme. Mr. John Rowell, of Bradninch, is Master and huntsman. The South Molton - twelve couples of nineteen-inch pure harriers, kennelled at South Molton - hunt over a wild moorland country in North Devon and Somerset, lying within the limits of the Exmoor and West Somerset foxhounds. The South Pool harriers (Mr. H. F. Brunskill's) number twenty-four couples of nineteen-inch harriers, which, with kennels at Buckland-Tout-Saints, hunt three days a week a broken and varied country within a radius of ten or twelve miles from Kingsbridge. This country consists of mingled grass and plough with some woodland. It is hilly, with small enclosures, and is happily untroubled by wire. No foxhounds hunt over the South Pool territory. Mr. Sperling's, otherwise known as the Lamerton, (eighteen couples of eighteen-inch pure harriers,) kennelled at Lamerton, near Tavistock, hunt two days a week over a wide and strong country, fortified by big banks and walls, lying in West Devon and Cornwall, in the territory hunted over by the Lamerton foxhounds. This country is mainly pasture and moorland, and wire is not obtrusive.

In Cornwall, to complete the tour of England proper, are to be found three packs of harriers, hunting over much of the wild, solitary moorland country of that remote and beautiful extremity of this island. The Fowey, with kennels at Par Moor, possess a very wide territory along the northern coast line of the county, thirty miles long by seven wide. This comprises pasture, plough, and some moorland. The Four Burrow foxhounds hunt over a portion of this country, which has little, if any, wire. The pack comprises thirteen couples of twenty-one-inch pure harriers, which hunt two days a week. Mr. J. de C. Treffry, the Master, is his own huntsman. Mr. Baron Lethbridge's harriers, a private pack, established by the Master in 1888, carry on their operations in a fine wild country, also in North Cornwall, comprising much of the

Bodmin and West Moors. Wire is said to be, unfortunately, on the increase, The pack, kennelled at Tregeare, Egloskerry, where the Master resides, consists of eighteen couples of eighteen-inch pure harriers, entered in the Studbook. They hunt two days a week, Mr. Lethbridge carrying the horn. The Trethill is another Cornish pack, hunting in the south-east of the county, between Rame Head and St. German's, with kennels at Trethill, near St. German's. Fifteen couples of seventeen-inch pure harriers compose the pack, which hunt on Wednesdays and Saturdays under the mastership of Major J. D. A. Roberts, who owns the hounds and is his own huntsman. This may be styled a foot-pack, and mounted followers are not encouraged. The country comprises mostly plough and pasture, with a portion of the fine Liskeard moors and some big woods. It is hilly and enclosed with high banks, and, unfortunately, a good deal of barbed wire is to be found in places. Hares are plentiful, especially near the large woodlands.

Here concludes my survey of English packs. I now pass on to Wales, Ireland, and Scotland.

[1] Since these lines were written, I regret to learn that these harriers have been given up.
[2] Mr. Bayden to the deep regret of many friends died suddenly this year (1903).
[3] The Brookside Harriers have been recently given up. The country is now to be amalgamated with that of the Brighton Harriers, and for the future Major Welch, Master of that pack, will hunt the whole. The style of his hounds will, henceforth, be "The Brighton and Brookside Harriers."
[4] Mr. Bragg has recently had to retire on account of ill-health, and Mr. L. T. S. Newberry is now Master of this pack.

Chapter Nine - Sport in Wales, Ireland, and Scotland

WALES

WALES, as I have said, has always been a good hare hunting, as it is a good otter-hunting, country; and it is a pleasure to find these two sports, as well as foxhunting, still flourishing there. Wire is, however, a constant and an increasing trouble in many parts of the Principality, and it will be probably found, in the long run, that the small occupiers of Wales will be more difficult to deal with in this respect than the farmers and graziers of England, with their larger holdings and wider views. Whatever the future may have for mounted packs in Wales, foot-harriers and beagles will, it is certain, find hunting-ground there for many generations yet to come.

First in order among the Welsh harrier packs now in existence, I take the Anglesey, which have a history dating from about the year 1856, when the late Major Hampton Lewis hunted part of the country. Since 1871 the pack has been a subscription one, hunting nearly the whole of Anglesey. The country consists of about two-thirds pasture and one-third plough. Wire is somewhat of a difficulty. The pack, kennelled at Tyndonan, Llangefni, consists of twenty couples of cross-bred hounds (twenty-one-inch), some of them entered in the harrier Stud-book. They hunt two days a week, with an occasional by-day after Christmas. Once a week a deer is hunted. Mr. J. Rice, the present Master, has held office since 1891. The Brecon harriers have been in existence some thirty-two years. They hunt both hare and fox, taking the field twice a week. The pack, with kennels at Brecon, consists of sixteen and a half couples of cross-bred

From a photograph by Elliott & Fry, Baker Street, W.

THE CRICKHOWELL HARRIERS

Stud-book harriers (nineteen and a half to twenty and a half inch). These hounds hunt a rough wild country, half moorland, the rest pasture and plough. It is not considered a good scenting country, and hares and foxes are alike stout, the foxes notably so, holing in rocky fastnesses, which render them hard to bring to hand. The pack is a subscription one, and the subscriptions reach about 150 per annum. The Crickhowell country consists of an area of about eight square miles in the south of Brecknockshire. Most of this is wild sheep-walk, with a small proportion of grass and plough. There is not much wire. The pack, a subscription one, comprises sixteen couples of seventeen to eighteen-inch Stud-book harriers, which are kennelled at Crickhowell, seven miles from Abergavenny. Mr. J. A. Doyle has mastered the hounds since 1889, having acted as joint Master from 1887 to that year. This pack is hunted on foot. The Glanyrafon are a private pack, established in 1863, and owned and mastered by Mr. Edward Bennett, of Glanyrafon, Llanidloes, Montgomeryshire. They number eleven and a half couples of eighteen-inch pure harriers, which hunt three days a week. The country consists of "bleak hills, intersected by cultivated valleys." Wire exists, but it is well marked. The country is innocent of foxhounds. Mr. Lloyd Price's hounds, which hunt in mid and northern Carmarthenshire, have been in existence since 1853, when they were established by the late Colonel Jones, of Velindre, who hunted them for thirty-seven years. Upon the death of Colonel Jones, in 1890, Mr. Lloyd Price bought the hounds and has mastered and hunted them ever since. The pack consists of seventeen couples of eighteen-inch pure harriers, which are kennelled at Bryn Cothi, Nantgaredig, South Wales, the residence of the Master. They hunt two days a week. The country comprises pasture, much moorland, a little plough, and a considerable area of woodland. Hares, which are very stout, are short in number, and wire is unpleasantly abundant. Mr. Lloyd Price has instituted a number of wickets, however, which allow passage through the hateful obstacle.

The Merthyr Old Court is a small private pack of Welsh harriers, seven couples in number, which hunt twice a week from the Chase, Merthyr Tydvil, where the Master, Major L. P. Jones, resides. The Mostyn and Talacre is, I believe, a new pack, established at the beginning of the season, 1902-3. Certainly it has never before appeared in any harrier list. Lord Mostyn and Sir Piers Mostyn are joint Masters, Lord Mostyn carrying the horn. Thirteen and a half couples of seventeen and a half to eighteen-inch harriers compose the pack, which is kennelled at Mostyn Hall, Mostyn, North Wales. The Mostyns have always been a great hunting family. Sir Thomas Mostyn, who hunted the Bicester and Warden Hill foxhounds from 1800 to 1831, is still remembered in Warwickshire, Northants, and Oxfordshire, and the Masters of this new Flintshire pack are pretty certain to provide good sport in the country round Mostyn Hall. The Plas Machynlleth is yet another private pack, hunting in North Wales, and owned by Lord Henry Vane Tempest. The hounds, numbering ten couples of eighteen-inch pure-bred harriers, take the field twice a week, with David Hughes as huntsman. The Plas Machynlleth is chiefly a mountain country, with a good deal of wall and fence to negotiate. It lies in Montgomeryshire and Cardiganshire, and has an area of some ten miles by five. A cob is described as the best nag for the district, but the foot-hunter can usually see almost as much of the sport as the mounted man. Lord Henry Vane Tempest may be said to do his duty manfully in the way of providing sport for his neighbours. In addition to hunting hare on Tuesdays and Fridays with this pack, he maintains a small pack of ten couples of hounds which pursue the fox on Mondays and Thursdays, the same huntsman officiating with both packs.

Mr. Vaughan Pryse, of Bwlchbychan, Llanybyther, South Wales, is one of the oldest supporters of harriers, I suppose, in the Principality. Now in his eighty-third year, he not only masters a pack of harriers, which he established so far back as 1858, but hunts them himself, and has done so for forty-three seasons. This is something like enthusiasm for the noble science! Mr. Vaughan Pryse's country, which lies in the shires of Cardigan and Carmarthen, consists of pasture, plough, and moorland. It has, unhappily, been of late years sadly spoiled by wire and wire netting, which latter is run along the tops of the banks. The pack consists of twenty-three couples of eighteen and a half-inch Stud-book harriers, which show only a remote cross of the foxhound.

Mrs. Pryse-Rice, of Llwyn-y-brain, Llandovery, who owns a pack of harriers in South Wales, is another among the very few ladies in the kingdom, who not only master but hunt their own hounds. Her country lies in Carmarthenshire and Brecknockshire, and consists of moor, pasture, and woodland, with a little arable land. On the hills a good deal of wire is to be found, but not much of it is barbed. Mrs. Pryse-Rice's pack was established in 1894, when her husband gave up fox-hunting. It consists of twenty couples of twenty-inch Stud-book harriers, which hunt hare and fox twice a week. This is a very smart pack; Mrs. Pryse-Rice has been frequently successful with her hounds at Peterborough. Sport is good, the pack is everywhere welcome, and although wire exists the farmers will usually take it down when asked to do so.

Wales is a country of private packs, and the Roath Court is yet another of those owned and maintained entirely by the Master. These hounds hunt in Glamorganshire, within the country hunted by Lord Tredegar's and the Glamorgan foxhounds. Mr. Charles Williams, of Roath Court, Cardiff, the Master, established the pack as far back as 1862, and has maintained them ever since. His hounds number eighteen couples of twenty-inch cross-bred harriers, which take the field two days a week.

IRELAND

In the Sister Island sport of every kind is pursued even more enthusiastically than in this country, and from thirty to thirty-one packs of harriers are usually in existence. Many of these packs are as smart and as workmanlike as the best of those on the eastern side of St. George's Channel, but here and there, in remote parts, you may still chance to light upon queer, go-as-you-please establishments, which remind one that the ways and customs so humorously described by Charles Lever and Miss Edgeworth are not quite extinct. Reduced gentlemen and squireens, whose packs are not recorded in Baily's or the "Field" Hound List, still keep a few couples of hounds, and entertain their guests with impromptu hunts, very much after the

From a photograph by Jones & Harper, Ludlow
MRS. PRYSE-RICE AND HER HARRIERS

fashion of Sir Harry Scattercash, in "Sponge's Sporting Tour," in pursuit of fox, hare, or any other kind of quarry that maybe found available.

I was talking with a friend, no great while since, on the subject of kennel and hound management among harrier packs in Ireland. "Don't pry too closely into these things," he replied; "I have known packs of harriers which thought themselves well housed in a ruined stable, and where the hounds scavenged for their food just wherever they could pick it up." That is, of course, a libel upon most of the Irish packs of harriers, but still it is undoubted that, whether in fox-hunting or in the chase of the hare, things are not always conducted in quite so orthodox a fashion as we are accustomed to over here. For one thing it is the custom of the country, and for another money is not so plentiful. Even in England and Wales, some of the smaller packs of harriers, and foxhounds, too, are not always managed on the grand scale. It is impossible that they should be.

I have, among the correspondence I have acquired during the preparation of this volume, some notes by a gentleman - one of the best all-round sportsmen I have ever met - who has in his time tested every phase of sport in Ireland, and an extract may, perhaps, give some idea of the more unorthodox methods I have hinted at. "I have forgotten," he says, "the year I took over the --- harriers, but it must have been about 1873 or 1874. I absolutely knew nothing about hounds at the time, but I was talked into it by men who didn't care a rap what sort of master they had, so long as they got some one to keep the thing going for the 100 a year which was promised. The first pack I got together were composed principally of an extremely nondescript lot I bought from a man at Longford who shall be nameless. They had evidently been used to run drag, and were a wild, quarrelsome lot of brutes. Added to these, drafts from two or three kennels made up a pack which only an ignoramus like myself would have fed for two days. How I got through that season I don't know, but I hope my subscribers liked it! Next season I made a somewhat better effort and bought a pack from a Mr. Blennerhassett, from somewhere in Kerry. There were really some very nice hounds in this lot, more than a half being a sort of badger-pied, evidently a cross with the Kerry beagle; but they were really good hunters, and I managed to account for a good many hares with them before parting with the hounds three years later. After an interval of two seasons I again took the hounds, but as the late master had not kept them up in any sort of way I shot most of them and started afresh. This time I went in for small foxhounds, getting them chiefly from the Duke of Buccleugh's pack and the Fife, then in the hands of Capt. Anstruther Thomson.

"For some seasons I got some very handsome under-sized hounds from the latter and had with them really very fair sport; and as we were always prepared, as some sporting correspondent says, to hunt anything, from an elephant to a flea, we had some rather curious experiences. One of the most amusing hunts we had was after a greyhound, on whose line I clapped the pack; the dog made a point for home and saved his scut by getting to ground in his master's cabin. I don't know if I am wise in telling you how I arranged some very good sport with dogs? When I wanted a good gallop, which was not very seldom, I either got a dog hired, or sometimes, when the owner was obdurate, borrowed one from some four or five miles away from where we wanted a hunt. The dog was taken across country to the meet, put into a sack in which ferrets had been lying for a week or so. He was kept thus for, say, half an hour, pretty well frightened, then turned out at the appointed time in some wood close by, and after letting him get a fair start, I used to draw the wood for a fox. It was quite wonderful how and with what speed the dog used to make his way home; he seemed to avoid human beings, and it was difficult for any one not in the know to believe they were not hunting a fox. I used to tell the field we were sure to find in that particular wood, and my prophecy on these occasions always came off triumphantly."

I do not publish these "Experiences of an Irish M.H." by any means as holding them up for imitation by embryo masters of hounds, but as a picture of what still goes on in the Sister Isle, and perhaps even elsewhere nearer home occasionally. These were, after all, the ebullitions of high spirits and hot youth, and my correspondent would himself be now the first to repudiate their encouragement. But, after all, "bagged dog" is little worse than "bagged fox," which is, to this hour, by no means an unknown quantity, even among solemn and reputable English packs.

Turning to more serious hunting matters, we find County Meath, the home of the finest fox-hunting in Ireland - some say in the world - supporting also three packs of harriers. Of these the Ballymacad hunt from kennels at Cross-drum, Old Castle, the residence of the Master and huntsman, Mr. E. Rotheram. Twenty-two couples of twenty-two-inch fox-hounds form the strength of this subscription pack, which hunts two days a week over a wall and ditch country situate in Meath, West Meath, and Cavan. Although classed as a harrier pack, I understand that the Ballymacad have obtained leave from the Meath Hunt to draw certain of their coverts, and now hunt chiefly fox. The Drewstown, kennelled at Drewstown, Kells, is another Meath pack, owned by Mr. G. B. McVeagh, who himself hunts them two days a week. The hounds consist of fourteen and a half couples of pure, old-fashioned, eighteen-inch harriers. They are, I am informed, an extremely nice lot of hounds, light and very fast. The country is a very good one, consisting almost entirely of grass, and extending westward beyond Meath into West Meath, and ranging in Meath itself from Kells close up to Navan. The Tara is the third pack of harriers in Meath. These hunt a fine grass country for about ten miles round about Tara, Dunsany and Navan. The kennels are at Dunsany Castle, the residence of the present Master, Lord Dunsany, who took over the hounds from Mr. W. Hope Johnstone last season. The pack consists of fifteen couples of nineteen-inch pure harriers, the majority of which are entered in the Harrier and Beagle Stud-book. This is a subscription pack, hunting two days a week. Lord Dunsany hunts his own hounds. Mr. William Dove, a first-rate, all-round sportsman, with whom I hunted big game in South Africa some years ago, was Master of the Tara harriers from 1898 to 1900, having some years before that mastered the South Mayo harriers. In both cases he hunted his own hounds. He has sent me some notes on hare hunting in Meath, which I think worth printing, as throwing a good deal of light on the character of the Irish hare. Meath, apparently, is nothing like so good a harrier as it is a fox-hunting country. Before his time the pack was mastered by Mr. G. V. Briscoe, of

Bellinter, and was known as the Bellinter. Mr. Briscoe himself was a first-rate man with harriers, and could kill a hare as handsomely as any huntsman. When Mr. Dove took over the hounds, he formed a new pack, which was called the Tara. "I bought," he says, "some Stud-book harriers from Mr. Doyne of Wells, in Wexford, whose hounds have been in his family for many years and have been bred from packs such as Lord Hopetoun's, the Anglesey, etc. ...I also bought drafts from the Aspull and Boddington packs, and altogether got together a very fine-looking lot. Mr. Henry Thomson, of Newry, kindly lent me his pack, so that I was really too full of hounds. We had very good sport, though I did not kill many hares, but that does not appear to be uncommon in Meath. As far as my recollection serves me - (this note was written from abroad) - fourteen brace of hares was about the best season I have known with the Tara harriers. Why this should be I don't know, but hares are, as a rule, bad, and dodge in and out of the big fences. A good hare was generally killed. There is a curious difference between a hare that has been hunted in Meath and one in the more open country in the west; the latter gets away smartly and keeps going, but the Meath hare runs to the first fence, dodges in and out, and seldom goes two fields away. Though we stuck as much as possible to the legitimate game, yet we came across a number of outlying foxes and had some fair runs; but as, of course, the country was not stopped they generally went soon to ground." An outlying deer was also occasionally hunted by these harriers.

County Dublin supports two packs, Mr. Brooke's and the Fingal. Mr. G. F. Brooke's pack, kennelled at Summerton, Castlenock, the residence of the Master, muster sixteen couples of twenty-and-a-half-inch Studbook harriers, which hunt two days a week. The country, which lies in the Meath

From a photograph by Elliott & Fry, Baker Street, W.
TARA HARRIERS, 1899

and Kildare Hunt territories, is a big one, extending from the Dublin Hills to Dunboyne, and from Dublin to Kilcock. Pasture and plough occupy three-fourths of the country, the rest being moorland. The Fingal, with kennels at Whitestown, Balbriggan, number sixteen couples of twenty-inch cross-bred hounds, hunting two days a week. Mr. R. T. Woods has been Master since 1881, with a subscription. The country, consisting mainly of pasture, lies in the north of County Dublin and the southern part of Meath. The Louth fox hounds hunt over this region.

Clare is another Irish county which boasts two packs of harriers. The Clare hounds, mastered by Mrs. Stacpoole, of Eden Vale, Ennis, have been more or less connected with this family since 1867, when the late Mr. Richard Stacpoole started them. He hunted these harriers until 1879-80, when the Land League stopped hunting over a great part of Ireland. The pack, consisting of eighteen couples of twenty-inch crossbred harriers, is now hunted by Mr. R. J. Stacpoole, son of the late Mr. R. Stacpoole. The country, Mr. Stacpoole tells me, is "very varied, comprising very rough crag-land, hilly country, low-lying corcass land, in which the jumping is all wide trenches, and good pasture land. The best of the country hunted over lies near the village of Six Mile Bridge." The hares in this country, although smaller than the average, are very hardy and stand up for a long time before hounds. The supply of them is fairly good, in some places too good. One of Mr. Stacpoole's best runs in recent years happened in the season of 1901-02, when, from a meet near Ennis, a hare was found which gave the pack a grand hunt, which, measured on the map, is over seven miles and three-quarters. As the country was very hilly, the distance covered could not have been less than nine miles. It is always interesting to have the opinion of Masters in varying districts, and especially Masters who hunt hounds themselves, on the subject of hound blood. Here is a note by Mr. R. J. Stacpoole, who has at different times hunted the Clare harriers for a good many seasons. "I prefer," he says, "a cross-breed between harrier and foxhound, as I think they are more hardy and do better over the rough country we have in parts of Clare. I think the pure harrier cannot stand the wear-and-tear work that the cross-bred can, and the latter seems to me to have more dash than the former. I am very fond of the black-and-tan Kerry beagle; it is a beautiful hunting hound, particularly on a poor scent, and gives splendid tongue; but it has the fault of want of dash, and it is a delicate hound generally. I have often had two or three of these hounds in my pack, and always found that they could lead the 'crossbreds on a poor scent, but with a good scent they required the latter to make them go the pace." The Clare harriers, which are a subscription pack, hunt practically the whole of Clare, which is untouched by foxhounds. No wire exists in the country.

The Derry Castle harriers have also their headquarters in Clare, at the residence - Derry Castle, Killaloe - of the Master, Captain C. W. Gartside Spaight. This pack numbers fifteen couples of twenty-inch cross-bred hounds, which hunt two days a week. Their country lies in Tipperary and part of Clare, being divided by the Shannon. It consists of a strip nineteen miles long by about five miles wide, nearly all of it pasture.

County Cork maintains three packs of harriers. Of these the Funcheon Vale, mastered and hunted by Mr. R. Grove Annesley, consists of twenty couples of twenty-inch harriers, hunting two days a week from kennels at Annesgrove, Castletownroche. The Glanmire, fourteen and a half couples of twenty-one-inch pure harriers, are kennelled at Glenmervyn, Glanmire, and

99

are hunted by Mr. R. Hall, the Master, twice a week. The third Cork pack is the Dromana, with kennels at Laurentinny, Clashmore, Youghall, mastered and hunted by Mr. G. Denneley, Junr.

The two packs of County Roscommon are the Rockingham and the Roscommon. Of these, the former, kennelled at Knockadoo, Boyle, which consist of eighteen couples of twenty-one-inch dwarf foxhound bitches, are hunted two days a week by Mr. E. S. Robinson, joint Master with Mr. A. B. Walker. The Rockingham succeeded to the Plains of Boyle harriers in 1895. They are now a subscription pack. The country is a good one, nearly all pasture, untouched by foxhounds, and having no wire. The Roscommon hunt a big pasture country, thirty-three miles by twenty, in Roscommon and Galway. About a fifth consists of moorland, while a tenth is occupied by plough and woodland. Like the Rockingham they are unvexed by wire or foxhounds. The hounds, twenty couples in strength, are kennelled at Rookwood, Athleague, and hunt two days a week.

In Down four packs are to be found, the East Down, the Newry, the Iveagh, and the North Down harriers. Of these, the East Down hunt mostly over a plough and bank country, varied by a small proportion of pasture. The kennels are at Downpatrick, and the hounds, twenty couples of nearly pure-bred nineteen-inch harriers, which find entry in the Stud-book, are hunted two days a week by Captain R. Ker, the Master. The Newry, twenty couples of twenty-two-inch cross-bred hounds, hunt two days a week in Down and Armagh. The Iveagh, kennelled at Gilford, put into the field twenty couples of eighteen-inch to nineteen-inch harriers. The North Down harriers, kennelled at Ballynickle, near Comber, consist of fifteen and a half couples of twenty-inch dwarf foxhounds, which take the field two days a week. Mr. J. B. Houston, M.P., has been Master since 1881, and the pack is hunted by Alfred Rees, a professional huntsman. The pack, which succeeded the Dufferin harriers, which had previously hunted the country for nearly twenty years, is very popular, and shows excellent sport. Mr. J. G. Allen is deputy Master.

In Louth are found the Dundalk and Littlegrange packs, each hunting two days a week. The Dundalk consist of twenty-one-inch foxhounds (twenty couples), while the Littlegrange, kennelled near Drogheda, show eleven couples of eighteen to twenty-inch pure harriers. The Dundalk hunt in Louth only; the Littlegrange in Louth and Meath.

Sligo, with the Sligo County and Mr. O'Hara's, is another two-pack county. The Sligo, seventeen and a half couples of twenty-two-inch foxhounds, hunt two days a week from Oakfield, near Sligo, under the Mastership of Lieut. - Colonel Campbell. Mr. O'Hara's, with eighteen couples of twenty-two-inch cross-bred harriers, is a private pack, hunting from Annaghmore, Collooney, where the O'Hara family have maintained hounds for generations. Both packs hunt over a good grass country and are little interfered with by wire.

Antrim is the last in my list of Irish counties maintaining two harrier packs. The Killultagh, Old Rock, and Chichester, with kennels at Crumlin, consist of twelve couples of twenty-one-inch harriers and foxhounds. They hunt over a good country, largely of old pasture, with about 25 per cent, plough. Of late years wire and a growing scarcity of hares have tended somewhat to the depreciation of sport. The Route harriers' country lies partly in Antrim, partly in Londonderry. The kennels are situate at Ballymagarry, near Portrush, where are maintained twenty-four couples of twenty-two-and-a-half-inch cross-bred hounds. Hunting is carried on two days a week, Major J. A. Montgomery acting as Master, with Captain F. J. Montgomery to carry the horn.

I now turn to a number of counties in which only one pack of harriers is to be found. In Armagh, the Tynan and Armagh take the field under the Mastership of yet another lady Master, Miss Isa McClintock, who employs a professional huntsman. These hounds, now kept by subscription, were maintained for many years as a private pack by the late Sir James Strange, Bart. The kennels at Fellows Hall, Tynan, the residence of the Master, contain fifteen and a half couples of twenty-one-inch cross-bred hounds, which hunt two days a week. Captain Brisco's harriers hunt three days a week from Clogrenane, Carlow - where they are kennelled - in Carlow, Kildare, Queen's County, and Kilkenny. The pack consists of fifteen couples of twenty-two-inch foxhounds, hunted by Captain Brisco, to whom Mrs. Brisco and the kennel huntsman act as whippers-in. In Cork the Knockmacool carry on operations from the place of that name under the Mastership of Mr. Richard Beamish, who hunts them. Fermanagh, with harriers of the same name, Kildare with Colonel Crichton's, Londonderry with the Derry, Queen's County with Mr. Moore's, Wicklow with the Shelton Abbey, Tyrone with the Seskinore, and Wexford with Mr. Doyne's, are all one-pack counties.

In Tipperary are to be found the Scarteen Beagles, a famous pack of black-and-tan hounds, which have a very ancient and most interesting history of their own.

Mr. Clement Ryan, the present Master, tells me that the ancestors of the Scarteen Beagles came originally from the South of France, and were first owned by Mr. John Ryan, of Ballyvistin, who hunted them from 1735 to 1789. His son, Thaddeus Richard, succeeded him, and hunted them until his death in 1823. During his time the family moved from Ballyvistin to Scarteen, the present family seat. John and Thaddeus Ryan never kennelled the hounds, although the latter certainly kept over twenty couples. Since 1823 the pack has always been kennelled. Upon the death of Mr. Thaddeus Ryan, his son John succeeded him, and by him the pack was hunted until the year of his death, 1863, since which time his son, the present Master, Mr. Clement Ryan, has hunted them. The pack were maintained at Scarteen until 1890, but are now kennelled at Emly House, the residence of the Master. The country was well stocked with hares until the year of the great "Foot and Mouth" epidemic, about 1873, when hares were all but exterminated. Since then Mr. Ryan has turned out several lots of hares, and there is now a fair supply. Hares in the Scarteen country seem always to have been small and hardy, and possessed of great running powers. Mr. Ryan first enlarged deer in 1884; since that time he hunts hares up to November and deer for the rest of the season.

"I prefer," says Mr. Ryan, "the beagles to any other blood, on account of their keen scent and wonderful tongue; the music of the black-and-tan pack is superior to anything you will hear elsewhere. My hounds are pure beagles, and have neither harrier nor foxhound blood, nor is there the slightest bloodhound cross in them. Their long ears, heavy jowls, and deep tongue lead people to suppose that there is a bloodhound strain; but this, emphatically, is *not* the case. They are identical with the Kerry beagle, whose origin is also French; and when I require a cross I always get it from Kerry.

"In 1870 I got four and a half couples from Sir Maurice O'Connell, of Lake View, Kerry, when he was dispersing the pack which had been for generations in the O'Connell family. In 1881 I got three couples from Chute, of Chute Hall, Kerry, who was then giving up his old family pack. The Scarteen hounds are, and always have been, black-and-tan. They are twenty-three inches high; the kennel consists of eighteen couples, and I usually hunt fifteen couples."

It is, I think, an almost unique record that, since 1735, this pack should have been hunted by four Masters only, viz., the present owner, and his father, grandfather, and great-grandfather. This gives an average of forty-two years to each Mastership. The Scarteen country is a very big one, consisting of endless grass pastures, with big banks, strengthened with stone, so wide upon the top that, as a friend remarked to me, you can almost drive a coach-and-four along. At all events, they are wide enough to afford well-used foot-paths to the country people.

As regards the Kerry beagle, my friend, Mr. W. Dove, sends me some interesting notes. He has seen them chiefly at Waterville, County Kerry. He describes them as "a big hound of about twenty-one or twenty-two inches, rather long-eared, and heavy-headed, showing a good deal of the badger-pie and black-and-tan. They seem to pick up a living anyhow, and although those I saw were supposed to belong to people living up in the mountains, yet they always seem to turn up in Waterville at some hour of the day to scavenge for a living. I am told that they are got together to hunt on Sundays. Another Sunday pack is to be found, or was a few years ago, in Ennis, County Clare; those I saw were as pretty little eighteen-inch hounds as one could wish to see. I am told that ten to fifteen couples could be got together on Sunday, and were collected by the huntsman for the day sounding his horn through the town. If the pack were all like the few couples I saw running about, they were bound to show sport."

This is a very curious and interesting phase of wild Irish sport, which, it seems to me, is worthy of mention in a book on hare-hunting. The Kerry beagle has, I am afraid, a much poorer time of it after his hunting than his well-fed brethren of England. Instead of going into a comfortable kennel to find an excellent supper, clean straw, and other luxuries ready for him, he is dismissed by the huntsman, on returning to his village, with a "Go home, ye divils!" or some such rough farewell, and slinks away, poor brute, to pick up a scratch meal as only an Irish dog knows how. Yet the good hound, with the pluck and energy of his race for he is a good-bred one hies to the summons of the horn on the next hunting-day, as eager and as keen as ever.

SCOTLAND

In Scotland, for some reason or other, hare-hunting has never obtained much foothold. At the present time no more than three packs of harriers are in existence north of the Tweed. Of these, the Aberdeenshire, mastered by Mr. G. Pirie, are kennelled at Stoneywood House, Bucksburn. Eighteen couples of twenty-inch Stud-book harriers compose the pack, which hunts two days a week over a nice country, consisting chiefly of pasture with some moorland and plough. The Cambo harriers, owned and mastered by Sir T. Erskine, of Cambo, Kingsbarn, Fife, and hunted by Mr. T. H. Erskine, number twenty couples of nineteen-inch Stud-book harriers, and hunt over arable country in the eastern portion of Fife. Wire is far too prevalent in all this locality. The Marquis of Linlithgow (until lately known as the Earl of Hopetoun) has maintained a pack of harriers in Linlithgowshire for seventeen years. Lord Linlithgow is an enthusiast in hound breeding, and, in addition to a good pack of harriers, supports a kennel of bloodhounds, and a little pack of ten-inch pocket-beagles, which hunt rabbit. The harriers, kennelled at Hopetoun House, consist of twenty-five couples of twenty-one-inch Stud-book harriers, which hunt three days a week. They are practically dwarf foxhounds, showing Belvoir colouring, and are very handsome. Their country consists of mingled pasture, plough, and woodland, a good deal of it, except upon Lord Linlithgow's own property, being troubled by wire, which is by no means well marked. Mr. Adam Cross hunts the pack.

The Lanarkshire, mastered and hunted by Captain W. B. Rankin, had, till a year or so back, kennels at Haughhead, near Hamilton, whence they hunted two days a week. They have now been given up, and a pack of beagles hunts in their stead. This country had long been hunted by harriers, Lord Hamilton of Dalzell and others having maintained hounds there. Colonel Robertson Aikman hunted the country very successfully from 1888 to 1901, sometimes alone, sometimes with a joint Master. The territory, which lies in Lanarkshire and Dumbartonshire, consists of a fair extent of pasture, with a third plough, and some moor and woodland. A good deal of wire exists, and this, no doubt, has led to the final extinction of harriers in this region, and the substitution of foot-beagles. Concerning Scottish hare-hunting Colonel Robertson Aikman sends me the following note, in answer to an inquiry of mine:

"Hare-hunting in Scotland differs little from that in England. My own experience was very good sport and good scent in Lanarkshire, which is a first-rate natural hunting country (in the northern half of the county), but is spoilt by the opening up of the mineral field. Wire fencing and railways innumerable were the consequence, and fox-hunting became impossible some twenty years ago, and now riding to any hounds is practically impossible.

"The reason there is little hare-hunting in Scotland is partly due to the fact that Scotsmen who are fond of hunting, and in a position to do so, go south for their sport, it being more plentiful there and more easily obtained. It is also partly owing to so much of Scotland being naturally unsuitable for hunting, as well as to the prevalence of wire and the importance attached to shooting."

Chapter Ten - Concerning Kennels

KENNELS, their situation, building, and management, are matters of the very highest importance in the economy of a pack of harriers. Active as hounds are in the field, and long as are their hours abroad on hunting days, they spend, after all, a very large proportion of their time in kennel, and it is, therefore, a supreme necessity that they shall be well and comfortably housed. Somervile recognised this fact, of course, and in his poem are to be found interesting passages on kennel and hound management. As to the situation, his direction can scarcely be bettered. Let it be, he says,

"Upon some little eminence erect,
And fronting to the ruddy dawn; its courts
On either hand wide opening to receive
The sun's all-cheering beams, when mild he shines,
And gilds the mountain tops."

Instead of fronting east, however, it is still better that kennels shall face south or south-east. Somervile also makes a point of shade and a stream of running water. Beckford, who devotes an excellent chapter to the subject of kennels, speaks of a little brook running through the middle of his grass court. A running stream naturally indicates damp, and a majority of modern masters of hounds would, I am convinced, be against the practice of including a running brook as part of the kennel equipment. A well and pump, or, better still, a water-pipe system and taps, if waterworks are adjacent, are far better.

Soil is a very serious consideration. Nothing is more troublesome or more difficult to eradicate than hound lameness, which, after all, is only another name for rheumatism. Hound lameness depends in very many instances, though perhaps not in all, upon the nature of the soil upon which kennels are fixed. This should not be porous; gravel and sand are above all things to be avoided. Clay is far preferable to either, and marl or chalk are, perhaps, the best of all. Mr. Otho Paget, whose beagles are well known, in an interesting note to the edition of Beckford which he edited, says: "Kennels should never be built on gravel. Clay certainly holds moisture, but at the same time it prevents any moisture rising from below. There is always water beneath gravel, and the heat of the hounds' bodies will draw it up from any depth...If kennels are already built on gravel, the floor should be taken up, the ground excavated and three feet of clay puddled in. Of course spouting should be attended to, and if there is any high ground above the kennel floor, drains should be made to carry off surface water." In place of puddling in clay, as thus suggested, I think a good foundation of concrete would be even better. Above this, again, would be a cement or asphalt flooring. As to the buildings, brick or timber are preferable to stone, which is apt to absorb moisture and is, for modest harrier kennels, an expensive luxury. Mr. Southerden, of the Hailsham Harriers, who has built his own kennels, which, having been familiar with for some years, I can pronounce entirely successful, sends me the following note: "I am greatly in favour of wooden buildings, with thatched roofs; they are drier and warmer in the winter than any other materials, while in the summer they are cooler. Outside, a coat of tar preserves the wood. My idea for size of a kennel for twenty hounds is a modern building of about fifteen feet by eight feet (Mr. Southerden has two of these kennels, one for his dog hounds the other for the bitches), with a movable bench, two feet nine inches wide, on each side, which leaves a passage of about two feet six inches, which is wide enough to enable hounds to get on and off the bench. Use only one bench at a time, so as to enable the kennel man to always have one clean, limewashed, and sweet. The bed should be composed of fresh deal shavings, if they can be procured, as they are better and more economical than wheat straw. [1] Attached there should be an enclosed run, the width of the building, and about fifteen feet in length; the whole of this space should be floored with Portland cement.

"Cleanliness is of the utmost importance, and kennels should be swept out with an abundance of water at least once a day, and occasionally a little disinfectant should be used. Always keep the floor of the kennel and the run well above the ground level, and the building should be so placed that the door should face as near south as possible, and arranged so that half, or rather more, of the upper part can be closed in bad or cold weather, leaving the bottom part open to the yard. Air must be given according to the season of year and the state of the temperature, and it is necessary to plan the building accordingly; but draught on the benches must be avoided. For fencing in a good space (the grass yard), where hounds can be let out for exercise every day while the kennel is being cleaned, I prefer stout wire netting, six feet high, to any other, as it does not obstruct the air or light."

To these remarks I should add that the lower part of the Hailsham kennel-yard fencing is protected by corrugated iron, which prevents gnawing, and is useful as affording more privacy to hounds and sheltering them from wet and wind. I append a plan of these kennels, which I may say are in every way suitable for a pack of twenty couples of harriers, managed in the modest and inexpensive, but perfectly effective, manner required for foot-hunting.

It is a good thing to have a spare kennel, into which hounds can be turned while the other kennels are being cleaned. The benches should, of course, be open i.e., made of spars for greater cleanliness, and it is recommended, and I think rightly, that they should be sparred down to the ground, so that hounds, and especially nervous hounds, shall not be able to creep under the beds of their fellows. The benches should be raised twenty or twenty-four inches from the floor. When the washing of the kennel is performed, it is advisable, after sluicing and brushing, to use a mop, so as to leave as little damp behind as possible.

The grass yard is a great feature of the kennel system. In this hounds take air and exercise when they are not out for road work, and it is, therefore, highly desirable that it should be as large as possible. It should be protected by six-feet railings, preferably open, or, as Mr. Southerden suggests, by strong wire-netting, well railed up. In order to guard against accidents, it is necessary that the kennel doors should be carefully closed, and bolts, which a servant must stop to fasten, are recommended in place of ordinary latches. A good sized feeding-house is preferable to feeding hounds outside the kennels. Here are placed the troughs, which in some establishments are made with perforated covers, which, when let down, afford a seat for the men. The boiling-house should be placed at one end of the building or even a little apart, with a yard of its own, if expense and convenience will allow it. This building should be especially well ventilated, so as to allow of the escape of steam. In it are placed

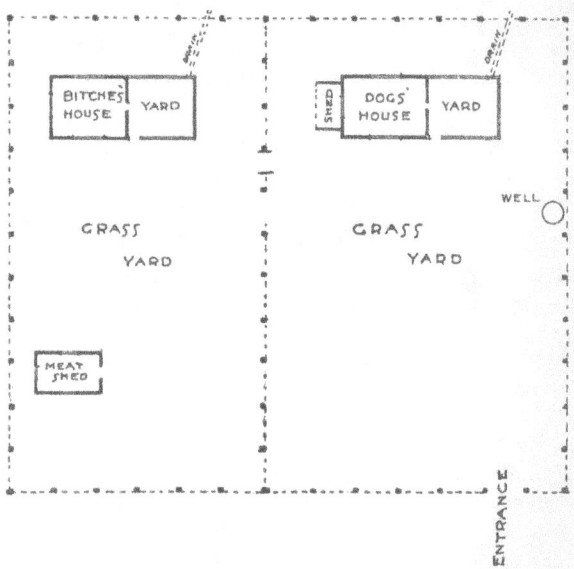

PLAN

OF INEXPENSIVE HARRIER KENNELS

TIMBER & STRAW-THATCHED.

To Accommodate 20 Couples.

Total Cost £70 to £75.

(Including Well)

NOTE. The Grass Yards are enclosed by Wood Uprights & Wire Fencing, 16 guage, 2 inch mesh.

two large boilers, preferably of cast iron, set in brickwork. One of these serves for meat, the other for meal. The size depends, of course, much upon the strength of your pack. A boiler of fifty or sixty gallons suffices for a fair-sized pack of foxhounds (forty couples). Coolers, six or eight feet in length, by four or five feet wide and one foot in depth, stand in the boiling-house. This part of the building will, of course, be floored with brick, or, preferably, asphalt or cement, and a drain inserted for the passage of blood, water, &c. In some kennels it is so arranged that, as the hounds come in from hunting, they pass to the feeding-room through a shallow foot-bath filled with warm broth, the effect of this bath being that they spend some time thereafter in licking their feet, and so healing their wounds and cleansing themselves at the same time. A bucket of hot broth to the same quantity of cold water is about the usual proportion of the bath mixture. With some of the larger and more imposing packs of harriers, it may be thought necessary to follow the foxhound plan and have a spare hunting kennel, into which the hounds, intended to hunt the next day, are drafted. An apartment to be used as an infirmary, and another in which to place such bitches as may require temporary seclusion, are also necessary. The meal should be kept in the driest place possible; a small coal-shed should not be forgotten, as well as space for straw. An open shed for hanging flesh, standing somewhere away by itself, and well fenced in, is required.

If larger and more complete kennels are thought necessary, and expense is not so much a consideration, the following accommodation may be provided:

1. Young hounds' lodging-room and court.	6. Straw court after feeding.
	7. Infirmary for sick hounds.
2. Hunting pack lodging-room and court.	8. Bitch house.
	9. Boiling-house.
3. Two principal lodging-rooms and courts.	10. Cooler-house.
	11. Coal-house.
4. Covered court before feeding.	12. Store-room for meal.
5. Feeding-room.	13. Straw house.

I give here a plan of harrier kennels, suitable for twenty-five couples of hounds.

It should be seen, of course, that the boiling-house be kept scrupulously clean, as, indeed, should every part of the kennels, and that the feeding-troughs be well scoured, and put away in their proper places when used. The feeder, who frequently, in small harrier establishments, also combines the offices of kennel huntsman and whip, should be kept carefully up to the mark in these respects, as upon him depends so much the health and well-being of the hounds. In the airing yards, it is to be remembered, should stand stone, slate, or iron drinking-vessels, in which fresh water is always to be found.

Beckford used to have a small hayrick standing in his grass yard. This he thought of use to keep hounds clean and improve their coats. "You will find them," he says, "frequently rubbing themselves against it; the shade of it is always useful to them in summer." A hayrick, however, is not an appurtenance that can be managed in the grass yard of every kennel. Hound gloves, which are commonly in use among huntsmen, are good substitutes for Mr. Beckford's hayrick. The grass yard itself should be looked after closely. The grass should be attended to and encouraged, for, after all, grass is one of the best, as it is the most natural, of medicines for every hound. The yard is to be kept clean and tidy, and, to ensure this the kennel huntsman, or feeder, should go over it at least once daily with his broom in his hand. Every hole worked by a hound should be filled up, and no bones or other refuse should be suffered to lie about.

In some kennels, where hounds are fed almost entirely on raw flesh, and there is little cooking to be done, the duties of a feeder are very considerably lightened; but in the great majority of establishments hounds are fed upon cooked flesh and meal, with the occasional addition of vegetables. [2] Horseflesh is the usual food of hounds, and part of the kennel huntsman's or feeder's duty will be in seeing that such flesh is duly forthcoming. The Master, himself, especially if he happens to move about the country, can often hear of the necessary food-supplies, or is able to make some permanent arrangement with a horse-knacker. The flesh should be boiled for hours until it parts readily from the bone. Digesters are recommended for this process, and although they add to the preliminary cost of kennels, they undoubtedly pay their way. The scent from the digester, which is not a pleasant one, can be carried off by a pipe so contrived as to lead into an adjacent drain. The flesh, when boiled, is taken out and set to cool; the broth is then divided between the boilers, which are filled up with water till nearly half full. Into this is poured the meal, which may be oatmeal, or Indian meal, or a mixture. Old, well-matured oatmeal is undoubtedly the best and most strengthening food; it is also the dearest. With the oatmeal may be mingled a small quantity of wheat flour. As to the period of boiling, Indian meal takes much the longest and requires two hours; oatmeal an hour; wheaten flour, if it is used, about half an hour. So soon as the stirabout is cooked it should be ladled out into the coolers. After a little cooling it is stiff

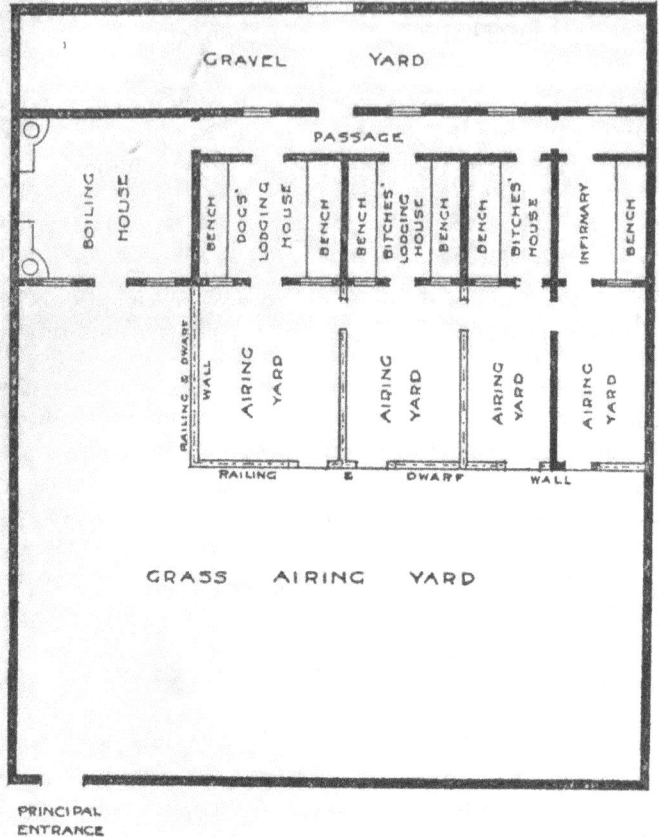

108

enough to cut with a spade. For the invalids, or light feeders, it may be suitably reduced with broth; but for strong hounds in hard condition it can be eaten of a pretty solid consistency. Before the feeding-hour the meat is cut up small, and with the stirabout placed in the feeding-troughs, well mingled together. It is the huntsman's duty, if there is a professional huntsman attached to the pack, to superintend the feeding operations. His hounds will be in such good order that, when he throws open the door of their kennel court, they pause until the names of those first wanted are called for. As many hounds as can comfortably feed at a trough are thus drawn. To any one not accustomed to the wonderful discipline of a well-managed pack of hounds, it is extremely interesting to note with what order and decorum these big and ofttimes fierce creatures await the summons to their meals. The more delicate feeders are attended to first, or fed apart, perhaps, and it is one of the peculiar duties of a good huntsman to see that each hound gets a fair and square meal. About a pound of the stirabout and from a quarter to half a pound of flesh are recommended as being a fair day's allowance for a single foxhound during the hunting season. A harrier can do with a trifle, but not much, less. Once a week it is advisable to boil with the soup some kind of vegetable, greens, turnips, &c., as before mentioned. In summer the feeding is, of course, lighter; little flesh is given, and more Indian meal, which is cheaper than old Scotch oatmeal, may be provided. The paunch of a cow, containing grass half digested, is recommended by Stonehenge as a good and cooling food. On intermediate days thin porridge, instead of the stiff stirabout, may form the dietary. Plenty of vegetables may at this time be used, boiled in the broth, and given towards evening, in addition to the morning meal.

The time of feeding varies a good deal. Some packs feed as early as seven or eight o'clock in the morning. Eleven o'clock is a favourite time. I know one or two packs which make their meal at two. With harriers, where the establishment is usually on a modest scale, the time of feeding must depend a little more than is the case with a pack of foxhounds on the convenience of the kennel huntsman. On the day of hunting, hounds are, of course, not fed until they come in from their work. Some Masters prefer that they should then wait an hour before being fed. In the meantime they may be sluiced with warm water and sprinkled with broth, the latter practice inducing them to lick one another clean. In cold weather, however, too much washing is not good for hounds. The late Earl of Suffolk, who kept harriers for some years, preferred, in summer, that his hounds should not be fed till they came in from their evening exercise, maintaining that they slept better after a late meal. Some Masters, on the day before hunting, so arrange that the hounds that are to go out next day feed later, say at four o'clock. This I think a sensible practice. It is a long fast, otherwise, especially for the more delicate hounds, and there are always some of these in every pack. It is, however, often maintained that hounds require twenty-four hours to empty themselves before hunting, so as to be fit and keen; with the majority of packs they are fed at the usual time in the morning.

As regards food and feeding, the opinions of Masters vary a good deal. Mr. Eames, of the Cotley Harriers, sends me the following interesting note: "I can never understand how they kept condition right in the old trencher-fed packs. My grandfather, I have heard, always fed on flesh and barley-meal, and he used to get some wonderful sport. I always feed on best Government old ship-biscuits the two days before hunting; with flesh or boiled vegetables, &c., on the other days. I found my hounds stand the work on this food better than on any other I have tried." An ex-Master of much experience writes to me: "I fed my hounds on Indian meal stirabout, with plenty of strong soup and vegetables in summer; when I had plenty of skim-milk from the dairy the hounds got that, and seemed to do very well on it. When they were getting into work I changed to half oatmeal and half Indian meal, with plenty of strong soup, and vegetables when I had them."

Photograph by R. B. Lodge, Enfield
SALLY
A MOTHER OF HARRIERS

Photograph by R. B. Lodge, Enfield
AT THE KENNELS

Some few packs feed entirely on raw flesh, and, when they are accustomed to it, do very well. I know one pack, the Hailsham, which are maintained on this diet, intimately well. Certainly no hounds can be healthier or in better condition. They hunt three days a week, and are seldom sick or sorry. Mr. Southerden, who owns these hounds, says: "I feed almost exclusively on raw flesh, which is thrown down to the hounds on the grass in great joints, so that they can tear the flesh from the bones. It does not do to throw down small pieces of meat, or hounds will swallow it without masticating. Of course, when fed on flesh hounds require much more exercise than when fed on meal, and it is absolutely necessary to give them plenty of fresh water to drink, and to sprinkle a good dusting of flowers of sulphur in the water which they lap up. Some people use stone brimstone, but my experience is that the flowers are by far the best for the purpose. The water should be emptied out every morning and a fresh supply given. Hounds should be fed only once a day on flesh, after they have had their walk; when wanted for work next day, it is well to feed about two or three o'clock in the afternoon, when they require nothing more before the next night, after returning from hunting."

No one who keeps hounds, whether they be harriers or foxhounds, can afford to be without a copy of Beckford's classic on hunting. Even at this distance of time it is an invaluable book. I annex a few passages on feeding:

"My hounds are generally fed about eleven o'clock; and if I am present myself I take the same opportunity to make my draft for the next day's hunting."

"Hounds that are tender feeders cannot be fed too late, or with meat too good."

"Hounds, I think, should be sharp-set before hunting; they run the better for it."

"If hounds are shut up as soon as they come in from hunting they will not readily leave the benches afterwards, for if they be much fatigued they will prefer rest to food."

Hounds, as Beckford advises, should be fed immediately they come in from hunting. His hounds were usually fed twice on the days they hunted. "Some," he says, "will feed better the second time than the first; besides, the turning them out of the lodging-house refreshes them; they stretch their limbs, empty their bodies; and, as during this time their kennel is cleaned out, and litter shaken up, they settle themselves better on the benches afterwards." Many packs of harriers are, however, only fed once in the day, even after hunting, and manage to do very well upon it. Hound feeding is a most important function and requires great attention and judgment. The Marquis of Cleveland, who flourished some seventy or eighty years ago, and hunted foxhounds for fifty years, never sat down to his own dinner till he had given his hounds theirs. This great fox-hunter, also, invariably noted down the events of each day before retiring for the night, and published them at the end of the year for the benefit of his friends. There is no doubt, I think, that the publication of a carefully kept hunting diary is an education in itself, and is often of the greatest assistance to others. I have been lately reading a book, entitled "A third of a Century with the High Peak Harriers." [3] This is the diary of Mr. Nesfield, for thirty-three seasons Master of that pack. It is an admirable little volume, well worthy to be read by all admirers of hare-hunting.

[1] Straw is commonly used; but it should be kept dry.
[2] Various kinds of vegetable are used: cabbage, greens, turnips, parsnips, beet, &c. All of them are good, in season.
[3] Buxton. C. F. Wardley. "High Peak News" Offices. 1802. Price 10s. 6d.

Chapter Eleven - Hound Management

HAVING dealt with the housing and feeding of hounds, it is now necessary to inquire further into the conduct and management of the pack. The breeding of hounds is a matter demanding infinite care, nicety, and judgment; a good kennel huntsman, who understands his business, and uses his brains, and has, into the bargain, a bent for hound management, is a rare treasure, not by any means easy of discovery. There are, however, such men, and, when found, their services are to the Master of harriers, always anxious to improve his hounds or to keep a good pack up to the mark, of the greatest value and assistance. Harrier breeding has been described as one of the most perplexing of all sciences, and, especially in the case of the Old English harrier, the results of mating a good dog hound and a good bitch are not by any means so certain to produce the desired puppy of perfection as might be supposed. Even when breeding from the foxhound strain, the results are often vexing enough. A well-known master of harriers, mating a twenty-one-inch pure-bred Belvoir dog hound with a bitch of similar breed, under twenty inches, has had a litter comprising some hounds which reached, at maturity, twenty-four inches, while others stood no more than sixteen inches. That master's standard was twenty inches, so that, for the purposes of his pack, one of the most symmetrical in the kingdom, such a litter would be useless. Pure harriers will sometimes throw back in extraordinary fashion, their puppies exhibiting rough coats, smooth coats, slack loins, bad feet, and elbows out; with these may be found mingled perfect puppies of the right old-fashioned sort so much desired in certain kennels.

But, after all, the great thing in breeding is to mate from good workers, well-nosed, low-scenting hounds, stout and of good constitutions, and, if possible, good road-hunters. Looks in the sire and mother must count for a good deal, but looks alone, without the right hunting qualifications, are not supremely desirable. Certain strains always seem to produce valuable hounds. These strains are treasured, and rightly so, in every kennel. In a small pack of harriers or beagles, especially where a good deal of work has to be got through with comparatively few couples of hounds, the master and kennel huntsman will mate their hounds from the well-nosed and hardy ones rather than from the smarter looking ones. In mating, the breeder will, of course, always attempt to correct faults or weak points in either of his hounds. Careful selection in these matters counts for a good deal. Mate for size, avoid much in-breeding, and strive for good crosses; here are three cardinal maxims. It is not desirable to breed from a bitch much after six or seven years. Her best time is then past.

The mother with whelps should be kept as quiet as possible, in some secluded corner of the kennels or, if there is no such convenient place, in some comfortable outhouse or loose box. The kennel huntsman, or feeder, or whoever attends her at this time, should be well known to her. The mother should not be permitted to bring up more than four or five of her litter, even if she is a good milker. If the litter is a large one, and it is desired to save another whelp or two, a foster-mother must be procured. This is often a matter of some difficulty. Spaniels and sheep dogs have been recommended as good wet nurses in such emergencies.

The whelps are usually weaned after six or seven weeks, if the mother has been able to support them so long. Their food at first should consist of a mess of milk, oatmeal, and good dog biscuits, mixed with a little warm broth. Some kennel

THE HOLCOMBE HARRIERS, LANCASHIRE

huntsmen give, in addition, a little minced meat, lightly boiled. Others add raw flesh, minced. If born in February or early March - February used to be considered the best month by hound-breeders - the puppies will be ready to be sent out to walk by mid-June.

A puppy begins to be fit to learn something of the business of his life by the time he is eighteen months old. Before that period he will either have passed his babyhood at the kennels, or have been put out at walk at the house of some resident, usually a farmer, or innkeeper, or other occupier, in the district. Harrier packs are not, however, so fortunate in this respect as are most of the foxhound establishments. The practice of walking puppies can be encouraged in various ways, and especially by the institution of prizes for the best puppy walked, together with a show and luncheon, when the prizes are distributed. During its youth the young hound will, after returning to kennel from the walk usually at the end of the hunting season which follows its birth begin its education. It will probably require medicine on its return to kennel; the change of habits and curtailment of freedom making a good deal of difference for some few weeks. It takes time, too, for the young hound to accustom itself to its new home and its change of master.

The huntsman will, in these early days, accustom the puppy to the use of its name, and regular exercise, and will break it gradually from riot that is, from running after sheep, deer, rabbits, and other quadrupeds. Riot is a terrible nuisance in a pack, and ought to be sternly repressed. Yet, even in first-rate packs of hounds, accidents will happen, especially in the early days of hunting. Here are a couple of entries from Mr. Nesfield's diary, which tell their own tale:

"6th November (1860) 'Trueman' and 'Ringwood' accused of sheep killing! *Hang them!*" "Saturday 10th October (1877) Under Nelson's rocks. A gale of wind. Hounds wild. Sheep all over. Killed two lambs and went home in a rage. 'Champion' the worst." "Saturday, 20th October. Sparklow. First regular day. Had one very good run, but thrown out by railway, and no kill. Foggy. 'Champion' again killed a sheep. He must be hung!" These harriers (the High Peak) were, however, at this time, dwarf foxhounds. Harriers proper are not so fierce, or so difficult to break from riot, as are hounds of pure foxhound blood. Sheep riot is especially dangerous, for, once a hound has tasted blood and the delights of this kind of sport, it is a matter of extreme difficulty to break him of the habit. Some authorities recommend as a cure, other than the rope, the coupling of the offending hound with a tough old ram, who will knock him about well and put the fear of sheep into him. I have read, however, of this remedy even proving unavailing. A proud Master who had recommended the cure to a friend took the latter to the ram's shed to exhibit the triumphant result. Upon opening the door they discovered the hound surely enough, but the ram had practically disappeared, his fellow prisoner having slain and devoured him! For an old hound killing sheep, there is, as Beckford says, but one remedy, "*The halter.*" Another cure suggested for young hounds running sheep is to tie up the offender securely by his feet, place him in a lane or gateway, and drive a flock of sheep right over him.

It is better at first to keep the young hounds in a separate kennel if it can be managed. When taken out to exercise, a young hound should be coupled with an old steady hound, and, preferably, dogs with bitches. Harriers in kennel are, at least as quarrelsome as foxhounds, and need looking after in this respect. I have known a harrier in the kennels of a Sussex pack torn to pieces by his fellows; and a draft hound from the same kennel, sent to another pack, was slaughtered by her new messmates. It sometimes happens that the whole pack, or nearly all of them, take a dislike to a particular hound. If this is the case that hound had better be drafted, or his end may be a bloody one. Young hounds need feeding twice a day. The ceremony of rounding ears, if it is followed, should take place before the weather is hot. Six months is a proper age at which rounding may be performed. This may be done with scissors, or with a special instrument (shaped like a crescent), and a block and mallet. Among many, probably the large majority of, harrier packs this custom is, however, not followed, and hounds run with their ears as nature made them. Personally, I think a hound, especially a harrier, looks much handsomer with his ears unrounded. In some harrier countries, however, where coverts are abundant and thorns and gorse troublesome, rounding may be thought necessary. But even among certain foxhound packs of the present day, the hounds' ears are not rounded.

The hours of exercise of a pack in summer are, of course, considerably longer than in winter, when they are hard at work. At this season they are more usually walked. Two hours in the early morning and the same in the evening are desirable. For getting hounds into condition towards the hunting season, and for the exercise of the hunting season itself, there is nothing like road work, which hardens the feet and renders the hound so much the more capable of resisting the wear and tear of a long day of hunting over all sorts of country. Bicycles are excellent things to exercise hounds with; the pace is more easily regulated than with a horse, and the hounds encounter less dust as they follow the huntsman or whip. Cycles are also very valuable auxiliaries in the case of packs of foot-harriers or beagles. The Hunt servants get comfortably to the meet, and the hounds can be taken along at a steady pace without pushing them too fast.

For the purpose of getting hounds into shape, and accustoming the young entry to the ways of hunting, a few by-days will probably be taken in September. By this process the pack will be a little more shipshape, and less inclined to riot and wildness, when it makes its bow to the public at the first advertised meet of the season, which usually takes place towards the second or third week in October. At first young hounds will straggle in the field, and a good deal of patience will be required. The whip should not be too often used. Much punishment at this stage frightens and discourages the young entry. The huntsman must, and usually does, possess his soul in patience, and the juveniles begin pretty soon to understand something of the great game in which they are destined to take a part. It is interesting, indeed, to note their growing keenness, and how almost imperceptibly they begin to fall into the ways of the old hands. Instinct, breeding, and usage finally accomplish their work, and the young hound is now an integral part of the pack, beginning to take his place.

It is an oft-debated point, and I suppose always will be to the end of hunting time, whether or no harriers should be kept to hares alone, or should be allowed, as they often are, especially in countries where hares are scarce, to hunt fox and deer. Beckford himself, a very high authority, is clear upon the question. He says, "Harriers, to be good, like all other hounds, must be kept to their own game: if you run fox with them you spoil them. Hounds cannot be perfect, unless used to one scent and one style of hunting. Harriers run fox in so different a style from hare, that it is of great disservice to them when they return to hare again: it makes them wild and teaches them to skirt. The high scent which a fox leaves, the straightness of his running, the eagerness of the pursuit, and the noise that generally accompanies it, all contribute to spoil a harrier." I am bound to say that I am old-fashioned enough to agree entirely with Beckford's reasoning. I have watched harriers run both fox and deer, and, in my opinion, their real qualities and capacity for hunting their proper quarry, the hare, were thereby materially detracted from. It is, I believe, undoubted that scarcity of hares has something to do with the practice of some masters in hunting fox when they come across them, and of others - and this is a fairly common practice - in hunting deer occasionally after Christmas.

Upon a question so much debated, it seems to me only fair to give the opinions of one or two other authorities. I believe the perusal of their experiences may be found of value to all those interested in harriers, beagles, and hare-hunting. Mr. J. A. Doyle, Master of the Crickhowell Harriers, Brecknockshire, writes me as follows: "My experience is that good harriers will hunt a fox as keenly as any foxhounds. It is a real treat to them to get a scent on which they can confidently drive forward. But for the next few days on a hare they will be flashy, and over-run the line, forgetting that they must be always in readiness for their hare turning." "Tantara" (a Master of Harriers), whose excellent little book on hare-hunting I have before referred to - its contents are so good that it is a pity it is not three or four times as long again - makes the following observations: "A pack of harriers, when properly managed, does immense good to foxhounds by driving outlying foxes from the hedgerows and out-lying spinnies into those coverts that are usually drawn by foxhounds.

"It has been often said that running a fox with harriers upsets them. It may be the case when constantly practised, but it certainly is not so if it happens only a few times in the season. I have run a fox in the morning with a pack of harriers, and hunted hare in the afternoon, and I certainly saw no difference in their manner of hunting on the day in question.

"It can easily be seen by the hounds themselves when they are on the line of a fox by the extra drive, by the partial absence of music, and by the way they raise their hackles, [1] but there is one thing harriers will not do, and that is break up a fox, though I have seen them tear one badly....Hunting a deer, however, has a bad effect on harriers, as it makes them wild, inclined to flash, and sometimes it inclines them to be unsteady at sheep."

Upon the whole, I am firmly of opinion that, if all masters and huntsmen of harriers were polled, their consensus would be that running fox or deer is by no means a good thing for a pack of harriers. Harriers, if they are good ones, by the way, will run down and kill a deer easily enough. On October 9, 1875, the High Peak harriers hunted an outlying buck from Mr. F. Potter's, through the Harthill Woods, then past Beech Plantations, over Gratton Ponds and Smerrill Grange, and pulled him down in the road in an hour and forty minutes, after a magnificent run. Mr. Nesfield, the Master of that period, when speaking of this run, used to mention, as a curious fact, that harriers, only entered to hare, and in full work, should have hunted and stuck to a deer through woods abounding in hares.

Harriers, although they run the hare fiercely enough, are not all of them, by any means, keen in the breaking of it up. It has been noticed, times out of mind, by all harrier men, that not infrequently the best hounds are quite indifferent about the worry. On the other hand, it would be futile even for a slack huntsman to trust to hounds not breaking up and devouring their hare. If they are alone they will do it. In hunting with foot-harriers, when hounds have got away and killed by themselves, I have a good many times arrived on the scene to find but a patch or two of fur and the skull remaining. Collectively, hounds must have blood, or they may lose some of their zest and keenness. For this reason if a huntsman, as will sometimes happen now and again in a poor hare country, has a run of bad luck, even a chop - usually counted a disaster - is better than no hare at all.

Hound ailments must, necessarily, be a source of constant anxiety and constant watchfulness in all kennels. Exercise is, of course, as with human beings, one of the first preventives against many complaints. The summer work I have already touched upon. In winter, when hounds are in full work, they should never have less than an hour and a half of steady exercise, preferably on the road, on the days when they are not hunting. Distemper remains to this hour the disease most dreaded and most dangerous to young hounds. All sorts of prophylactics and patent cures have been proclaimed, from time immemorial, yet up to the present day this ailment remains unconquered. In some seasons it is far worse than in others. During the spring and summer of 1902 the ravages of distemper were more fatal than they have been for a generation past. Some packs lost practically the whole of their young hounds, and many others, throughout the length and breadth of the country, suffered very severely. The ailment was complicated by much influenza and, under the influence of the two, the young entry were swept off like flies. Paralysis in these cases frequently set in, and nothing could save the unfortunate patient. Distemper is also frequently complicated by jaundice, or "yellows," as kennel huntsmen prefer to call it. Jaundice, it is to be remembered, is not seldom induced by over-feeding and lack of exercise. Young hounds, by the way, when at kennel, should have the run of the grass yard the whole day, in addition to their ordinary exercise. For influenza, calomel is still one of the soundest of all remedies, if exhibited in the early stage of the illness and provided the hound is in good condition.

Beckford mentions with favour a remedy said to have been of great service in his time, viz., an ounce of Peruvian bark in a glass of port wine, taken twice a day. He mentions also, in his humorous way, the case of a stag-hound, which, treated in this manner, drank three bottles of port in five days! "You may think, perhaps," he adds, with a twinkle, "that the feeder drank his share, and, probably, he might, had it not been sent ready mixed up in the bark." At all events, the hound recovered. Beckford's chapters on disease and distemper are even now well worth reading. But, indeed, what part of his book is not? I believe that port wine and quinine are likely to do as much good in distemper as any other remedy of the present day.

"Stonehenge's" remedy is as follows: "Compound tincture of bark, three ounces; decoction of yellow bark, fourteen ounces; to be given twice or thrice daily, in doses of three table-spoons. A table-spoon of castor oil and syrup of buckthorn is often advocated in the early stages." Warmth, dry quarters, port wine, and essence of beef are valuable aids, which must never be neglected; but, as a rule, nature takes her own course, and is not to be denied. For this and other diseases help may be obtained by recourse to some good modern book on the dog; but the safest and most effectual precaution is to call in at once the services of a good veterinary surgeon. Many of them nowadays are specialists in dog diseases. Most kennel huntsmen have their own patent nostrum for distemper, and in a mild season these may apparently succeed; but when the disease is really, as in 1902, at its worst, no known remedy seems to be of much avail.

For mange, a fruitful source of trouble in kennels, there is no better remedy than a mixture of lard and black brimstone. Kennel lameness I have already referred to. This is one of the most troublesome of all hound complaints. In a large number of cases it proceeds from damp or exposure and is nothing else than rheumatism. But there are instances of kennel lameness which, it seems, nothing can account for. The kennels may be improved, the site changed, and yet the disease will appear. Mr. J. S. Gibbons sends me the following note on this often mysterious disease: "I think I have had as much, or more, experience of it than any one in England; I am glad to say I have completely got rid of it now, but the result of my several years' experience of it and trying every sort of remedy and experiment is that I don't think that either I or any one else knows anything really about it at all."

Boiled herrings daily for a fortnight, a couple to each hound, are said to be an excellent remedy. Spirits of nitre or salicylate of soda are often advocated. A dry kennel with a false floor, allowing free current of air, is probably the soundest of all alleviatives for this disease.

It is the custom with the Masters of some of our best harrier packs of the present day to print each season a little book, setting forth the particulars of the pack and a list of the hounds. This is a commendable plan, which serves in after years as a very useful record, in case, as often happens, some reference back is needed. The first page will be as follows - I append an example from the Aspull Harriers' lists:

The second page may contain a note of advice from the Master to his subscribers and others as to their conduct in the field, the avoidance of damage, and so forth. On the remaining pages will follow the complete list of hounds comprising the pack. Thus:

13th Season.

A LIST OF THE ASPULL HARRIERS.

1902–3.

MR. CARLTON CROSS'S.

FRANK BILLEN, K.H. . . . . 1st Whipper-in.
TOM GODDARD . . . . 2nd   ,,

Kennels . . Martin House, Whittle-le-Woods, Chorley, Lancashire.

Telegrams :—" Whittle-le-Woods," ¾ mile.
Station—CHORLEY, 3¾ miles.

Age.		Name.	Sire.	Dam.
			Major Wickham's	*His*
7 years old .	.	Dissolute	Dealer	Diligent
		1st Peterboro', '96, Unentered couples		
		Cup ,, '97, Best three couples		
			Eamont	*Their*
7 ,,	. .	Treachery	Sovereign	Termagant
			Holm Hill	
7 ,,	. .	Gunner	Guardian	Lunacy
			Eamont	
7 ,,	. .	Concord	Rodney	Costly
			Eamont *Major Wickham's*	
7 ,,	. .	Watchman	Roderick	Woful

The list will begin with the oldest hounds and proceed by degrees to the youngest. An analysis of the whole pack on the last page will fitly conclude the little volume. The expense of printing a few copies of such a booklet is trifling. Some Masters print on the left-hand page, which is left blank, a record of prizes gained by the hounds named on the right-hand page.

The naming of hounds is a serious business, which ought to be undertaken with care and thought. Some packs are named without any regard to the fitness of things. Hound nomenclature should be sonorous, and to my mind the old-fashioned names are far preferable to some of the modern intrusions. How infinitely to be preferred, for example, are such names as Bravery, Champion, Stormer, and Statesman, to Squeaker, Sally, Thwacker, and Gaslight, all of which I have encountered. I have known a cricket enthusiast name three hounds out of one litter, Grace, Abel, and Ranji. Grace and even Abel one could pass well enough, but Ranji always jarred upon me as a hound name. I confess to a great weakness for old-fashioned hound names. I always remember, as a youngster, a Pytchley puppy

From a photograph by R. B. Lodge, Enfield

GOING TO A HOLLOA

From a photograph by R. B. Lodge, Enfield

A STERN CHASE

named Pantler, one of the most engaging yet mischievous rascals that ever went out to walk. His name has stuck in my memory ever since. It is a very ancient, probably now an almost extinct one.

The whelps should be named from the initials of either sire or dam, and it should be the care of the person selecting them to see to it that the names in one litter are not too much alike, so that each puppy shall easily recognise his own name when called. In the Appendix "B" I have given some lists of hound names, which may be found useful by those in search of a fair vocabulary of nomenclature. These comprise hound names from "Thoughts on Hunting" (1780), and from the Duke of Beaufort's, the Duke of Rutland's, Mr. Musters' (the Pytchley), and Mr. Osbaldeston's (the Quorn) packs in 1826.

[1] This is one of the infallible signs.

Chapter Twelve - Hunt Servants and Their Duties

IT has been well said that it is as difficult to find a perfect huntsman as a good Prime Minister. The huntsman of a pack of harriers needs certain qualifications which are not necessary and, indeed, would be undesirable, in one who pursues the fox. His sport is a more leisurely one, and there is not the same need in it of youth, and fire, and occasionally, even, of impetuosity. Beckford counsels a huntsman *d'un certain age* for harriers, and assigns to him, very properly, the qualifications of quiet and perseverance. He adds: "I know no family that would furnish a better cross than that of the *silent gentleman,* mentioned by the *Spectator;* a female of his line, crossed with a knowing huntsman, would probably produce a perfect harehunter."

Yet in many respects the huntsman, whether he pursues hare or fox, ought to be possessed of similar attributes. These are strength, activity, courage, enterprise, good spirits, perseverance, firmness, and decision. The man who cannot make up his mind, but listens to the suggestions that are poured in upon him at every check, will never make a good huntsman. He needs also a keen eye, a quick ear, and a good voice. He should be even-tempered, not readily cast down by disappointments, or too easily elevated by success, and he should be smart and clean in his person and civil in his address. The qualities of intelligence and good memory are also extremely desirable in that rare union of perfection, a good harrier huntsman. He must of necessity be a capable horseman.

No man, whether he be amateur or professional, can hope to succeed in this most difficult of all occupations unless he has his heart and soul in the business, and is prepared for much hard work and long hours in the field. If, as is often the case with harriers, he combines the offices of huntsman, kennel huntsman, and feeder - with the assistance, probably, of a lad as whipper-in and helper - it must be admitted that his life is one of a good deal of labour and of much care. Still, he has compensations. In many ways the existence of a huntsman is a very enviable one. He lives a healthy, open-air life; he loves (or he ought to love) his work; and very frequently he enjoys pleasures so keen and so thrilling that there are few joys in life, indeed, to be compared with them. If he has had a good day, and killed a brace of hares after a first-rate display of hunting, he jogs homeward suffused with a glow of satisfaction such as falls to few human beings in this vale of care. The huntsman, too, has a position in the world, and is an object of consideration and interest, usually of admiration, upon his countryside. Even the care of hounds, though it may involve a good deal of work and anxiety, is an extremely interesting one. In fact, if a man is fond of his business, as he ought to be, and usually is, the pleasure of hunting a pack of hounds, whether they be harriers or fox-hounds, far outweighs the pains and difficulties, though the latter, too, must sometimes occur.

A quiet huntsman is a necessity with harriers. There is no great hurry, the hare is always above ground, and it is essential that hounds shall be disturbed as little as possible in their work. Too often a noisy huntsman, or a shouting whip, gets hounds' heads up, and sport is thereby spoiled. I like to hear a harrier huntsman with a good and cheerful voice. Yet he should be chary of using it; now and again, when hounds need encouragement, a few words are useful; and it is essential that hounds should understand and obey notes of command and reproval when they are scattered, or running riot or heel. A good ear in a harrier huntsman is a most excellent thing. He should be able to distinguish the note of every hound, and he can then tell in a moment, as he hears a whimper or a challenge, whether the line is right or not. If scent is good - and whether it is or not is very quickly apparent - hounds will hunt themselves, and require no aid from the huntsman until a check happens. Even then the huntsman will allow them plenty of time to make their own casts and hit off the line for themselves. In drawing he will take care that hounds do not stick too closely to his heels, but spread out to their work, not leaving the finding of the hare to some more painstaking or more sagacious human being. Some cheery words of encouragement, when drawing, are by no means out of place.

The use of the horn is, in hare-hunting, by no means so frequent or so necessary as in fox-hunting. [1] A good huntsman will take care not to sound it unduly, as some men do, apparently for the mere purpose of making cheerful sounds. I love the sound of a horn as much as any man; there is to me something inexpressibly inspiring in it, as there is in hound music. But in hare-hunting you can easily have too much of it. Some few Masters, especially with foot packs, hold that the horn is unnecessary and only distracts hounds. I confess I do not share that opinion. I believe that at times, even with harriers and beagles, the horn is very useful, especially in getting hounds out of woodlands and in cases of riot, or when hounds are running heel or have split and are following two hares. And where the pack is entirely at fault, and the huntsman has made up his mind to go to a holloa which he knows to be a reliable one, a few blasts from his horn are useful in getting hounds to him and hurrying them on at best speed to the point from whence the holloa proceeds. For these and other reasons, I believe in accustoming harriers and beagles to the sound of the horn, and in the huntsman seeing that, with the assistance of the whip, they come quickly to him when he uses it. In the matter of lifting hounds, the huntsman will, of course, not fail to remember that golden rule, never to lift hounds when running. There are often temptations to cut off corners, and to close up more speedily on a sinking hare, but it is the safest and, indeed, the only sportsmanlike policy to let hounds hunt it out themselves.

Punctuality is the soul of hunting, as it is of most other important affairs of life. The huntsman, therefore, whether he be professional or amateur, will see to it that his hounds arrive at their meeting-place in good time, yet are not over hurried. To most meets harriers are enabled to go on foot. If they are driven to very distant meets, a long van, open or covered, such as is used by a tradesman for the purpose of his business, makes a very good vehicle. The hounds are best kept in by an arrangement of strong wire netting, or even of calf net which prevents them from jumping out. Such a van may sometimes be hired for the few occasions when hounds have to be conveyed to the meet. A small pack of harriers is not often possessed of a van of its own.

It is absolutely necessary that a huntsman shall be of sober habits. He is usually a popular character, and has temptations in the way of drinking, and it is essential that he should have the strength to resist them. And his Master will see to it that his Hunt servants take hounds to the meet and get them to kennels in good time, without loitering.

Some huntsmen are consumed with the ambition to make a big score of kills during the season. Up to a certain point, keenness for blood is a good thing. In some places that I know of hares are so numerous that it is necessary to keep them down, always, of course, by fair hunting. But excessive keenness to make a record tally of kills is undesirable and ought to be checked. I have known a huntsman so eager in this respect that he fell into the unfortunate habit of butchering, rather than of hunting down fairly, many of his hares. He had a very keen eye for a hare in her form and a very acute knowledge of likely resting places. By this means he was enabled, while apparently drawing innocently enough, to chop many a hare that might otherwise have given a real good run. It is a miserable practice and ought to be put down, either by the Master, or by the representations of subscribers to the Hunt, with a firm hand. Discrimination must, of course, be exercised in such cases. A hint that too many hares are chopped may have the desired effect.

As to the number of hares killed in a season, this must depend greatly upon the nature of the country as well as upon the qualities of huntsman and pack.

The Rochdale harriers, as I have said, kill about a hundred hares in a season. That is a big total. During a period of thirty-two seasons - from 1860 to 1892 - the High Peak harriers, under Mr. Nesfield's mastership, hunting two days a week, killed exactly a thousand hares in one thousand two hundred and thirty-five days. This give them an average of a trifle over thirty-one hares per season. In their best season they killed fifty-seven hares; in their two worst eight and eleven respectively. Of course frost and hard winters have to be reckoned for in such estimates. In fair, average winters these hounds killed from thirty-five to fifty hares in a season. Considering that the pack was composed practically of dwarf foxhounds, very fast and very good hunters, the number of hares killed seems small. On the other hand, it is to be remembered that in north Derbyshire there are more interruptions from hard weather than in southern counties. The foot-pack with which I see a good deal of my sport (the Hailsham), kills usually from fifty to sixty-five hares in a fair season. Big scores are not always to be taken as proof of the finest hunting. After all, a rattling good hunt, with a hare pulled down at the end of it, is far better than a muddling day with two or three hares chopped, or killed in short feeble chases.

A good harrier huntsman is not to be picked up readily. His education must, necessarily, be a slow and a gradual one. Only years of constant practice in the field, united with an acute mind, keen faculties, and a strong frame, can equip a man properly for such a post. An old gentleman, seventy years of age, who had hunted with all sorts of hounds,

From a photograph by Mr. J. Coster

KENNEL HUNTSMAN AND WHIP CYCLING TO THE MEET

was once congratulated upon his perfect science in the art of hunting hare. He protested vigorously that the life of man was too short to allow of any one attaining perfection in this difficult art. It is certain that a man may hunt hounds for thirty or forty years of his life, and yet in his next essay learn some new wrinkle in his art. There are innumerable things which may arise during the progress of a day's hunting to alter the chase and spoil a success-ful run. A huntsman must have his wits constantly on the alert. Even if his pack be a good one, it is by no means odds on his handling the hare in front of him. Rather are the odds usually the other way. Every hare has its particu-lar idiosyncrasies and tricks. The change of atmosphere, or of soil, or of wind, a burst of sunshine, the coming up of a storm, the vanishing of frost, the crossing of a stream, all these and fifty other causes, which may operate against success, have to be carefully noted, and their effects guarded against. The taint of sheep, curs which may course the hare, fresh hares springing up, foot people heading the quarry, are always fruitful sources of trouble to the huntsman. On a good scenting day things go merrily enough, as a rule. It is on a bad scent that the huntsman has to prove his mettle and, by his skill, his resource, his observation, and his knowledge of hunting, prove that he is ca-pable of assisting his pack amid difficulties, and extricating them from what may look like an *impasse.* As a general rule, it is better that the huntsman, especially if he is not a veteran at the game, should prefer to trust to the nos-es and instincts of his hounds rather than to his own knowledge.

123

The huntsman, whether professional or amateur, will need a whipper-in to aid him in getting hounds to the meet and taking them home again. With only one servant with them, hounds straggle or may run riot. In the field, the whipper-in is by no means so important a personage with a pack of harriers as with foxhounds. Usually a steady sharp lad, who will obey orders and use his head, is sufficient for the post. He will be needed to keep up stragglers, to whip off when required, to prevent hounds running heel, or tying on the scent, as old-fashioned harriers sometimes will do, as well as for opening gates, turning hounds to the huntsman, and so forth. It is most important that the whipper-in shall understand clearly that neither his whip nor his voice are to be used too freely. I have often noticed a harrier whip bellowing out at a straggling hound or a skirter, and so getting up the heads and distracting the attention of the rest of the pack, when, by the exercise of a little activity, he might have got round to the recalcitrant and, by the mere threat of his whip and a single word, have sent him to join his fellows. Quietness in the whip is even more essential than in the huntsman. Beckford goes so far as to say that he should not dare even to stop a hound or smack a whip without the huntsman's order. The modern master or huntsman would scarcely agree with this dictum. The whip, in hare-hunting, ought to be even more self-effacing than his brother of the foxhounds. Like the huntsman, he needs a sharp eye and a good ear, and especially the gift of observation. Often the hare claps back, having run the foil, and the whip, whose place is in the rear, if he is keen and observant, will note her sneaking home to her old quarters. When hounds and huntsman come up again, or if the hounds have come to a fault, the whip will then be able to inform the huntsman that his quarry has returned upon her old line.

Both huntsman and whip will be in the habit of counting their hounds; and, especially, when emerging from a covert, it will be the whip's duty to bring along stragglers and recover lost hounds. It may sometimes happen that, where the Master hunts the pack himself, he may depute his whip and a groom to get hounds to the meet and take them home after hunting. In such a case, especially on the homeward way, when it is essential that hounds shall be got to their kennels and supper as soon as possible, the whip, having often assisted to correct riot in his hounds, will, young though his age may be, re-member to check any tendency to riot in himself and his assistant. He will perform his duties in a conscientious manner, and not be tempted to linger at inns on the way. Not for him on these occasions are the snug temptations of the alehouse, the fascinations of red-cheeked damsels; he must get his hounds to kennel and forswear all other distractions. There is nothing worse for hounds, after a hard day's work, than for the Hunt servants to get into the habit of calling at inns on the way home. While they are inside drinking, the hounds, already weary and exhausted, are becoming chilled.

Like the huntsman, the whip will cultivate civility, which costs nothing and tends greatly to the popularity of a pack of hounds. Smart, pleasant, well-spoken Hunt servants, who know their duties and their places, and are popular in the district in which they hunt, add not a little to the prospects of goodwill from farmers and labourers and the chances of finding a hare. Many a shepherd, who knows the seats and runs of hares usually better than any man on the land, is to be conciliated by a pleasant word from the Hunt servants, a piece of silver occasionally from the Master, or a pint of ale from a supporter of the Hunt.

The feeder, who, with many harrier packs, usually doubles the part of kennel huntsman, is, of course, an important personage in the hunting establishment. Upon him depends practically the welfare of the pack, and thereby the prospect of sport. A good feeder, who knows his business and has the wit to consider the idiosyncrasies and weaknesses of his charges, to note their constitutions, and look after their appetites, is a treasure indeed. Many a delicate hound or poor eater is kept fit for work and has its constitution gradually built up by a careful and painstaking feeder. A careless man lets his hounds rip; the stronger hounds get more than their share, and the weak and delicate hounds suffer. There is much even in the very cooking of the hound food.

The loss of a good and successful feeder is often a serious inconvenience to a pack of hounds, which will lose condition and run down astonishingly in the hands of a successor who is careless or does not understand his business.

In the case of small harrier packs, therefore, which are run on modest lines, it is essential that the huntsman, who practically has, with the help of a lad as whip and understrapper, to manage the business of the whole pack, including hunting, feeding, and all other kennel management, shall be not only efficient in the field but a careful kennel man and a competent and observant feeder. Such a Hunt servant has much upon his hands far more than many people can possibly imagine and he needs not only fair wages but due consideration from his master and the subscribers. In most cases where the same man carries on these offices I have known even a youth double and treble these difficult posts and perform them all more than reasonably well he is a real enthusiast who loves nothing in this world so well as his hounds and hunting. But for this love of sport, wild life, and the open air, it would be difficult to find a man willing to devote such long and laborious days, especially if he be with a foot pack, to the business of hunting. For my part, I have a great admiration for Hunt servants. They are, as a rule, an estimable class, hard-working, civil, keen, and hardy, a credit to the Anglo-Saxon race. If we bred thousands like them, and taught them to shoot, what magnificent mounted infantry they would make. Hunt servants are relics of the good old days, when men lived much more in the open air; when England had still leisure to be merry; when the pestilent custom of crowding into towns and deserting the country was not; when motor-cars and other abominations were undreamed of; when country gentlemen were content to live quietly upon their own acres, and the farmer was not pursued by carking care, as he is now, but could make a livelihood comfortably out of his holding. Few men go through more exposure, or live harder lives with less complaint. How many of us, I wonder, realise what it means to hunt a pack of hounds, even harriers, thrice a week; the dark mornings of work, the labour in the field, the late evenings on tired horses or afoot, the care and anxiety for their hounds, the drenching days, the frosts, snows, and storms that these men endure, and endure cheerfully.

"Stonehenge" has some excellent and pithy things to say on the subject of Hunt servants and harriers. Concerning the huntsman he says: "As with the poet so with the huntsman, *nascitur non fit.* He should be a very different person from the huntsman of a pack of foxhounds. Sometimes a young man succeeds in this task, but more frequently he fails from want of temper and patience; and the age which is best suited for the sport is that at which man usually has arrived at some degree of control over his natural impulses. Still, there are some exceptions to this rule, and I have seen harriers exceedingly well hunted by very young men. [2] But whatever the age of the huntsman, he should be quiet, persevering, cautious, and free from meddling, and should trust to the noses of hounds in preference to his own head...few are so framed as to fit them for the management of harriers until they have sown a crop of wild oats in other and more exciting amusements. The chief art of the huntsman here (in hare-hunting) is in breeding his hounds and in drafting them so that they shall be 'suity' and pack well; for when once they are in the field, little or no interference is necessary. They should be as handy as kittens, and should scarcely require a whipper-in, and indeed some of the best packs I have ever seen have been without that appendage. By constantly taking out hounds in summer, and breaking them from riot, and by feeding them after drawing each by name, and otherwise getting control over hounds in the summer season, it is seldom that any occasion occurs for the office of the whip. [3]

"If the huntsman rides well to them, he is always near enough to them to interfere when this is wanted; and the hounds are not cowed by the needless display of power, which, if placed in the hands of a whip, is sure to be exercised.

"But the critical eye of the Master is always employed, though he may otherwise be idle, in watching the actions of each hound, and noting his hunting and his pace, also in detecting skirting and babbling, and in deciding all the various qualities which will lead him to draft certain hounds or to breed from others. This is interest sufficient for any man; and to a real lover of hunting it is a most delightful amusement...Harriers or beagles may easily be handled when well matched; but it is in the matching that the huntsman's power is shown. He therefore requires a great knowledge of individual character in the hounds, so as to select those only which exhibit what he wants in great perfection to breed from, and to cross with those which will develop still further those good qualities or suppress the bad ones." "The whipper-in (adds 'Stonehenge') should be a mere groom, solely intended as a second pair of hands to those of the Master; and he should never be allowed to use them without orders." This is somewhat too sweeping. I would prefer to assume that, at the beginning of the season, the whip is well drilled by his Master or huntsman into the nature of his duties, which are simple enough. If the Master had to shout to him every time he might use his whip or turn a hound it would be unendurable for both parties.

In drawing hounds for the next day's hunting, the huntsman will see to it that no sick, sorry, or lame ones, or bitches out of order, are included. From twelve to fifteen couples make a fair hunting number, but where the pack is small, ten or eleven couples will suffice. A hound that is badly lamed or injured during hunting can usually be got to kennels in some passing trap, or it may be even left behind in a stable, comfortably provided for, till next day. Many huntsmen run through their pack the same night, to look them over for cuts, thorns, and other slight injuries. Cases of lameness will, of course, have been noted during the day. It is, however, sometimes too dark in kennels to see properly to extricate thorns and dress cuts, and the huntsman may attend to these matters in the morning.

In the field the huntsman is perpetually plagued by busybodies, excitable sportsmen, and meddlers, with suggestions as to going to holloas, casting this way or that, and a score of other details, which he, of course, understands far better than any person out. All these things are very distracting and at times very annoying. The level-headed huntsman, however, will, for the sake of peace and in the interests of hunting, usually offer a civil reply to such suggestions. He will, at the same time, pay little or no heed to them, but pursue his own plan of hunting in his own way. Occasionally it may happen that a huntsman has been left in covert, or may have had a fall, or been thrown out, and may require information. He will, in such an event, know exactly how and from whom to get the news he requires. Spectators ought always to remember that the more the huntsman is left alone the better will be their sport.

[1] Occasionally even a fox-hunting huntsman has been known to ride without a horn. "Nimrod," in his Yorkshire Tour, of 1827, mentions "Old Carter," huntsman to Sir Tatton Sykes. "I was much pleased," he says, "with his venerable appearance, his grey locks denoting many years experience in his profession...he was not without his peculiarities and prejudices – one of which was that he never carried a hunting-horn." I have myself known a harrier Master who had a strong objection to the horn; and, for a season or two, his huntsman never carried one.
[2] I can testify to the same prodigy, but it is rare indeed.
[3] With this I do not agree. A whip is necessary, if he be only one of the field who understands the duties.

Chapter Thirteen - Cost and Equipment

THE expense of maintaining a pack of harriers must, of necessity, be a matter of great elasticity, varying in accordance with the ideas of the Master, the length of his purse, and the general turn-out of the establishment. Some few packs of harriers, which perhaps are rather extravagantly managed, and maintain a larger number of hounds than are necessary for hare hunting, may cost as much as £700 per annum, or even a trifle more. If you wish to turn out your men in a style rivalling that of a good pack of foxhounds, as I have seen more than one Master do, you may, and probably will, make a big hole in a thousand pounds. But this is quite unnecessary. With harriers you can see just as much sport with a pack that costs not more than £250 a year, or even less, as with a pack of very high-bred dwarf foxhounds, the Master and two men mounted on expensive horses, unnecessarily good for their work. At the far end of the scale of cost, you may place some of the humbler foot-packs, which can be run upon extremely inexpensive lines. I am acquainted with a pack of nineteen or twenty couples of foot-harriers, for example, which cost to the subscribers a year or so back no more than £120 per annum. In this case, however, the kennels, which belong to the Master, are occupied rent free; the kennel huntsman is employed about the same gentleman's garden, and gets part of his

BALANCE SHEET.

RECEIPTS.	£	s.	d.	EXPENDITURE.	£	s.	d.
Subscriptions, as per List of Subscribing Members	147	7	0	By Licences for hounds *	6	15	0
Balance from last year, less accounts unpaid	2	3	0	,, Huntsman's wages	32	15	6
				,, Keep of hounds	38	12	6
				,, Rent of kennels	8	0	0
				,, Repairs at kennels	5	10	0
				,, Rent of land	1	0	0
				,, Railway fares and expenses for huntsman and hounds, when from kennels	12	5	6
				,, —— & Co.'s account	6	0	0
				,, Postages for balance sheets, &c., and wires	2	17	11
				,, Coal account (16s. 6d. and 17s. 6d.)	1	14	0
				,, Entries into Harrier and Beagle Stud-book	1	11	0
				,, Entries for Show	1	4	0
				,, ——, chemist's account	0	16	4
				,, Advertisements	0	15	0
				,, ——& Co.'s account	0	8	0
				,, Mr. —— account	0	6	8
				,, Straw account	0	16	11
				,, Cheque forms	0	1	8
				,, Balance	28	0	0
	£149	10	0		£149	10	0

* *i.e.*, for nine couples of working hounds.

wages in that way; and, the pack being fed almost entirely on horse-flesh, there is no big bill for meal. At the same time, this pack is thoroughly well done; the kennel huntsman and whip are neatly turned out in proper costume, with caps, green coats, breeches, gaiters, and so forth; and there is even a small surplus available towards prizes at a local Root Show. This convinces one that packs of harriers can be, and often are, hunted at astonishingly low cost, compared with the enormous figures to which the maintenance of foxhounds now runs. On the following page are the accounts of a pack of ten couples of foot-harriers in the north of England, which show how very cheaply sport can be obtained in a wild district where hares are plentiful and there are many good friends to hunting.

This account is for the season ending May 1901. It will be observed that there is a balance in hand of £28, which, deducted from the figures at foot, £149 10s., leaves £121 10s. as the cost of maintenance of this particular pack. Still lower in the scale of expenditure is the cost of a small pack of beagles, say ten or twelve couples, which can be kept going, allowing for wages of a sharp lad, who will act as kennel huntsman and whip, at £70 per annum, or less.

Even in the case of a pack of mounted harriers, the expenditure is often surprisingly little. The late Earl of Suffolk and Berkshire, who thoroughly understood the science of hare-hunting and kept harriers himself for years, has borne testimony, in the "Encyclopaedia of Sport," to the economy with which a mounted pack can be managed. "For most of the many years," he says, "during which I kept harriers, their food cost me about a penny a day per hound, but their solitary attendant was a curious old-fashioned retainer with unusual notions of thrift. A second horseman whipped in, and a horse had to be reserved for this express purpose." Lord Suffolk's pack of fifteen and a half couples cost him for maintenance no more than £114 10s. per annum. This sum was made up as follows:

"Keep of hounds, kennel-man's wages, medicine, and other incidental expenses, £83. The keep of horse for twenty-one weeks (he was only debited to the pack during the hunting season) at £1 1s. per week, £22 1s. The allocated portion of groom's wages for same time, at 9s. per week, £9 9s. This was the lad who whipped in." "Things were roughly, perhaps very roughly, done, but we had capital fun for all that," is Lord Suffolk's concluding remark on the maintenance of this extremely inexpensive pack.

These examples will suffice to show that harriers can, under certain conditions, be managed at surprisingly low cost. Where, however, things are done on the grander scale and with less regard for the policy of cutting matters fine, the cost of harrier-keeping mounts to considerably higher figures. Some thirty years ago an authority upon hunting put the expense of an average pack of harriers twenty-four couples thus:

"By great economy," it is added, "and the dispensing with the whip, and using one horse only, with twenty couples of hounds, only about half this sum will suffice, especially with beagles."

	£	s.	d.	£	s.	d.
Twenty-four couples of hounds at 1s. 6d. per week per head . .	187	4	0			
Tax on ditto	28	16	0			
Medicines, &c. . . .	4	0	0			
Three horses for seven months, at 15s. per week . . .	63	0	0			
Ditto ditto for five months, at 7s. per week	21	0	0			
Tax on ditto	3	0	0			
Veterinary surgeon . . .	3	0	0			
Shoeing	7	10	0			
Saddlery	12	0	0			
				329	10	0
Helper and whip, at 12s. per week .	62	0	0			
Tax on ditto	2	0	0			
				64	0	0
Total cost				£393	10	0

There are various criticisms to be suggested at the present time on such a statement of accounts. In the first place is. 6d. per hound per week would be considered an excessive sum for the feeding of a pack of harriers. A recent authority has reckoned the outside cost of oatmeal for hounds at 11d. per head per week; if mixed with Indian meal it would come out at no more than 8d. or 9d. per head per week. The cost of horseflesh may be put at 2d. per head per week, on the assumption that each horse costs a sovereign. Thus the cost per hound per week for oatmeal and flesh would amount to is. id. per head; while, if Indian meal were mixed with the oatmeal, the cost would be reduced to 10d. per hound per week. Taxes (male-servants), 15s. per man, have to be reckoned for, and hound licences at 7s. 6d. per hound. The wages of helper and whip in the foregoing account are put at far too low a figure for the present day. In providing for a combined kennel huntsman and whip at least £1 per week would now have to be allocated. For a pack of fifteen couples of harriers, hunted by the Master, with the assistance of a kennel huntsman, the cost of hunting two days a week on a quite modest scale might be put pretty much as follows:

This is cutting the thing rather fine; yet I believe that, with great care and economy, a pack of harriers, run with a

	£	s.	d.
Maintenance of fifteen couples of hounds, at 1s. per head per week	78	0	0
Hounds' bedding, implements, repairs, &c. . .	15	0	0
Taxes and licences—hounds and one servant .	12	0	0
Medicines, &c.	3	0	0
Maintenance of whip's horse, seven months at £1 per week (say, £30), five months at 10s. per week (say £11)	41	0	0
Master's horse, seven months at £1 per week .	28	0	0
Veterinary surgeon	2	0	0
Shoeing	3	0	0
Saddlery and repairs	7	0	0
Wages of kennel huntsman at £1 per week .	52	0	0
His outfit	15	0	0
Incidental expenses	14	0	0
Total	£170	0	0

single Hunt servant (mounted), could be maintained for this figure - £170.

In these two last estimates no allowances have been made for rent of kennels or maintenance of puppies. I am assuming that the master, as is very often the case, provides his own kennels. But, on the other hand, I give no credit for certain small incomings, such as sale of hides and sale of draft hounds. These accounts are merely given as indicating the main expenses of a very modest hare-hunting establishment.

A fashionable pack of harriers, run on very liberal lines and turned out huntsman, whip, and all very much after the style of a foxhound pack, may be expected to reach something like the following figures:

This would be running

	£	s.	d.
Huntsman's book (including wages of himself, whip, and feeder, and cost of flesh) . .	300	0	0
Meal and biscuit bill	140	0	0
Rent of kennels and premises (to include all Hunt servants)	35	0	0
Maintenance of three horses	160	0	0
Liveries, saddlery, &c.	50	0	0
Dinner to farmers and others, who walk puppies .	20	0	0
Expense of young hounds	25	0	0
Various incidental expenses—straw, rail, travelling, shoeing, taxes, &c.	60	0	0
Total	£790	0	0

a large pack, say twenty-five couples, on extremely liberal, not to say extravagant, lines, and comparatively few Masters of harriers would be tempted to remain long at the head of hounds if their hare-hunting cost them anything like such a sum. It will be noted also that allowance has been made for a huntsman, his wages and horse, which are items much more often than not saved by the Master hunting his own hounds. Some few packs may, and no doubt do, actually cost their owners and subscribers as much as £700 or £800 a year. But these are in a very small minority indeed; if it were otherwise, hare hunting, which is a cheap sport, could not possibly flourish as it does in these islands.

It may be taken, I think, as a reasonable estimate, that a pack of harriers, hunted on horseback, can be maintained in modest, but perfectly presentable, fashion for £250 per annum. For £300 per annum the thing can be done yet more comfortably. A foot pack, as I have shown, can be run well on £125 per annum. In the case of the more reasonable estimates I have given, rent of kennels is sometimes included, in others it is absent. There is very frequently some kind friend to the Hunt, a Master or ex-Master, who has, at one time or another, built or adapted kennels, which he either lends to the Hunt or lets at a very low figure. In the same way the pack of hounds is often lent, practically for an indeterminate period.

It is, of course, always to be remembered that, to a man starting a pack of harriers where none have previously existed, there must be a good many heavy expenses to begin with. The pack has to be got together, and even a scratch pack of twelve or fifteen couples of draft hounds will average probably from £1 10s. to £2 per hound. Kennels may have to be erected, or adapted from outhouses or old farm buildings. This may run into all sorts of figures. He is a lucky man who can obtain practically new kennels for less than from £100 to £150.

Horses need not be anything like so extravagant an item for hare-hunting as for the chase of the fox. The class of hunter needed with harriers is a handy, confidential mount, which can jump well and cleanly and has a good mouth. There is so much turning with a horse, that your hard-mouthed, free-going, impetuous animal is useless. Even in fox-hunting, it is a *sine qua non* that huntsmen and whips shall have handy mounts, though they should be at the same time good gallopers and bold, clean fencers. With harriers, pace is not so much an essential. Now and again, it is true, hounds will run like wildfire, with a straight-necked hare, and even a first-rate hunter can scarcely live with them. But for average hare hunting, a sound, handy, easy-mouthed horse, a good and temperate fencer, and a fair galloper is all that is needed. Still, it must be remembered that if the Master, who acts as huntsman, means to follow his hounds, he must have a horse that can jump; and in the course of his career he may have to face some very queer and awkward places indeed.

At the same time, it is to be said that some packs of harriers are hunted, and hunted respectably, by Masters getting well on in years, who perform but little fencing, and yet, by their knowledge of the country and of the hare's habits, and by the use of gates, are usually there, or thereabouts, when the kill happens. As for the whip, he may be adequately but not expensively mounted. In Hunts where economy is the vogue, a lad, mounted on a useful cob that can gallop and jump, is often found performing the duties of his office quite reasonably well. Some Masters provide themselves and their whip with second horses, but this is a distinctly uncommon practice in hare-hunting.

In the case of the more affluent of harrier packs, the men are turned out, save that the colour of their coats is green instead of

From a photograph by Mr. J. Coster

THE FOXBUSH HARRIERS

scarlet, in almost exactly the same style as are their brethren with foxhounds. In quieter establishments, the rules of costume are not adhered to with quite such nicety. But with the majority of packs the kit and turn-out are usually smart and workmanlike. Britons, wherever their sport is concerned, love to have things done decently and in order; and, even in the case of establishments where one knows that the Hunt is run on economical lines, it is often noticeable how smartly, yet neatly, the whole thing - men, pack, and horses - is turned out.

With foot-harrier packs, and, very often, even in the case of beagles and bassets, huntsman and whip, if the thing is done respectably, are usually attired in velvet hunting-caps, short green coats, breeches, gaiters, and lace-up boots. White breeches look very smart at the outset, but they soon become soiled, and whipcord, or the thinnest velvet cord procurable, is preferable. For running on foot, of course, the clothing must, all round, be much lighter and thinner than that worn on horseback. Strong green serge is a very good material for jackets, and is much more porous than Melton or other smooth cloths. White breeches of jean or some thin cotton material are, as I say, smart looking, but when, as often happens, the huntsman or whip jumps into a dyke or has to cross a stream, and they get wet, they are certainly chilling garments afterwards. Even khaki is preferable.

Not long since I came across a large coloured print, entitled "The Merry Beaglers," in which a pack of beagles of about the period of the early forties, or perhaps a little earlier, was portrayed. The original painting must have been by no means a bad one. The beagles are of a good stamp and look smart, keen, and up to their work. But it was the costume of the three gentlemen - evidently huntsman and whips - depicted with them that most attracted my attention. They were attired in tall hats, such as our ancestors played cricket in in those days indeed, our ancestors seem to have done everything in tall hats at that time; they even rowed at Henley in them! In addition to the tall hats, big collars, and ample neck-bands, they wore short green jackets and apparently cord trousers, the latter, if my memory serves me, strapped under the boots. Although a fearful and wonderful costume for running down hares in, yet these were no doubt good sportsmen in their day, and saw and enjoyed many a cheery hare hunt. This old print must, I think, be a rare one. I have only once come across it. Certainly we men of the twentieth century are far more sensible in our sporting dress than were our forefathers of the late Georgian and early Victorian period.

With harriers, the costume of the field is very much of the "go as you please" order. The tall hat - that fetish to which fox-hunting men still bow the knee - is seldom exhibited, and tweeds are much more frequently seen than anything else. For running on foot, tweeds, knickerbockers, and stockings, or knickerbocker-breeches and gaiters, a flannel shirt, and a cloth cap are by far the most useful outfit. Ladies - who enjoy sport with foot-harriers, beagles, or bassets as much as any man - are now more suitably equipped than they used to be. In a wet country, where dykes were frequent, I have noticed that a girl, the best lady runner I ever saw out with a foot-pack, had adopted putties, which seemed a sensible precaution. It is astonishing how ladies in these days will brave weather, mud, hills, ploughing, and other obstacles in their determination to see sport. It is by no means an uncommon thing now to see a lady in at the death of a hare, which has been fairly run down by foot-harriers or beagles.

For the pedestrian, the cost of hunting with a pack of foot-harriers is, beyond a trifling subscription - say £1 1s., which ought in fairness to be paid, if the sportsman goes out often - practically nil. A packet of sandwiches suffices for lunch, and a drink on the way home is the only occasion for which the hand need go to the pocket. Occasionally, with foot-packs, a cap may be taken for the huntsman and whip; on such an occasion a shilling will not be grudged by any fair-minded sportsman.

Subscriptions to mounted packs vary a good deal. In some few instances the full membership of the Hunt - which is limited - may be as much as £20 to £25; but, as a rule, from £3 3s. to £5 5s. may be taken to be a fair subscription for a man hunting once or twice a week.

Chapter Fourteen - Some Notable Runs and Curious Anecdotes

IN the case of every pack of harriers, aye, and of beagles, too, in almost every country, you will find, if you begin to inquire with particularity, the memories of some great and astounding run, which has remained always keenly treasured by the sportsmen of the district. If the accounts of these runs could be carefully collected and printed they would form, I am convinced, a very excellent volume. Some few of the great runs of the past have, happily, been preserved from utter oblivion by being printed in some old sporting magazine or in the local paper of the period. Before passing to some among the more remarkable runs of the present day, I think it may interest my hare-hunting readers if I recall one or two famous chases of the past.

While making inquiries for the purpose of this book concerning the origin of hare-hunting in the Peak district of Derbyshire, I came, on several occasions, across various references to a certain renowned Squire Frith, who hunted a pack of fine, old-fashioned harriers many years ago in that wild and picturesque district. And, in particular, I found repeated allusions to a most memorable hunt which the Squire and his good hounds accomplished. Oral tradition is useful, but it is not always very reliable or very particular in its details. After a good deal of inquiry, I have managed to unearth the details of this great run, partly from the *Sporting Magazine* of 1826, partly from the accounts procured for me, from oral tradition, by a brother [1] living in Derbyshire. Squire Frith, of Bank Hall, near Chapel-en-le-Frith, kept harriers for many years in the eighteenth and early part of the nineteenth century. He was a very famous old sportsman, who, after fifty years of the chase, was, in the year 1826, still to be seen mounted on a square-built cob, ambling over the fine turf of his native hills with the Buxton harriers, which he gave up in that year. Many a good run had the old gentleman seen with his staunch hounds; but the finest of all was his great chase of close on forty miles from near Chapel-en-le-Frith to the neighbourhood of Congleton in Cheshire. Squire Frith seems always to have stuck to harriers, but, like many other sportsmen of his time, he hunted an occasional fox as well as hare. In December, somewhere about the year 1786, word came to the Squire that a fox had been marked to earth and "made in," as they call it up north, near a cottage called Hole House, by Castle Naze Rocks, not far from Chapel-en-le-Frith. Next morning, December 8, when the Squire turned out with his hounds and field, the frost had rendered the ground much fitter for foot-work than for hunting a fox over the rugged and steep moorlands and through the rocky dales of North Derbyshire. All the earths round had been stopped, and the fox was duly unkennelled and the pack laid on. As sometimes happens in frost there was a ravishing scent, and a marvellous chase ensued. The fox took them by Taxal, near Whaley Bridge, over the Duke of Devonshire's moors, skirting Axe Edge, the highest range in the county, on to Macclesfield Forest; thence by Tagsneys, Crookward, and Langly and Gracely Woods, to Swithingly, where they sustained a short check. Hitting off the line again they followed him to Horsly and Gawsworth, and finally ran into and killed this wonderfully stout fox at Clouds Hill, near Congleton. The fox had stood up before his pursuers for just under forty miles. The horses got their riders back as far as the "Cat and Fiddle" Inn, on Axe Edge, the highest inn in England, but were so beaten that they had to be left there for the night.

This is by far the finest and longest run with a pack of harriers that I ever heard of. Few, if any, packs of foxhounds have ever beaten it. It made so deep an impression on the country-side at the time that some rustic bard composed a song, commemorating this great hunt, which song was sung at all popular gatherings in the Peak district for more than fifty years after. There is still an old man living in this district who used, as a boy with a fine voice, to go all round the country to sing it at various assemblies. [2] During this run Squire Frith rode his well-known horse, Blackjack, a very notable fencer in that country of stone walls, and always well up with hounds.

I have made some reference to "Parson" Froude's pack of old English harriers, from which is descended in great part the present pack of Sir John Heathcoat Amory. In the year 1825 Mr. Froude and his pack while trailing for a hare, came on a wild red deer, a hind which had wandered from Exmoor Forest. With this hind the pack had an extraordinary run of four hours; with the exception of a check of five minutes hounds were pushing their quarry hard the whole time. They ran through ten parishes, and although the deer sought to baffle them by taking soil on two occasions, they pressed her from scent to view, and finally killed her near Tiverton. It was recorded at the time that although these harriers had to undergo a desperately severe chase over a strong country every hound was up at the death, and all returned to kennel without being overdone. This must evidently have been a real good pack of hounds. They are stated to have been chiefly bred from their own kennel for a score of years previously, were grey and white in colour, twenty-one inches in height, possessing plenty of bone, and standing on a good deal of ground. In the same year (1825) the Dorset Vale harriers killed two foxes in one day after runs of an hour and forty-five minutes and an hour and thirty-three minutes respectively. These harriers apparently hunted hare and fox indiscriminately and were as good upon one as the other.

In the winter of 1820 a stag was turned out at Silverly, near Newmarket, before Mr. Bryant's harriers. The pack that day consisting of six couples only. There was a big field out. With this stag these harriers ran over a stiff country for a distance reckoned at twenty miles and, pulling him down, killed him. The pace must have been more than good, for of the horses following two were killed outright, while others were not expected to recover. Somehow or other in those days hunting-men killed their horses far more frequently than is the case at present. Whether they rode them unfit, or whether, as I am inclined to think, they pushed them more recklessly and more unmercifully than they do now, it is certain that a large number of horses died in the hunting-field each winter. Such a thing is comparatively rare nowadays. For one thing, I believe riders are more humane, and a beaten horse is not ridden and spurred to his last gasp as used to be the case.

Before I quit the subject of harriers and deer, I will mention a good run with a Ward Union deer, in which my friend, Mr. W. Dove, and his pack, the Tara Harriers, took a leading part. This was in the season of 1898-99. "An occasional outlying deer was," writes Mr. Dove, "left out on our side of the country, and, being rather too far for the Wards to come for it, the Master used to give me leave to hunt them. This we did with much success, having one really great run in my first season, from Corbalton Hall vid Sclater's Gorse, Kilmoor, and Newton Sticks, to beyond Ashbourne, when she jumped up from a ditch. From there she ran in view through the village of Ashbourne; on then past the Ward kennels, where she evidently tried to get into the paddock, over the Sutherland farm, as if for Lagore, *via* Creakenstown. Here a hare got up in front of hounds and, getting through wire, we could not stop them for some time. Having succeeded and got them on the road for home, they again hit off the line of the deer and ran nearly back to Corbalton. Here we saw her in front of hounds dead beat. She got into a ditch in the next field and died while being taken out by two men, whether from the effects of the run or from striking some wire with which she had come in contact I don't know. She was a celebrated deer, Drogheda Lass, and had given the Wards many fine hunts. We found that, though the best point was only nine miles, we had covered between twenty-two and twenty-three miles of the finest country in Meath." These instances serve to show that, when hunting deer, harriers are fully as capable as foxhounds of showing magnificent sport. From my own point of view, although I should much have liked to have seen Parson Froude's harriers pull down a wild Exmoor red deer after a run of four hours I prefer to see harriers hunt hare, which is to my mind their true and natural vocation. Mr. Dove tells me that in one of his harriers' runs after outlying deer their hind swam two miles down the centre of the Boyne river, a curious performance. This was a very cunning deer, which used constantly to take to the river.

Coming to the real thing, one of the finest hare hunts of which I have record, is that of a great run with the Cotley harriers during the time of the grandfather of the present Master, Mr. Eames. "They found," writes Mr. Eames, "a hare on Cotley Farm and killed her at Wellington Monument, which is over twelve miles as the crow flies." Mr. Eames suggests that this is a record run with a hare. I, for one, am not disinclined to agree with him. More than twelve miles as the crow flies is, in truth, an extraordinary run with a hare. A glance at a map of Somersetshire will show that hare, hounds, and huntsman must have passed through a large number of parishes during the course of this wonderful run.

The best run I have ever myself seen with a hare, whether hunting on horseback or on foot, happened with the Hailsham harriers on November 24,

1900. We met at Pevensey, the day being dull but fine, with a mild, light breeze from the south-east. Quickly finding a hare, hounds pushed her out on to the marshes parallel with the sea. After running up wind for threequarters of a mile or so, the hare turned short back, and, running right through a number of spectators, amid much noise, holloaing and hubbub, sustained, I suppose, such a fright that she set her face straight for the inland country, and neither turned nor dallied for another yard. Heading northward, straight across the wide marshes, she quitted her own country and, crossing Manxey Level, passed Horse-Eye, and swam the Hurst Haven, a broadish stream which runs into the sea on this part of the Sussex coast. Now leaning a little towards Hailsham she presently changed her mind, bore right-handed and sped on for New Bridge and Herstmonceux. Coming round the castle she was disturbed by some villagers and ran on to Wartling Hill, where, on some ploughing just below the church, a check occurred. Scent, from the very beginning of the hunt, had been a burning one, and hounds ran with a beautiful cry

From a photograph by Fred. A. Bourne, Eastbourne

HAILSHAM HARRIERS

and with the greatest fire and resolution. The field had, from the severity of the pace and the straightness of the run, been left far behind, some stopped by lack of wind, others by the broad and deep dykes scattered over the marsh; and at Wartling Hill, as we trotted up towards the hounds, only five or six were left to fight it out. Among these were Mr. Rupert Williams, the then joint-Master and huntsman, James Holmwood, the kennel huntsman, the writer, and two or three others.

As we got within hail, the hounds, which had for some time been busily casting about for themselves, put up the hare, which had here squatted on the plough, and, with a wonderful burst of music from their deep voices, raced away in pursuit. The pace was now again so great that we were left quickly in the rear. The hare now took us through Wartling Wood, thence left-handed over Mr. Curteis's park at Windmill Hill, then crossing the road between Herstmonceux village and Boreham Street, she sank the beautiful valley towards Bodle Street and reached Cowden Wood. The pack was pressing her with such vigour that she had little inclination or time to linger. She now pushed on to Causeway, thence to Fareham Bridge, Promts Wood and Cattell's Wood. From Cattell's Wood, with the ravening pack closing up and now near at hand, she pressed uphill towards Cowbeech Mill. Hounds were now close at her scut and she was tiring fast. She got as far as Foul Mile, some little way beyond Cowbeech, and was there run into and killed. Two labourers, who happened to be close at hand, saved the hare from the pack and handed her to two gentlemen who had joined in the hunt near Windmill Hill. The five survivors of the beginning of this great run, toiling on foot far in the rear of the hounds, and occasionally guided by their voices, were a mile or so behind when the end came. We presently picked up the hounds as they returned to Herstmonceux. This was a quite extraordinary run, lasting two hours and three quarters. From point to point this stout hare took the pack seven miles; as hounds ran the distance measured thirteen or fourteen. In this instance the pack hunted and killed their game entirely unassisted. At times, especially as they raced across Windmill Hill Park, they were running mute, a somewhat remarkable thing in a pack largely of Southern Hound blood and renowned for its music. The hare had traversed no less than seven parishes; and we were so far from our head-quarters and so leg weary that we chartered a trap and drove back the six miles from Herstmonceux village to Pevensey. It is very seldom, indeed, that, even with a pack hunted on foot, I have seen hounds get so completely away from their field as upon this occasion.

Colonel Robertson Aikman tells me that the best run he had in Lanarkshire, where he hunted hare many seasons, was on January 26, 1891. They ran from Cleddans Gate to the moor beyond Cumbernauld and killed in forty-five minutes; as hounds ran the distance was eight miles, while from point to point it measures six miles. In Derbyshire, with the High Peak harriers, his present pack, Colonel Robertson Aikman's best day happened on January 10, 1903. As hounds ran the distance traversed was nine miles, the cream of it a six-mile point from below Parsley Hay, Monyash Side, to Middleton Hall, accomplished in thirty-five minutes. The whole run occupied one hour. This has always been an excellent part of the High Peak country for runs, and the hares all over this district are wonderfully tough and hardy some of the very stoutest in England, in fact. Here is an entry from the diary of Mr. Nesfield, so long Master of the pack, in 1865: "Tuesday, 19th December, Monyash. Found near Mellands'; ran brilliantly to Abbot's Gorse, down the road to Hurdlow Wood and Wharf, over the heather hills to the left, thence leaving Cronkstone Grange on the left over the hill, back to the heath. Here the two foxhound bitches 'Ruby' and 'Fairmaid' distinguished themselves; they took up the scent and killed in Cronkstone Wood; two hours, twenty-eight minutes." "How many foxes," adds his commentator, "could stand before Belvoir bitches like this!" Two days after this great run, the High Peak, meeting at Gotham Gate, found near Cliff House and had a wonderful run of an hour and ten minutes. At the end the hare fell dead, one hundred yards in front of the pack. Instances of hares falling dead before hounds in this way, after a very severe hunt, are not common, still, they do occur. Colonel Aikman tells me of a similar incident which happened in a run in Lanarkshire on October 31, 1898.

The hare dropped dead two fields in front of hounds after a long hunt. These cases happen, I fancy, more often where hares are hunted with dwarf fox-hounds, or with harriers containing a good deal of foxhound blood, than with ordinary harriers. I imagine that the severity of the pace is greater and the hare is much more pressed throughout.

Before I quit Derbyshire hare-hunting I will make mention of an extraordinary instance of endurance in a hound. Towards the end of the season of 1892, while hunting to the south of Newhaven, one of the High Peak bitches, "Dauntless," was lost. Fairclough, the huntsman, feared she had fallen down one of the several disused lead-mines, and tried every one he could find. He obtained no response, however, and reluctantly gave up the search as hopeless. A month and a day later a farmer, having lost a lamb in this part of the country, also examined the same mines and presently heard a faint whine. No ladder could be obtained of sufficient length and a miner went down the shaft on a rope. He found the hound just alive, but unable to stand or see. In spite of this extraordinary period of starvation and exposure the bitch recovered both her health and good looks. [3] As illustrating the extraordinary lack of scent in a squatting hare, I make one more quotation from Mr. Nesfield's diary. "Thursday, 23rd October (1873). Elton; had a capital run and kill; one hour thirty-five minutes. It was a soaking rain...She clapped (squatted), and I watched no less than four or five hounds actually tread on her without finding her out. Not a particle of scent till in motion."

Mr. Hawkins, whose harriers I have already mentioned, sends me a brief note of a very fine run with his pack in Northamptonshire in 1902. This took place in the territory of the Grafton and Pytchley Hunts, some of the very finest fox-hunting country in Britain. After killing a brace of hares in the neighbourhood of Stowe Nine Churches, where they met, his harriers put up a stout jack hare in Heyford parish. Him they hunted at a fast pace by the village of Stowe, thence along the northern side of Stowe Wood. Breasting the hill above Weedon hounds left that place on their right and, racing down the hill over Everdon Vale, pulled down their hare a mile short of Badby Wood. "The distance as the crow flies was seven miles, and the pace was good throughout." I know this country well, and the Grafton followers would esteem themselves lucky if they had chased and killed a fox over such a line.

In Gloucestershire, Mr. J. S. Gibbons's harriers, the "Boddington," show excellent sport. Many good runs with points of five miles or so, writes Mr. Gibbons, have been enjoyed during his mastership of the country. Here a are few of them. "Found at Swindon, ran well across the Vale, straight up the hill, and killed on the top of Cleeve Hill. Twice in one season a hare ran from Boddington to Wallsworth Hall, a point of nearly five miles, losing, through changing hares, at the finish; probably the same hare gave both these runs, as the line was precisely the same. In 1901 two long runs occurred in one day, one hare being found at Haydon and the other at Boddington, and both being curiously lost at Tredington village, after a four- and five-mile point in each instance. Perhaps the best run over the Vale we ever had was last season, when a hare from the Leigh was killed close to Cheltenham, after 45 minutes fast run over some of the best of the Vale country."

"The longest run I have had," says Mr. Carlton Cross, Master since 1890 of the Aspull harriers, Lancashire, "was a 6-mile point, but it was not as fast as one in the season of 1900-1901, when we ran 6½ miles in a horse-shoe in thirty minutes, over a grass country; in both cases we never changed. As to the distance a hare can run, I have known them go three times round our point-to-point racecourse, which is three miles round." A nine-mile hare-hunt is no bad thing, and Lancashire hares are evidently good enough for any harriers; for the Aspull is a very smart and well-bred pack of modern harriers, with a good deal of foxhound blood about them. Mr. Cross, among other interesting notes with which he has been good enough to favour me, tells me that he is one of those who hold with giving plenty of hares to hounds. He does it and believes in it. I think the majority of harehunters, who give their killed hares to neighbouring farmers, are satisfied with the keenness of the pack without more blood than is afforded by the entrails, &c. I have for years watched the demeanour of hounds at the death, and whether they run into and kill and devour the hare themselves, as sometimes happens, or whether the hare is taken from them and saved, I have never been able to discover that their keenness thereafter was greater one way than the other. Still, Mr. Carlton Cross holds the contrary opinion, and thinks that it is "most necessary" that harriers should have plenty of hares.

Mr. Cross sends me a very amusing instance of the mysterious disappearance of a hare at the end of a run. All hare-hunters, I am afraid, can bear testimony to being robbed of the fruits of a hard run in some such manner; but the experience of the Master of the Aspull harriers is almost unique. He had run a hare and lost her. Riding up to an old woman who was passing by, he asked her if she had seen anything of the quarry. She answered that she had not, and went on her way. Mr. Cross never noticed her umbrella, but the old dame had actually picked up the hare, deposited it in her umbrella, and got clear away with it! Well, to an old and poor woman one would not grudge a spent hare now and again, but it is rather maddening, as one discovers afterwards, when some poaching lout with a dog picks up the hunted hare at the end of a hard run and makes off with it, thus robbing the pack of its well-earned blood and some honest farmer of a capital dinner.

This incident with the Aspull harriers is, however, not quite unprecedented. More than a hundred years ago a country woman, passing down a lane, came face to face with a hare hotly pursued by a pack of harriers. The hare was so intent on the clamour of her followers that she never observed the woman, who, "with great presence of mind," as the chronicler puts it, stooped and held out her apron, into which the hare straightway ran and was captured. [4]

Fox-hunters of the present day constantly complain, and with great show of reason, of short running foxes, and the poor hunts but too often obtained. It is certainly quite the exception in these later years to experience a really great run with a pack of foxhounds, even in the best of our hunting countries. Various causes are assigned for this state of things. Some allege that cubs are too much left alone; others, that the young foxes are slain in the cubbing season in too great numbers; while others, again, hold that we breed our hounds too much for speed and pay too little attention to the quality of our foxes. Others, again, assert, and I think with a good deal of reason, that in many countries there are far too many foxes, and that constant changing robs the pack of many a good run which might otherwise have been obtained. Again, the enormous fields, of both horse and foot people, have undoubtedly a very deterrent effect on the quality of sport shown. At meets in fashionable countries foxes have but too often small chance of getting away with a fair start, and are so headed and mobbed that they can yield no sport and die an unworthy death. Happily, one does not find the same state of things obtaining with harrier packs. The sport, conducted usually in a quiet and enjoyable manner, with small fields and comparatively few foot people, escapes, thank heaven, the unhappy popularity of fox-hunting, and flourishes as successfully as it did two hundred years ago, when Sir Roger de Coverley and his fellow squires rode out with their Southern hounds.

To me it seems - and I have followed very closely the history and the records of hare-hunting that sport with harriers at the present day yields as good runs as ever it did. Hare-hunts are not so frequently published in the *Field* as are runs with foxhounds. Yet, as I write this chapter, I take from the current number of that excellent publication, details of a first-rate run with a pack of harriers, the Dart Vale, mastered and hunted by Mr. Leigh Densham. On February 9, 1903, these hounds found a hare near Afton Tor, and ran her by way of Loventor and Waye Barton back to Afton, where they changed in some big woodland. Hounds were now taken away and at Weekabaro Cross roads got on to the line of a travelling hare, which gave them a magnificent run of an hour and ten minutes, when hounds ran into her at Barton Pines. In this run, which occurred without a check, a six-mile point was made, and the pace was so good that at one time the pack were nearly a mile ahead of the rapidly tiring field, most of whom, however, by judicious riding managed to get on terms again. A run like this is surely good enough even for fox-hunters.

In the same number of the *Field* I read an account of two runs in one day with the Downham harriers; the first, thirty-five minutes and a kill with a real straight-necked hare; the second, a very fine forty-five minutes and a kill in the Fens. Yet again, in the same paper, is an account of a great run with the Culm Vale Foot-Harriers, an hour and forty-five minutes and a kill, and another run of an hour and thirty-five minutes. These instances, taken from but three accounts of sport with harriers in the same week, prove, surely enough, if proof were needed, that hare hunting in these early years of the twentieth century flourishes exceedingly. I have seen a great deal of sport with fox-hounds, and I admire that sport as much as any man, but I honestly believe that at the present time and in the present state of fox-hunting, the harrier man gets more sport and better value for his time and money than does the fox-hunter. I don't say this for a moment with the view of making hare-hunting more popular. Heaven forbid! I, and all other hare-hunters must, I am convinced, pray that the sport may go on and prosper under its present quiet and placid conditions. If it becomes popular, as has fox-hunting, it will be ruined. Its very strength and its very pleasures lie in the fact that it is pursued chiefly upon quiet country sides, in the old-fashioned manner, and with small fields.

Some harriers are, individually, extremely keen on foxes if they come across them, and as a rule most packs, collectively, will, once they get on the line of that animal, hunt him with great fire and vigour. Some hounds will, on the contrary, never look at the drag of a fox, and seem to dislike it instinctively. Some, again, will hunt readily either hare or fox. Mr. Doyle, of the Crickhowell Harriers, sends me a curious incident in connection with his pack. They were hunting (on foot), by arrangement, in Monmouthshire, just after frost, and were sent to draw a certain foxcovert which the Monmouthshire Hunt had never drawn that season. "As might have been expected," he continues, "we found a fox there. They drove him straight for about six miles, then swung round to the right for about two more, and then ran into him, no one up. I only learnt long after how it ended from a casual passer-by, who saw the kill from his gig. We utterly failed to find the hounds, and went home with a few which had been tailed off and straggled back. Next day my whip found the hounds at a homestead, where a benevolent farmer had housed them for the night. On their return journey they found and killed a hare. Two were missing, Landsman and Wanderer. We found Landsman about a month afterwards at the Ross kennels. Wanderer, I hope, returned to his original home." Landsman, it is to be noted, was very keen on a fox, and if by accident they got on to one, it was no easy matter to whip him off. In this case it seems probable that the extreme keenness of one harrier for fox led the whole pack into a grand hunt, in which, however, they slipped their field and had the fun entirely to themselves. Another harrier, on the contrary, says Mr. Doyle, "would not go ten yards on a fox. One such hound in a pack is a treasure in a country like ours, saving one from all doubt."

Of one of his harriers (the above-mentioned Wanderer) Mr. Doyle writes: "One of the best hounds I ever had was a rough Welsh hound. He suddenly turned up we knew not from where. He had rather humpy shoulders, but was otherwise very well made, with better legs and feet than the generality of his breed. He had a rare nose and a lovely voice, and hunted hare or fox with perfect impartiality. He had, too, a mysterious knack of anticipating almost always correctly - a hare's doubles, and, when he got older, and somewhat slow, cutting off corners." One wonders if this good Welsh hound ever found his way to his own kennels after the memorable fox-hunt above referred to. Perhaps he thought he had then done enough for the Crickhowell, and did, in fact, betake himself to his old quarters.

I confess to a partiality for Welsh hounds. They are seldom bad ones. Some years ago the Pytchley Hunt had curiously enough, a couple of these rough hounds running with the pack. They were wonderful workers, and held their own gallantly with one of the best packs in the country. "Brooksby" several times made mention of them in his hunting notes of that period. It was a singular experiment, but it proved, at any rate, that the Welsh hound, with his rough coat and not always perfect shape - according to modern ideas - is good enough to hold his own in the best of company.

I have already mentioned the fact that hares will occasionally go to ground when hard pressed, just as they will betake themselves to that unfamiliar element, the sea. The Crickhowell last season ran a hare to ground in a cleft amid some rocks. A terrier was put in and killed her, and the hare was later on got out with some difficulty. Some weeks afterwards, another hare went to earth in the same place; after much digging and shifting of boulders, this one was found fast jammed between two rocks at least six feet below the surface.

Among the most fruitful sources of danger to harriers and foxhounds alike are railway lines and sea cliffs. Many a good hound has, unhappily, fallen a victim to one or the other. Colonel Robertson Aikman's harriers, in March 1889, had one of the most extraordinary escapes on record. Three or four couples of them were not only on the line as a train came by, but actually went under the whole length of the train in motion and escaped unhurt. This was a rather wonderful day with these hounds as, in addition to the train episode, they ran a hare into the river Clyde and killed her there.

Every one familiar with harriers has seen a hare run through the jaws of a pack, as it were, and escape with her life. Colonel Aikman tells me of a remarkable instance of this with his pack in Derbyshire last year. When on the moorland at Sparklow he saw two hares sitting. They got up and hounds were running them in view through a narrow way, with a wall on either side. A third hare jumped up, as hounds went over her, and ran right through the middle of the pack for thirty or forty yards, passing each hound before he saw her.

I once witnessed a very curious incident while out with the Foxbush Harriers. It was a good many years ago, when Mr. Kemp himself always hunted them on foot. We found a hare, and had a capital run with her and lost. Almost immediately we got on to a fresh hare and enjoyed a real good run with her also. Presently she began to tire, and hounds closed up rapidly and were running hard for blood. We had by this time returned to the place where we first found her. Just at this moment some of the hounds picked up the first hare, which was by this time so stiff that she was scarcely able to move. We had at this moment then the strange gratification of running into both our hunted hares simultaneously. They were actually killed within a few yards of one another.

I have already made some mention of the frequency with which hares when hunted take to rivers and streams. I came recently on some old accounts of sport with the Blackmoor Vale Harriers (Dorset) in the year 1832, in which some extraordinary feats of swimming are recorded. On February 24 these harriers met on Lydlinch Common, and, finding a jack hare near Bagbere, had a great run with him. He swam the river Lyddon four times, and finding the pack still pressing him unpleasantly crossed yet a fifth time. Thence he ran to Stourton Caundle, where he swam the Caundle stream, and yet once more crossing the river was killed on the border of Lydlinch Common, after a magnificent run of an hour and thirty minutes. During this run twelve miles of country were covered, seven of them nearly straight. A second find this day furnished a run of one hour thirty-five minutes, with a kill at the finish, this hare having swum the Stour. On March 1 with the same pack their hare swam the river five times and was killed after a chase of an hour and twenty minutes. Another hare on the same day was killed after thirty-five minutes' hard gallop, while yet another yielded a run of more than two hours.

The Blackmoor Vale Harriers seem to have shown quite extraordinary sport in those days. I find accounts of the following runs between January 24 and March 1, 1832.

These seem to me to be extraordinarily good records, scarcely to be excelled by any pack at any period.

Date	Duration	Result
January 24	1 hour 45 min.	Kill.
,, 24	1 ,, 3 ,,	Kill.
,, 27	50 ,,	Kill.
,, 27	45 ,,	Kill.
,, 27	1 ,, 25 ,,	Kill.
,, 31	50 ,,	Kill. (Every horse left behind "out of sight and hearing.")
February 3	1 ,, 10 ,,	Hare picked up.
,, 3	55 ,,	Kill.
,, 3	1 ,, 45 ,,	Whipped off.
,, 7	1 ,, 15 ,,	Kill.
,, 7	1 ,, 5 ,,	Kill.
,, 10	1 ,, 30 ,,	Kill.
,, 10	1 ,, 40 ,,	Lost.
,, 14	1 ,,	Kill.
,, 14	2 ,, 30 ,,	Kill. (Over thirteen miles of country.)
,, 17	1 ,, 30 ,,	Kill.
,, 17	2 ,, 20 ,,	Whipped off at a fox covert.
,, 21	45 ,,	Kill.
,, 21	45 ,,	Kill.
,, 24	1 ,, 30 ,,	Kill.
,, 24	1 ,, 35 ,,	Kill.
February 28	30 min.	Lost.
March 1	35 ,,	Kill.
,, 1	1 hour 20 ,,	Kill.
,, 1	2 ,,	Whipped off.

[1] Mr. W. R. Bryden, of Buxton.
[2] I have printed this song in Appendix C, not for its metre, which is very halting at times, but as a curiosity in harrier annals. As a contemporaneous document, it is striking evidence of Squire Frith's famous run. One version of the song, gathered from oral tradition, says the fox was run to ground. In the version I give, printed in the *Sporting Magazine* so far back as 1826, it states distinctly that the quarry was killed. Possibly he was dug out and killed.
[3] This case is authenticated in "A Third of a Century with the High Peak Harriers," p. 40.
[4] "Annals of Sporting," 1823. Vol. iv. p. 233.

Chapter Fifteen - Hunting with Foot-Harriers

HUNTING with foot-harriers is a peculiarly English sport, which must have flourished in quiet country places for untold generations. It is typically English, as it seems to me, for the reason that it appeals to those athletic and outdoor instincts in which all Englishmen, and indeed all Britons, have been remarkable from the earliest times. And especially in the wilder and remoter parts of the kingdom, in localities unsuited for pursuit on horseback, is the foot-hunter to be found flourishing at the present day, just as he has flourished for hundreds of years past. The Fells of Cumberland and Westmoreland, the moors of Lancashire, the hills of Wales and the marshes and downs of Sussex still afford magnificent sport to foot-hunters, and throughout the winter attract small but enthusiastic fields, who follow each feature of the chase and watch the staunch harriers at their work with a keenness and enjoyment not to be excelled in any branch of British rural sport. As for beagle packs, to which I shall come in another chapter, they are nowadays very plentiful, and in almost all parts of England afford excellent hunting. Even in Ireland, that country of horses and horsemen, as I have shown, the hare is occasionally hunted with harriers on foot; and the peasants and small farmers of Kerry and Clare gather their trencher-fed hounds on Sunday mornings and range the mountains in pursuit of a pastime which affords them endless pleasure and excitement. In Cumberland and the lake country, the fox as well as the hare is hunted on foot, and among the rugged fells great sport is shown with either quarry. Whether John Peel hunted hare as well as fox, I know not; possibly he did. But at the present day the Brampton Harriers, hunting from near Carlisle, show first-rate sport with hare in Peel's old country. These hounds are now hunted on horseback as well as on foot; but when engaged in some of their fell country, they can be hunted and followed on foot only. Occasionally after a good day the field rest and refresh themselves at Caldbeck Inn, and, with the cheery fell-side farmers, wake the echoes of the very room where, years ago, the famous old hunting-song was composed. John Peel himself, it will be remembered, lived at Troutbeck "once on a day," but the veteran in his grey coat hunted his hounds many a time and oft above Caldbeck village.

Hunting on foot is a thoroughly democratic sport, which can be enjoyed by the country lad or girl, the farmer's son, the village postman, nay, the village cobbler, if he choose to put aside his last, just as heartily as by the squire himself, or any of their betters. The good farmer himself welcomes the hounds. Even if, in these bad times, he is not quite so keen on foxhunting as he or his forbears used to be, he can join heart and soul in the sport of the foot-hunter; and if he is too well up in years to follow the chase himself, can usually nick in here and there, or from some chosen eminence view the hounds pushing their hare with merry cry over the more open country. Foot-hunting is a form of sport I think much more adapted for hills, downland, or open marshes than in strongly enclosed country, where the view is hindered by big timbered hedge-rows. Perhaps the finest country of all, from a spectacular as well as a sporting point of view, lies in the wide, well-drained marshes of the coast line of East Sussex, where, from the low hills surrounding the great grass "levels," magnificent views of the whole panorama of the chase are frequently to be obtained, even if the spectator is not inclined to do much running.

Dyke-jumping is a particular feature of hare-hunting in this locality, and the man who can long-jump fairly well, has a sound wind, and is keen on the sport, can have some of the best hare-hunting in England. An athletic training stands one in excellent stead for this phase of the sport. Some of the dykes are so wide that a man must be able to clear fourteen or even fifteen feet to get over. To an athlete in light running costume and spiked shoes that distance, of course, sounds very little. But put the same man into winter clothing, tweeds, knickerbockers, and boots, and offer him a poorish take-off on heavy, and perhaps, greasy ground, and a leap of fourteen feet means a good deal. The man who can get over a Sussex dyke containing say twelve feet of water, would, in athlete's costume, on a fine day and from a good take-off, readily clear eighteen or nineteen feet. It is a real pleasure - I speak as an old athlete - to see a man going well over such a country, with a good pack of foot-harriers. This form of running is a considerably more severe trial than a jog trot with a paper chase; I have tested every possible style of running, and I speak from experience. I like to see a man run steadily after the clamorous pack, keeping well within himself, taking each broad dyke as it comes, and clearing it with a fine effort, and keeping the while an eye on the line of the hare. When hounds are really running hard on a good scenting day - I speak of eighteen- or nineteen-inch harriers - it is of course impossible for the finest long-distance runner in England to keep within hail. The judicious sportsman must, if he means to see the end, cut off a corner now and again and swing across the centre of the ring which the hare is almost inevitably making.

In such a country the man on foot is more than a match for a good horse. These deep dykes are too trappy to be ridden over, and the marshes of which I write are practically never attempted by fox-hunters. But even in more practicable country the good water-jumper on foot is, at a wide brook, more than a match usually for the average mounted man or woman. Few horses are really fond of water, and steeplechasers, like Chandler (whose mythical thirty-nine feet at Warwick by the way has never yet been satisfactorily proved), are few and far between. Jack Mytton and one or two others are said to have cleared nine yards of water on exceptionally fine hunters. I think such a feat is, for a real good horse - say, one in ten thousand - and a very bold rider, quite possible, but few mounted hunters indeed would make much of a show against a good Sussex dyke-jumper who is really "for it" and means going. I have known enthusiasts during some particularly exciting moment of a hare-hunt, when hounds are racing for blood and the end is surely coming, who will jump at anything. Nay, I have in mind a Master of foot-harriers, a fine long-jumper, who, sooner than not be with his hounds, will spring full-tilt into a river and get across somehow, if it is too broad to compass at a leap. Still, it is not all, even among the enthusiasts, who will proceed to such extremities. After all there are such things as chills, and one cannot take liberties with one's constitution perpetually.

As a maturer foot-hunter who, thanks to an athletic youth, can still stay comfortably at a steady pace over such a country, and still jump a Sussex marsh dyke with most of the youngsters, I advise the foot-hunter, unless he be a first-rate athlete in fine running trim, always to bear in mind some lines of Somervile. They contain most excellent advice, written of hounds, yet singularly applicable to the human hunter, who may be desirous to see the end of a really good run in which he is taking part:

"Happy the man who with unrival'd speed
Can pass his fellows, and with pleasure view
The struggling pack; how in the rapid course
Alternate they preside, and, jostling, push
To guide the dubious scent: how giddy youth,
Oft babbling, errs, by wiser age reprov'd;
How, niggard of his strength, the wise old hound
Hangs in the rear, till some important point
Rouse all his diligence, or till the Chace
Sinking he finds; then to the head he springs,
With thirst of glory fir'd, and wins the prize."

Even to the best runner in the world these lines may be useful. To the moderate performer and the veteran they contain advice on hare-hunting which it is impossible to better.

But hare-hunting on foot is not alone for the athlete and for youth. Many a man of middle-age, many a grey-haired farmer, many a lady, can watch the chase in all its diverse wanderings and enjoy a long day's sport without running a hundred yards. Thanks to that instinct which seems, in nine cases out of ten, to compel the hare to return to the neighbourhood of the very place where she was first put up, the spectators, especially in fairly open country or from a hillside, can often see as much of the hunt as the runners striding along with infinite labour and endurance in the wake of the hounds. Nay, it is not by any means an unusual thing to see those who have been merely watching and not following, nick in just as they see hounds running into their game, and actually be up at the death before the three or four stout runners and jumpers who have been steadily sticking to the line for an hour or more. Mr. Otho Paget, an enthusiastic hare-hunter, has said that hunting on foot is the only sportsmanlike way of pursuing this animal. I do not go so far with him as that, but I do agree that hare-hunting on foot, if a man is fit enough and athletic enough to run with hounds, is one of the very finest pastimes in the world. Personally, after having tested almost every kind of sport, mounted and on foot, I know few pleasures to equal it. On foot a man can, to my mind, see even more of the actual science of hare-hunting, one of the most beautiful and interesting chases in the world, than on horseback. A man on foot can go anywhere. He can penetrate woodlands and copses where a horse cannot follow. He can cross a big stream, either by leaping or wading, or a combination of both, where a horse is pounded; and he can penetrate into all sorts of odd corners and perplexing places where his mounted fellow cannot possibly make his way. In fact, much more frequently than not he can be almost always with hounds, watching each phase of the hare's flight and of the marvellous patience, instinct, perseverance, scenting, and stoutness with which the good harrier unravels yard by yard, mile by mile, that cunning puzzle which the little brown beast ahead has set before the pack.

From a photograph by Mr. J. Coster
HAILSHAM HARRIERS
THE DEATH

During the chase of a hare over wild moorland country or broad unfrequented marshes, or through big woodlands, you may often come suddenly upon some

From a photograph by Mr. J. Coster
HAILSHAM HARRIERS
GOING HOME

interesting feature in natural history. While hare-hunting in Sussex I have seen peregrine falcons and hen-harriers pursuing their predatory career while one was actually hunting; hoodie crows, with their quaint and rather murderous ways, are constant winter residents upon our marshes; they come to us punctually in October and depart at the beginning of spring, just as we are abandoning hare-hunting for the season. Mallards, wigeon, teal, and, in hard weather, wild geese and other rarer wild fowl are visitors to our marshes. The stately heron is always in evidence. Snipe constantly spring up before one as the chase sweeps on. The wide coast marshes have in truth at times many rare and singular visitants. I have seen occasionally, disturbed by the chase, redshanks, greenshanks, dunlin, whimbrel, and other wading birds. This very winter we had on Pevensey marshes a small flight or two of

148

Glossy Ibises, strangely infrequent wanderers from the rivers and lagoons of far-off Africa. They had lit there, no doubt, on their way south, and, as usually happens, some of their numbers fell victims to the gunner and the collector.

While penetrating the woodlands, whither the hare had carried us, I have more than once flushed a woodcock from his snug resting-place under a bush or a tree of wild holly, not far from the soft-banked, trickling streamlet, whence he has been extracting dainties overnight. To any one fond of wild life and of nature, there is a wonderful pleasure in such little discoveries as these. Most sportsmen have, I fancy, a natural eye for the wild beauties of the country-side, even in winter. In traversing a woodland through which a hare has run, while its depths are resounding to the cheerful and inspiring notes of the deep-voiced hounds, how infinitely beautiful are many of its features! The exquisite carpeting of russet-brown leaves, here and there, where some great beech has shed its garment, reddened by the deeper hue of that wonderfully coloured leafage; the delicate winter tracery of the birch trees, their silvery boles, the majestic contours of the oak, the dark pine standing solitary in her pride; the beautiful colouring of jay or woodpecker as, disturbed by the unwonted turmoil, they betake themselves to other retreats; all these objects, especially if a tender gleam of winter sun shines upon them and brings out their beauties, add zest and interest to the already abounding pleasures of the foot-hunter. There is not, I think, a more beautiful woodland picture in winter than a tree of wild holly, with its berries of vivid scarlet and its gleaming dark green leaves, burnished by nature to an almost mirrorlike smoothness. I know of such a tree in the woods adjoining Herstmonceux, which, lit up by sunshine, is a marvel of winter beauty. Not one of your thick, massive holly trees, solid old gentlemen of some centuries, but a slim, tallish, elegant creature, decked in harrier green and hunting scarlet, a typical lady of the woods. She will always remain, just as remains so many a good hunting-run, a living picture in the memory.

Strange and amusing incidents happen sometimes to the foot-hunter as he follows hounds. Only a few days since, with the Hailsham Harriers, a man jumping a broad dyke saw that he was alighting directly on top of a hare - not the hunted one - which happened to be lying on the bank. He managed to avoid her as he touched the ground, and the hare was so startled and so terrified that she plumped straightway into the dyke and, floundering across in the most ludicrous fashion, emerged like a drowned rat on the other side, and raced away in a very panic of fright. The scene was a most ludicrous one. It is a real pleasure to jump a good dyke, but these obstacles to the hare hunter afford infinite grief sometimes. I saw this winter an enthusiastic photographer, rushing to take a snap-shot of hounds and hunters as they passed by, make a stride for a plank which bridged the dyke. He omitted to remember that there had been a sharp white frost during the night and that the plank was doubly treacherous. His foot slipped and he plunged bodily into the dyke. Happily, he was an enthusiast in his work and, holding his camera above his head, he managed to preserve his precious cargo of plates. If it had been otherwise, this volume might have been shorn of some of its illustrations. The enthusiast stuck to his work pluckily for the rest of the day, in spite of the fact that he was practically wet through.

Shepherds on the Sussex marshes get from one part of the broad pastures to the other by means of occasional planks, usually very narrow and slippery, which span the wide and muddy "diks," as they are called locally, that drain the levels. These slender bridges are godsends to ladies and to the non-jumping division who, with the aid of a "bat" a long staff affected by most marsh-traversers in this part of Sussex are enabled to cross readily enough. The "bat" is quite a local institution among Sussex foot-hunters. A staff, usually of hazel, wild cherry, or ash, cut from some local woodland, it serves for various purposes. It is an excellent aid in crossing these marsh planks and beating coverts, and with a hat elevated upon its apex serves, in place of the noisy and disturbing view holloa, to call attention to the line of the hare. If you are not among the hurrying division, you may, leaning upon this excellent staff, gaze restfully and contemplatively from some convenient hill-side at all the features of the chase, stretching out below you. I confess to a weakness for the rustic staff of Sussex, although I belong, naturally, to the more active division of foot-hunters. The Sussex "bat" seems to be a very ancient aid to hare-hunting in these parts. I find reference to it in old accounts of the chase of the hare in the Weald of Sussex in the days when Southern hounds were used. In this part of the county, and elsewhere, especially about Horsham, much of the hunting seems to have been done on foot. Certainly at the pace the old Southern hound went, and with his absurd deliberation, the man on foot could have had no great difficulty in keeping up during the long five and six hour chases in which our ancestors seem to have delighted. "Bats" were, however, occasionally used for other purposes. In one of the last encounters between smugglers and preventive officers on the coast of East Sussex, a cargo was about to be run and the officers had assembled to prevent it. A number of smugglers and their local adherents, however, fell upon the officers with bats and so mishandled them that they drove them off, left one of their number for dead, and successfully ran their contraband. This happened no more than about eighty years ago, at Little Common, on the edge of the marshes, between Bexhill and Pevensey. The beginnings of some of the old-fashioned foot-hunting packs of harriers, in the days when hounds were trencher-fed, must have been often singular enough. Mr. C. Garnett, of the Holcombe Harriers, has unearthed a document, dating from the year 1773, which gives a curious picture of the internal economy of such a pack. The document from which my extracts are given embodies the rules of the Hunt for that season. The extracts run as follows:

HOLCOMBE. Nov. 25, 1773.

1st. Mr. Holt Brown to be the conductor of the Dogs for this season. No person in the society to call for the hounds to hunt in any particular Place, or at any Time without giving notice to the Dog-Lad in writing and his consent. Too (sic) days in a week till Old Candlemas to be hunting-days, the weather allowing it.

2nd. John Kay to be huntsman; to have wastecoat, Breeches, Stockings, and a pair of Shoos gratis; to have a Cap lent this season; to have is 6d per day of hunting; to have is extraordinary, for every Hair (sic) he shall kill; and to call the Dogs off the Chace at the request of the Dog-Lad or any other subscriber if he can, or else forfeit that day's Wages.

3rd. Every person who shall keep a Dog to enter it as one of the Pack (living in the Manor) and not to be at liberty to withdraw or dispose of it to any other Person wile the Society continue to hunt togr. and to have each an Hare if requested and possible to be got.

4th. Every Person who shall keep a Dog, etc. and attempt to destroy Hares etc. exclusive of and in opposition to the Society, in this Manor to be prosecuted according to the law, and the Huntsman or any other Person who can and shall convict them thereof to have 55 over and above the allowance of the Law from this Society towards their expenses and trouble in going to a Magistrate.

5th. If at the end of this season any money shall remain in the hands of the Dog-Lad, it shall be paid and delivered to his successor in office who shall be chosen by a majority of the subscribers; and if the sum subscribed shall happen to be deficient such Deficiency to be made up by the subscribers, in proportion to the sums they shall at first have subscribed towards the Hunt.

Witness our Hands JOHN SMITH, SAM. BRANDWOOD, JOHN ROGSTRON, ROBT. HOLT BROWN, BENJ. BUCKLEY, JOHN BOOTH, JAS. HOWARTH.

This quaint document - a thoroughly English production, grave, solid, and law-abiding - proves amply that even the supporters of trencher-fed packs took their sport quite as seriously as their modern successors, and allied themselves frequently by hard and fast rules, which regulated the conduct of their hunting even to minute particulars.

In hunting foot-harriers, it is better to keep the pack as near as possible to a standard of eighteen or nineteen inches. Eighteen inches is, to my mind, the ideal height for foot-harriers. It is, however, a difficult matter to keep down the standard to that desideratum; harriers, whether bred from foxhound or Southern hound blood, are inclined to produce hounds just a little bigger than is often wished for. The pack with which I hunt are nineteen-inch harriers, which, for foot-hunting, is the maximum that ought to be permitted. In fact, even for hunting hare on horseback, I would sooner hunt with nineteen-inch harriers than those of any other standard.

Hunting on foot is not only a most wholesome, but a most cheery, winter sport. The farmers and landowners are almost invariably staunch friends and supporters of a sport which affords a great deal of amusement and does them no harm. No one's fences are injured, the fields are small, and the pastime can be enjoyed by young and old, rich and poor, alike. The intrusion of the mere vulgar ostentation of wealth, too often seen nowadays, even in the hunting-field, is conspicuous by its absence. In fact, the vulgar *nouveau riche,* who is usually a self-indulgent sort of person, much more devoted to motor cars than to any other form of out-door exercise, can have little part or lot in a hare-hunt on foot, where activity, good wind, firm muscles, and clean living are essentials to success if a man really means to follow hounds. Here in truth the farmer's son is likely to be a better man than the youth nurtured on money-bags.

Besides being a most fascinating form of sport, hare-hunting on foot is a first-rate training for British youth. It makes them fond of the country, and renders them hardy, healthy, and vigorous. Every school-boy likes it, and it is a real pleasure to see in holiday time the youngster out for the day with beagles or foot-harriers. Besides drawing youth out of the towns, it teaches them to use their eyes and to train their minds to observation. To understand the run of a hare, even more than that of a fox, a man must use his wits, and the careless, the unobservant, and the fool can never hope to become either a good harrier-man or a sound fox-hunter. It is one of the misfortunes of latter-day sport that, in fashionable countries, the lad who goes out fox-hunting sees very little indeed of the real science of the chase, and can learn little of the working of hounds or the run of a fox. He learns, it is true, to gallop and to jump, but in ninety cases out of a hundred, what with the hurry and scurry of three or four hundred excited horsemen and the precautions of the Master, who has to manage and dispose his field before drawing a covert, somewhat like a regiment of cavalry, it is impossible for the budding sportsman to see much of the real and true inwardness of the sport in which he is supposed to be taking a part. If a man wants his son to learn something of the art of hunting hounds, he cannot do better than enter him, as a youngster, with a pack of beagles or foot-harriers, where he may glean the whole of the process of the chase from find to finish. Many a keen fox-hunter, who has ably hunted his own hounds, has picked up the rudiments of his art in this way, and has passed from beagles to harriers and from harriers to foxhounds.

In hunting harriers on foot, the same number of hounds are taken out, and the process of hunting is identically the same as when the hunter is mounted. In some ways, I am inclined to think better sport is often enjoyed on foot than on horseback. Hounds are necessarily often left more to their own devices; they get away from their field and have more opportunity to follow their own instincts, which are, usually, even more valuable to them than the huntsman's judgment. It is an old, and a perfectly true maxim with harriers, that the more they are left alone the better the sport is. It follows that, with foot-packs, the interference being less frequent, the sport shown is usually of very high quality, of its kind and in its own way not to be surpassed by any other open-air pursuit. There seems to me to be a great and growing appreciation of this form of hunting.

Chapter Sixteen - Some Runs with Foot-Harriers

IT may, I think, be not uninteresting if I attempt to depict one or two runs with foot-harriers. It is a dull, misty, November morning. Our meet to-day lies at a quiet old manor-house, lying in the very heart of the South Downs, and, as flints are plentiful and cycling among these hills is not of much assistance, we start fairly early and walk the four and a half miles to the try sting-place. Arrived there, we find the hounds already shut up in a stable and the score or so of hunters assembled inside the old house. We enter the ancient hall, a fine old lofty chamber, timbered with dark oak, and dating back from the later days of Henry VIII.'s reign. This is the oldest part of the mansion, the south front dating from about 1630. But it is all delightfully ancient, a fine, solid, well-built, ancient manor-house, in which generation after generation of sturdy squires and yeomen have been reared. Its present owner has done much towards the restoration of the old place, and it is now in good condition, fit for sheltering folk for a hundred or two of years more. The old Tudor hall is now used as a billiard-room, and the table is spread with all manner of good things, beef, ham, sandwiches, pies, and every kind of drink, from whiskey and soda to old ale and cherry brandy. Upon the snow-white table-cloth great dishes of ruddy-golden apples make a fine display; they are so typically English, and they contrast so pleasantly with the rich, dark panelling of the great chamber. In the wide-open grate burns a roaring wood fire, a notable and most comfortable addition to a typical picture of the country-side as one likes to see it. Refreshment over, hounds are unkennelled from their stable, and we proceed to draw up a long, open valley between two high folds in the down. Half a mile from the house, suddenly from among a thick crop of roots, a hare jumps up right in the middle of hounds. There is the usual scuffle observed on such occasions. The hare makes her escape from the open jaws of twelve couples of her foes as if by a miracle, and, setting her face for the down-side, away she tears, one ear down the other half cocked, as if to catch every tone of that terrible chorus behind her. With a grand burst of melody, hounds pack together and race off in pursuit. For a few hundred yards it is a mere confused scurry, hounds running in view, all clamorous to get at that little brown form fleeting away at such a pace in front of them. In this open down country this is a thing that cannot be avoided, and for that reason I, for one, prefer hunting in the marshes, and upon more enclosed land, to hare-hunting on the downs. However, the hare presently slips out of sight, hounds are brought to their noses, and we make the best of our way after them.

For two miles this stout hare keeps her face pointed straight for the south-east and the sea. We climb the down, trot some way along the top, sink another deep valley, and then the hare turns right-handed. Scent is, up to this point, first-rate, and hounds carry a marvellously good head, but there are indications that this excellent state of affairs may not continue. The mist is clearing, and there are gleams of sunshine. Belle Toute lighthouse shows at length, clear and spotless white against the green turf of the cliff edge. And, looking away down Birling Gap yonder, a coasting barque, with all plain sail set for the faint breeze, creeps out of the sea mist. Another lift of the white veil, and a tramp steamer ploughs clumsily eastward through the grey-green sea. But after an instant's check at the sharp angle of the hare's sudden turn hounds race away again. It is clear from their direction that the hare is ring-ing back to her head-quarters. A judicious line across the centre of the circle, which our quarry appears to be bent on making, enables us toiling footmen - those of us who are really running, no joke with harriers on these open downs - to nick in again close to the tail of the pack. Away we go again full cry through the valley from which the hare got up; away over down and into val-ley as before.

But now the change of temperature has wrought its inevitable result, and scent begins to fail considerably. Slow hunting is to be the fashion, and the hare gains some temporary respite. She needs it, surely, by now; for fifty minutes and more she has been rattled over the hills in a way that few of her kind - even the stoutest down hare ever bred - can stand for long together. Hitherto Stormer, a wonderful young hound, and some of the speedier of the pack have been doing most of the leading work. We come to a check on a wide piece of ploughing. Watch now as they cast themselves, spreading fan-like over the red earth, and, with noses close to the ground, searching staunchly for the slightest taint of the animal in front of them. See the pale old hound out yonder; how busy he is! That is old Captain, the best-nosed hound in the pack, a veteran of seven seasons, who, in such emergencies as this, is the most trusted ally alike of huntsman and of his fellow hounds. No harrier in Sussex is better on a road, or a dry plough, than he. Not a hound in England is more reliable or more truthful. Captain has it! His head goes up, he flings forth a deep note or two, and to him fly Sally and Pepper, two fa-mous blue-mottled bitches of the right Southern hound lineage. "It is right!" they cry, with still deeper and more melodious voices than that of Captain himself. The rest of the pack fling to them, and slowly, with encouraging mu-sic, they puzzle out the line of the hare. They clear the plough and sweep more briskly over some down grass again; and then, upon some more plough thickly sown with flints, scent seems to fail them altogether. The sun has done its work, and the hare has for the moment the best of it.

Here comes the huntsman's opportunity. He makes a circling cast forward. Hounds just touch the line, but lose it again. Now comes a holloa from the Master, who, with quick eyes, has, as usual, noted the hunted hare creeping round once more towards her old haunts. That holloa, and the wave of the Master's hat, is, in such an emergency, when we look like being run out of scent altogether, good enough, and, with a touch of the horn, away we go at best pace. If you do go to a holloa at all, don't dally, but take your hounds as fast as you like. A foot-huntsman, after all, can never blow his hounds on such an occasion. We pick up the line again, and, passing the Master, are cheered with the tidings that the hare is tiring fast. So, indeed, are some of us bipeds; but we push on, hope as usual springing eternal in the hunting breast. Hounds now carry the line slowly to a little shaw towards East Dean. The hare has certainly gone through, but beyond scent fails again lamenta-bly; it looks almost as if we were going to be beaten after all. A longish cast round, and we suddenly come upon the hunted animal, which has squatted and now springs away just in front of hounds. From a rather ominous quiet, we suddenly emerge once more into the joyous clamour of hound voices, all mad with the idea of running into their prey. It is very plain, indeed, that the hare is beaten. Her rest has but served to accentuate, her stiffness, and her gait now is far different from that wondrous display of speed with which she sailed away from us during the first hour of the hunt. The pack gains on her rapidly. Stormer leads the van; Champion, Dauntless, and Abel push him hard. Old Captain, knowing well that the end is near, is straining every nerve and is well up with the leaders. They close up rapidly. In three minutes it is all over. They are close upon her; she jinks feebly once or twice, and now, upon the smooth down turf, the leaders have pulled her down, and the whole pack are ravening at her. We are quickly up, the huntsman rescues the dead hare from the jaws of the hounds, and then with a blast or two of the horn and piercing who-whoops we proceed to celebrate the obsequies. An hour and forty minutes since we found; 'a capital run, the first hour of it very fast, the last forty minutes slow hunting, but none the less extremely interesting, and to the two or three youngsters who have watched it extremely instructive. And so, while the scattered little field collects again, we take a welcome rest of ten minutes in the good down air before drawing further.

Here is a phase of sport with foot-harriers in another part of East Sussex. The meet is at an old-fashioned inn, close to the walls of Pevensey Castle. At 11:15 A.M. we make a move for the broad marshes just outside the village, and, as usual in this locality, have not long to wait for a hare. Spreading out in line, we draw a marsh pasture or two. Suddenly there is a holloa behind. As so often happens amid the thick grass of this kind of pasturage, chequered here and there with tussocks and occasional patches of rush, just the kind of lying for a hare, hounds and field have passed over the very animal of which we are in search. The holloa is from a noted finder of hares, who, hanging behind as is his wont, has spied the hare snug in her form. His hat is up; we know that that signal is unfailing, and, with one cheery blast from the horn, hounds are collected and taken quietly back. When the pack is within sixty yards of him the finder turns back a pace or two, touches the still squatting hare with his long staff, and away she flies for dear life, as fast as those strong hind legs of hers can propel her. With their usual rousing chorus on these occasions, the hounds, mad with excitement, race after her. The hare flies a dyke, skims along the bank, slips under a gateway, and, descending the steep bank of another dyke, is presently out of view. Hounds are now brought to their noses, which is by far the best thing for them. It is at once apparent that scent is first-rate. The day is clear and bright, with but little wind; just the fresh touch of a gentle south-easterly breeze moves over the wide levels. Quickly picking up the line, hounds, running with immense dash and fire and with a grand and most tuneful cry, scour after the hare, which has set her face for the gentle slopes of Wartling Hill and takes over a succession of broad dykes that need a good deal of jumping. A cart or two, laden with enthusiastic farmers and their daughters, spin along the road on the left.

Two others, whose drivers have formed a different opinion of the hare's line, turn right-handed and bear across the marsh towards Sewers Bridge and Ninfield; these last are, as it turns out, in the right.

After running a long mile or more towards Wartling, the hare, headed unconsciously by a shepherd, suddenly swings right-handed, and now hastens over that vast sea of marsh pastures, which extend to Hooe and Little Common. Those on foot, who do not care for the labours and delights of running and jumping, now betake themselves to the middle road that towards Ninfield - where they can see the chase for miles round over the broad levels, here guiltless of tree, or hedge, or any thing that may impede the vision. A little band of ten or a dozen ardent pedestrians follow the clamouring pack, and prepare for a long run and an infinity of leaping. For half an hour or so it is a stern and a hard chase, and the runners have much ado to keep at all within hail of the pack. But relief comes at length. Hounds check on the high bank of a small marsh river - the Haven - where, before crossing, it is clear that the hare has spent a minute or two in running a puzzling foil, which, for a brief period, at all events, shall perplex her pursuers and give her breathing space and rather more law. Clever creature that she is, she has judged correctly. Hounds check here for close on five minutes, by which time the Master is up, and, it being evident that the hare must have gone over, the pack is holloaed and encouraged across. A welcome bridge, a little to the left, gives access to the runners, and the chase is hotly resumed. Over the road presently swings the pack, still bearing a little right-handed. More running, more jumping; these dykes seem interminable. The limits of the marsh are reached, and it looks as if the hare were going to climb the little hill towards Hooe. But no! her bent is still for the marsh. On, on over the never-ending pastures, till we are close upon the Sluice, where the marsh river finds access to the sea, and a little old-fashioned inn, notable in the old days as a favourite haunt of smugglers, nestles amid a few trees, solitary upon the levels. Still going righthanded, we come to a loose gravelly road and check once more.

Here hounds are at fault for a minute or two, until old Captain, our famous road-hound, proclaims the fact that the hare has betaken herself to the roadway. Slowly we pick it out up a little eminence, whence the sea, quite near at hand upon our left, gleams a clear steel-blue. Its surface, scarce broken by a ripple, is dotted with brown-sailed fishing smacks, which push with difficulty out into the Channel, so little does the faint breeze assist them. Two hundred yards from the flat shore line floats, on the calm water, a long string of scoters, the "black duck" of sea-fowlers. They are worthless for powder and shot, and hence, probably, their immunity; so fishy is their flesh that, in Catholic countries, they may be eaten during Lent or on fast days, a poor tribute, indeed, to their value as table-birds.

But there is little time just now to think of wildfowling. A glance or two at the pleasant sea-scape, with Beachy Head jutting boldly in front of us, and our eyes and ears are once more riveted on hounds and the line of chase. Captain and the leaders of the pack check for a moment at a gate, and then, plunging into the grass pasture again, tell us with a grand chorus of glad voices that the line is right and that scent is good again. At the same instant a far away holloa or two in front tell that the hare is running straight for Wall's End, the little sea-shore off-shoot of Pevensey village.

Scent is burning again, and, refreshed and heartened, the pack, now gathered well together, are running at a great pace, and with a grand cry. It is inspiring, indeed. Surely we are going to kill this stout hare, which has now been running before us for full three quarters of an hour! We toil on and are nearing Wall's End, when, suddenly, the line of the hare breaks off to the right. It looks as if she meant going back for the very field from which we first put her up; but no! for some reason, either because she was headed, or because she merely wished to baulk her pursuers, she has evidently doubled. It is a ticklish moment; but hounds, left judiciously to themselves, hit off the line. They are *not* running heel as some supposed. The hare has turned short back, run a foil close upon her old line, and, as hounds tell us by their patient and more careful work, has evidently dodged about here considerably before going away again. It looks like a tiring hare, and our spirits rise proportionately. They puzzle it out round two or three pastures, along dyke sides, close to the water, in and out, up and down, this way and that, until at length all is clear, and the pack is away again. We point now for the rich pastures between Pevensey and the sea, leaving Wall's End on the left, and then comes a distant holloa. It is from the very edge of the "Crumbles," a vast expanse of flat shingle, from which the sea has, centuries ago, receded. The holloa is from a coastguard; it tells us the plain tale that our hare is indeed hard put to it, or she would scarcely have resorted to that last shift of the unhappy chase, a run over this strange, trackless, and usually scentless stretch of shore line. The coastguard has seen her, truly enough, and tells us she is very beat and going slowly. Excellent news, indeed! The question is whether the "Crumbles" will to-day give us any scent at all.

That issue is soon clear enough. There is some scent, for a wonder; and, albeit at a much slower pace, hounds continue to hold the line. We struggle through the waste of pebbles, as best we can, for half a mile, and then, suddenly, the leading hounds, topping a ridge of shingle towards the sea, rush on with renewed energy and a wondrous clamour. They have a view, undoubtedly. We scale the little ascent and there, one hundred and fifty yards away, witness the last shift of the failing hare. Hounds are now close at her scut. She turns, twists, and dodges, with a courage and a perseverance surely deserving of a kindlier fate, and then all is over. She dies! she dies! as Somervile would have had it, in his blank verse; and, disappearing amid the final worry of the pack, we see the little brown form no more. Tired limbs are forgotten. With one impulse we rush up to the scene, as fast as legs can carry us, just in time to rescue the stiff and somewhat battered quarry from the jaws of her pursuers. She is, of course, quite dead. The usual triumphant cries are raised; the huntsman sounds cheery blasts upon his horn. In the far distance we already discern, coming to us as best they can across the marshes, such followers of the Hunt as are anywhere within sight or sound. A glorious run, quite in the old-fashioned manner, and worth, surely, a week of a man's - a town-dwelling man's - life! One hour and twenty-five minutes is the time, and hounds have killed their game practically unaided. We carry back the dead hare to the marsh, and, in presence of the rest of the spectators, complete the final rites.

In few runs, indeed, is the huntsman's assistance less often tendered. A too eager man might, and probably would, have spoilt all by interfering with the pack just at those two or three critical moments when the hare's clever and devious tactics had caused a check. And here let me offer just one word of advice to quite young huntsmen, especially with a foot-pack. Don't be afraid to trust your hounds. After all, they *must* know far more about this business of hunting than you or any other biped, even the oldest and most *rusé* member of the field. Do remember that they and their ancestors have, from almost immemorial time, been engaged in no other business in the world than the hunting of hare in this manner. Through a thousand generations have their progenitors been bred and selected and crossed, and counter-crossed, with no other object than to give them good noses, and stout limbs, and school them for the chase and for nothing else. Their instincts, their training, their selection fit them, far more than any other creature, certainly far more than the cleverest human hunter that ever raised a holloa or blew a horn, to pursue successfully the wonderful problem laid out upon the surface of the earth by probably the most resourceful beast of chase in the world. Do, then, give credit to your hounds! Give them time, give them room. Don't be afraid of the comment of the field, most of whom know very little about the sport of which they are spectators; but trust to your hounds, have infinite patience, and in ninety-nine times out of a hundred they will pull through.

Chapter Seventeen - Beagles and Beagling

W HAT is a beagle? "A small hound, with which hares are hunted," is the definition of an old-time writer on the chase. That is a fair description, but it does not carry one very far. The very name "beagle" is one which has puzzled all sorts of learned people, so much so that some of the dictionaries tell you that the origin of the word is unknown. The term seems to have been little in vogue before the time of Henry VII.; yet it is certain that these small and lively hounds were known, probably by some other designation, to our ancestors long before that time.

The revival of the beagle for hunting purposes within the last twenty years is of the happiest augury. It seemed, seventy or eighty year ago, as if these little hounds, although still used for shooting purposes, were in some danger of being lost to us. Here is what a sporting authority of that period says concerning them. "Much emulation prevailed in former times among sportsmen in the breeding of beagles, and it was then the greatest merit to rear dogs of the smallest growth. Amongst amateurs of hunting, beagles were so carefully selected in point of size that they seldom exceeded ten or eleven inches in height; and they were so well matched with respect to speed, that during the chase a good pack might be covered with a sheet. This is with all hounds a sure mark of excellence.

"Although beagles are slow in speed they are uncommonly eager; for, if the scent lies well, a hare has little chance of escape from them. Their slowness, however, is the principal reason of their being almost totally discontinued in packs; and that they are now seldom to be met with beyond a few couples, used in some of the southern counties of England to ensure finding more certainly in greyhound coursing."

This is an extraordinary statement, and although hunting with beagles had, in the early part of the last century, certainly gone out of fashion, they were never totally abandoned for hunting, or anything like it. Here and there, in quiet places, a few packs were still maintained and the blood kept up. And for shooting, especially in Sussex, beagles were always in favour.

"Hunting with the beagle," adds the same author, Mr. Brown, "was admirably adapted for ladies and gentlemen up in years; and, besides, afforded much amusement to rustics and other pedestrian hunters; for there were few male persons of any activity who could not keep up with them."

The latter part of this statement I take leave to doubt. When beagles really run, nowadays, it requires a pretty good man to keep up with them. Possibly the author had only seen hunting with ten or eleven-inch beagles, whose pace would not, of course, be very great over a rough country. But that beagles had been bigger and fleeter than these pigmies may be easily ascertained by reference to Beckford and other older authorities. From these we know that, before the advent of the foxhound, beagles were used a great deal for hunting foxes to earth, whence reynard was dug out and knocked on the head. That these small hounds, especially the north-country beagle, were fleet and lively is proved by the testimony of this writer, who advises the mating of them with the slow Southern hound, for the purpose of producing a good harrier. He, as I have shown, bred his pack of harriers in this way, and succeeded, after some years, in the difficult task of pleasing even himself.

An older writer than Beckford, quoted by Daniel, says: "The North-Country beagle is nimble and vigorous, he pursues the Hare with impetuosity, gives her no time to double, and if the Scent is high will easily run down two brace before dinner." "But," he adds, "it is only on a good scenting day these speedy hounds show themselves, for without the constant discipline of the whip, and perpetually hunting them down, it is impossible to make a good pack of them. [1] There is another sort preferred from their tenderness of Nose, and because they eat little, but without great care they are apt to chatter without any occasion." Concerning this small race, Daniel gives a curious anecdote. "Of this diminutive and lavish kind," he says, "the late Colonel Hardy had once a Cry, consisting of ten or eleven couple, which were always carried to and from the field in a large pair of Panniers, slung across a horse; small as they were, they would keep a Hare at all her shifts to escape them, and often worry her to death; but it was similar to that species of hunting where a Fox was hunted in Devonshire House Gardens, it might be endured as a novelty, but no one would ever wish to behold it a second time. The Catastrophe attending this Pack of Hounds is laughable, and perhaps a Larceny unique in its attempt. A small barn was their allotted Kennel, the door of which was one night broke open and every hound, with the Panniers, stolen, nor could the most diligent search discover the least trace of the Robbers or their Booty."

"Stonehenge," in the second edition of his volume on "The Dog," dated 1872, makes the rather astonishing statement that the true beagle was almost entirely displaced by dwarf specimens of the foxhound, or by crosses with it in varying proportions. That statement seems to me far too sweeping. I grant that dwarf foxhound blood has strongly invaded the constitution of the modern beagle, but, here and there, you may still find many a good beagle of the right old-fashioned stamp, probably blue-mottle in colour, or with strong traces of blue-mottle, and showing by its long ears, the contour of its head, its fine voice, and perhaps a certain throatiness, its descent from the Southern hound or some equally ancient type. As to throatiness, which is usually reckoned by modern judges so terrible an offence, I advise the novice who is getting together a cry of beagles or harriers either not to be too much frightened by the appearance of this fault. It may be taken as a sound axiom that a throaty hound is always blessed with a good nose. Tom Smith, the famous Master of Foxhounds, author of "The Life of a Fox," and "The Diary of a Huntsman," makes some extremely sensible remarks on this matter of nose and throat. "This rage for pace and shape," he says, "in some measure accounts for the great deficiency of nose, in comparison with what it was formerly. It is true that hounds may be, and are, nearer perfection in point of beauty. A throaty hound, for instance, is rarely seen in a pack, although very common some years back, when men thought more of hunting than of riding; but by getting rid of the throat the nose had gone with it, for a throaty hound has invariably a good nose; and that all hounds were so until the end of the last (eighteenth) century, nearly all sporting pictures of hounds will prove." In the case of beagles, therefore, and even of harriers, a master should pause before he proceeds to draft a hound because it is cursed (or blessed) with throatiness.

Beagles of the present day vary a great deal. We have what is practically a dwarf foxhound, with short legs, the rough-coated Welsh beagle, an excellent type, the old-fashioned beagle, which is a miniature and improved version of the Southern hound, the mixed beagle, constituting a variety of blends of foxhound, harrier, and the original breed, and the little sharp rabbit beagle, used for hunting rabbits and not for shooting purposes. This latter is the pocket beagle, standing no more than ten inches at the shoulder. The Marquis of Linlithgow has a kennel of these little creatures, which display extraordinary fire, spirit, and dash, and hunt rabbits in most amusing fashion.

As to colour, the beagle, like other hounds, runs in almost all hues, fox-hound colour, blue-mottle, lemon and white, hare-pie, badger-pie, black-and-tan, and red. If I had the choosing or breeding of a pack, I should prefer beagles of hound colour with a strong admixture of blue-mottle. The blue-mottle colour always indicates an ancient strain, and where you get that colour you have also good nose and cry, two highly important accessories in hare-hunting. Black-and-tan is a colour that, latterly, has been coming into vogue somewhat, where beagles are concerned, and judges at shows seem to favour it. It is not, however, in my humble opinion, so true or so characteristic a beagle colour as blue-mottle, or hound colour, or a mixture of the two.

As regards size, the tendency of the last score of years has been, I am afraid, to increase the standard. Some beagle packs now hunting, are distinctly too big and approach more nearly the size of harriers than that of beagles. A good pack of beagles, that is a pack of beagles which are not only well-looking, but can properly account for their hares, after a more or less prolonged hunt, ought not to be less than thirteen and a half inches or more than fifteen and a half inches. Some packs run to sixteen inches, but I believe that a fifteen and a half-inch beagle will be found, in nearly every kind of country, good enough to kill hares in sterling fashion. Personally, I incline to hunting with fourteen and a half or fifteen-inch beagles, which go quite fast enough to keep out of the way of the foot runners, and bring their hares to hand very satisfactorily.

Seventy or eighty years ago, as I have shown, it seemed almost as if hare-hunting with beagles was likely soon to become a thing of the past. Twenty or twenty-five years ago there began to be distinct symptoms of a revival of interest in this most excellent sport. But even then you might have counted the packs hunting in England on the fingers of your two hands. Then the interest began to spread, and to spread rapidly. By the year 1886-87 there were some eighteen packs established, and by 1895 there were no less than forty-four packs of beagles hunting in the United Kingdom. During this last season there have been somewhere about fifty packs, a goodly muster, indeed. [2]

I have said that hunting with foot-harriers is one of the finest of English winter sports. Beagling follows very closely upon its heels. In some ways, possibly, it is even preferable, because, with foot-harriers, a man must be an exceedingly good pedestrian and in the very best of trim to keep within hail of a pack of hounds standing eighteen or nineteen inches in height and blessed with plenty of pace as well as wonderful noses. For this reason, probably, it is that packs of foot-beagles so largely outnumber packs of foot-harriers, which last do not, I think, throughout the United Kingdom, number more than about a dozen, all told. Fourteen- or fifteen-inch beagles go quite fast enough for most people; they show first-rate sport; and they cost less to maintain than harriers.

England supports by far the great majority of beagle packs now in existence. Out of forty-nine or fifty that took the field in the United Kingdom during this last winter, Ireland is to be credited with seven, Wales with three, Scotland with but one. The rest are all hunted in England proper. While speaking of Wales, it is contended by some authorities that the rough haired Welsh beagle obtains his thick wiry coat from an admixture of rough-coated terrier blood. That seems rather a strong assumption, yet many good judges, including the late Mr. J. H. Walsh ("Stonehenge "), believed in it. "One reason," says "Stonehenge," "why I have supposed him (the Welsh beagle) to arise from the above cross (between the medium-sized beagle and the rough terrier) is, that he has lost in great measure the beagle tongue, and squeaks like a terrier, though not quite so much as that dog." Whether "Stonehenge" came across some special breed of this kind, I know not; but I am bound to say that not all rough-coated Welsh beagles are possessed of the squeaky terrier voice above referred to. The origin of this hound is, truly, lost in obscurity, but I, for one, am inclined to think that in most Welsh beagles of the rough-coated kind there can be very little indeed of terrier blood. The question of the ancestry of all our hounds

Photograph by R. B. Lodge, Enfield

BUSHEY HEATH BEAGLES

MEET AT ALDENHAM ABBEY

Photograph by R. B. Lodge, Enfield

BUSHEY HEATH BEAGLES

REGENT

Photograph by R. B. Lodge, Enfield

BUSHEY HEATH BEAGLES

PRIESTESS

is, however, a most difficult one, and no living person can pretend to say, with confidence, how exactly the different points and qualities of our various modern hounds were produced. The blending has been the gradual process of centuries. "Stonehenge" himself maintained that the deerhound, from which the Welsh harrier and beagle and the otter-hound were supposed by some to obtain their rough coats, was in itself the remote ancestor of the

162

wire-haired terrier. But discussion on this subject, which, after all, must be almost purely hypothetical, would be endless.

The number of a pack of beagles is usually considerably less than with harriers. Most establishments range from ten to sixteen couples. Here and there a few packs are to be found in stronger numbers, but they are not many. The Hulton, which hunt near Bolton, in Lancashire, muster seventeen and a half couples; Captain Croft's, hunting near Ware, consist of eighteen couples; the Seskinawaddy, a County Tyrone pack, number twenty couples; while the Innis Beg, hunting from Creagh, County Cork, hold the record (twenty-three couples) in point of numbers. A pack of twelve or fourteen couples will show plenty of sport, and very pretty hunting indeed is often to be had with a cry of beagles which numbers in kennel no more than ten couples, all told. With these small packs, of course, two days a week or three days a fortnight is the utmost that can be expected if hounds are to turn out for their work fresh and fit. At the Universities, packs of beagles have been maintained for years by some few Colleges. The Christ Church, Oxford, and Trinity College, Cambridge, beagles are well known. New and Magdalen Colleges, Oxford, have this last season - 1902-03 - combined to put into the field for the first time a beagle pack, which numbers twelve couples and hunts from Tilbury, near Oxford. Eton College has had its beagles for years, and it is to be hoped may continue to do so, in spite of the absurd outcry raised recently by certain members of the Humanitarian League. Clayesmore School, Pangbourne, has also started a pack, which consists of eleven and a half couples, and hunts the beautiful Berkshire country in the neighbourhood of the Thames. The Britannia Cadets have long possessed their pack of beagles and shown very good sport in Devon, in the Dartmouth district. Among soldiers, Aldershot Camp produces a pack of sixteen-inch beagle-harriers, which hunt the Aldershot district two days a week. Colchester Garrison has its pack; while, from Newcastle, yet another pack, the 5th and 68th R.D., has for some years been hunted.

I have sometimes heard it said that it is of little use going out with a pack of beagles, because they are too slow to get up to and run into their hares. That is an absurd mis-statement, which a little experience in the field would quickly falsify. I have had a good deal of sport with beagles at different times, and I have always seen a fair number of hares killed. Indeed, given a country where hares are reasonably abundant, the number of blank days with a beaglepack will be found to be surprisingly few. If you hunt with beagles less than twelve or thirteen inches in height, you must, of course, be prepared to find your sport slower and your hares consequently more difficult to bring to hand. But with fourteen-inch beagles, of the right sort, and well handled, almost as much sport is obtained as with a pack of harriers. The Chawston beagles, for example, hunting from Colesden Grange, St. Neots, had killed up to February 13, in this last season of 1902-03, no fewer than forty-nine hares, a capital record. As a sample of the kind of sport to be got with a good pack, I may state that, during the week this number was achieved, the following sport was obtained. On February 6, meeting at Colesden Grange, two hares were killed, after good runs, while a third made a three-mile point and saved her scut. On the 9th, meeting at Long Stow, near Kimbolton, some extraordinarily good sport was shown. The first hare found afforded a very fast run of an hour and five minutes, without a check. The second hare gave a run almost as faultless, also without a check. In both instances hounds ran into and killed their game in the open, after traversing a splendid grass country. A third run took place over plough, without blood, On the 11th, the same pack had a good run of two hours, chiefly over plough, killing their hare between Wyboston and Eaton. The Chawston are fifteen-inch beagles and maintain a high level of sport. These are but samples of the kind of thing to be seen daily with beagles in all parts of the country. As a rule, hares naturally take longer to bring to hand than with harriers, and runs of two hours and upwards may be pretty often expected.

The management of beagles is, on a smaller scale, identically the same as that of harriers. The kennels are usually on a very simple scale, and, more often than not, contrived from some disused stable or outbuilding. The same precautions against damp and kennel lameness must, of course, be taken as in the case of bigger and more important packs. Some packs are hunted without any pretence to regular costume; but even with a "cry" of little beagles it is more seemly that the Master and whip should appear in short green coats and velvet caps. It is very frequently the case that not only the huntsman, who is in nearly all cases the Master, but also the whip or whips, are amateurs, which, of course, tends considerably to the saving of expense. A steady lad as kennel huntsman and feeder, is, in such cases, the only paid servant needed; his wages should not amount to a very heavy item. With great economy a pack of ten or twelve couples can be maintained for as little as £70 a year, possibly a trifle less. In the field eight couples are sufficient, though a couple or two more are seen where packs are strong in number. As few as six couples even are occasionally employed, but with less than this number real hare-hunting is a matter of some difficulty.

The science and practice of hunting hare with beagles are, of course, practically the same as with harriers. The pace is, naturally, slower. Beagles, with their fine noses and low scenting propensities, are inclined to dally or "tie" on the scent, as it is called. For this reason, without unduly rushing them, it should be seen that stragglers and loiterers are kept up to the main body of the pack. With harriers, lifting hounds to the holloa is always to be discouraged; but with beagles a little licence may be allowed in this respect, unless, of course, they are running the line hard. And especially in long, slow, dragging runs, where scent is poor, and there is a chance of the pack being run out of it altogether, beagles may be now and again lifted to a holloa, if it is known to be a sure and a good one. When lifted they should be trotted briskly forward, and no time should be lost.

Some people have advocated the practice of having a mounted man with a pack of beagles, not to hunt them, but to hang about on the outskirts of the chase, watch the line of the hare, and head her away from any coverts or for-bidden preserves, to which she may be making. Personally, I do not hold with such a practice. I believe it tends, more usually than not, to the mounted man getting with the hounds and - unconsciously, if you like - trying to manage them himself. Mounted people with foot-packs almost always upset harriers or beagles, and should be severely discouraged. Of course, a friendly farmer, riding over his own fields to show the huntsman a hare, is on a different foot-ing. He is the last person to spoil sport; he understands the rules of the game; and without him hunting could not exist. But in my experience of beagles a mounted man is quite unnecessary, and, in fact, undesirable. It is possible that in the case of sixteen-inch beagles, which are practically almost as big as harriers, instances may now and again occur in which the pack gets clean away from its field and runs into a woodland, where pheasants are preserv-ed, or into a fox-covert, which ought not to be disturbed. In such a case a mounted man might have prevented mischief. There are, as a matter of fact, however, very few occasions, indeed, where the followers of beagles cannot keep their pack in hand. Where it is especially necessary that woodland shall not be disturbed - before a big shoot, for instance - a Master of beagles can us-ually so arrange his meets as to keep well away from the spot; or if he meets in the neighbourhood he can draw in the opposite direction and station some one near the covert to turn the hare, if it be possible, or whip off hounds.

In the case of both harriers and beagles, it is not only desirable but neces-sary that Masters of foxhound packs in the district over which it is proposed to hunt shall be duly consulted before any arrangements are made for bring-ing hare-hounds into the field. Foxhounds are to be conceded the right of priority; theirs is the more important branch of the sport; and they usually have vested interests, as it were, which are not lightly to be set aside. In the case of harriers, these are often as long established as are foxhounds - in some cases considerably longer - and the arrangements as to the hunting of the country have, therefore, been long since settled. But where a new pack of harriers or beagles is sought to be established, it ought always to be borne in mind that, in addition to securing the support and consent of the farmers and land-owners of the country over which it is proposed to hunt, an arrange-ment should be made with the Master of foxhounds hunting the district. It may not be nay, it is not absolutely the right of the Master of foxhounds to insist on this; in fact, with the consent of the tenant and owners, the Master of beagles and harriers can hunt where he pleases. But it is an unwritten law, and as a matter of courtesy, of policy, and of honour, the Master of beagles will interview the Master of foxhounds and come to an amicable understand-ing with him as to hunting hare. Some Masters of foxhounds are extremely tolerant in this matter; they believe in the principle of live and let live, and will even declare that harriers and beagles do good to fox-hunting by driving outlying foxes into the coverts where they are most readily found. A few fox-hunters, it must be admitted, are very difficult to deal with. With such, per-haps, the *suaviter in modo* treatment having failed, the remonstrances of a farmer or two, who have the right of refusal to *all* hounds, and who favour hare, may prove availing.

It is most desirable for both parties that an understanding shall be come to. And the foxhound Master, on his part, will be well advised to make honourable terms with the foot-beagler, who, after all, can do him little, or no, harm. As a matter of fact, the average fox-hunter who is, in the very nature of things, a good sportsman at heart, finds little objection to a quiet pack of beagles, properly conducted, the management of which will, of course, make their arrangements to hunt on the days when foxhounds are not in the same neighbourhood. Courtesy and good feeling between all parties, which are always desirable, are, one is glad to say, the almost invariable rule in these matters.

As regards greyhounds and coursing *versus* beagles, there is, naturally, some little friction at times between the two exponents. Harrier- or beagle-men, who have long hunted a particular country, can scarcely be expected to regard with equanimity the invasion of coursers and greyhounds. And, *vice versa*, old coursing men and it is to be remembered that coursing is a very ancient pastime cannot see without jealousy the incursion of harriers or beagles into fields which hitherto they had been taught to regard as peculiarly their own. Where hares are scarce, and the district is used both by coursing-men and hare-hunters, there must, necessarily, be friction. However, both factions are sportsmen, and some *modus vivendi* has to be found. I am inclined to think that, where hares are inordinately plentiful, as they are in some districts that I know of, harrier- and beagle-men are sometimes unnecessarily jealous of coursers. In such a district I am convinced that coursing does a great deal of good. It tends to the keeping down of hares, which are often a perfect nuisance to hounds and hunting, by the frequent changing they necessitate and the consequent exhaustion and dispiritment of the pack. And it tends also to move and disperse hares, to give them exercise, and make them yield better runs before harriers. This is certainly the result of pretty close observation of my own in certain parts of Sussex, where hares are strongly preserved and over abundant. There must, of course, be an understanding with farmers and coursers that greyhounds, which are more deadly in their pursuit than harriers or beagles, shall not be too often out, so as not to diminish seriously the stock of hares. All these are matters of arrangement. Sportsmen, whatever their favourite pursuit may be, are if we except certain types of pheasant-preservers usually reasonable enough, and hare-hunting and coursing can often go very well hand in hand. For instance, I have hunted regularly these last two seasons over a Sussex marsh, where, during each week, harriers and greyhounds of course, on different days enjoy magnificent sport.

[1] Beagles seem to have been much more unruly in the old days than they are at the present time.
[2] In Appendix "D" will be found a list of beagle packs for 1902-03.

Chapter Eighteen - Sport with Basset Hounds

HUNTING with basset hounds is a comparatively new feature in British field sports. It dates back little farther than fourteen or fifteen years, and, in fact, may be said not to have been really established on a businesslike footing until the Messrs. Heseltine began to hunt regularly in the year 1891. It is not a sport which, for various reasons, is ever likely to oust beagles or harriers from their ancient popularity. In the first place, bassets are much more difficult to get hold of and more expensive to buy. In the second place, although they have wonderful noses and are most determined workers, they are, from their very conformation, exceedingly slow, and take several hours, usually from two to three, sometimes even more, to wear down their quarry. This style of hunting, although to the chosen few who love hound work before anything else most interesting to watch, is, to the average modern sportsman, inclined to be tedious, and most men would, therefore, prefer to take their pleasure with a faster type of hound. Still, bassets have come to stay; they are now growing far more numerous than they were a dozen years ago; many fanciers have become greatly attached to them; there are a Basset Club and a Stud Book, and each season, among the list of packs of hounds hunting in these islands, there are to be found two or three packs of these bizarre-looking, but wonderfully handsome, hounds.

Before the year 1875, the basset hound was practically unknown in England. He had flourished for ages upon the Continent, chiefly in France and Belgium, as well as, to a lesser extent, in Austria and Germany, where he had been employed for various purposes connected with sport. But in England, prior to that year, the Earl of Onslow was, I believe, the only person who had ever kept bassets in this country. Lord Onslow had, in fact, a kennel of these hounds before the late Sir Everett Millais, who was, next to him, the earliest introducer of them, appeared on the scene. These had been presented to Lord Onslow by the Comte Tournon de Montmelas. In 1875 Sir Everett (then Mr.) Millais first exhibited one of these hounds, the celebrated "Model," which is still often referred to as a typical hound of this curious breed. The basset became quickly a fashion. Sir Everett Millais did much to encourage fanciers, and even wrote a monograph on the new importation, [1] and before very long by the year 1883 this hound had acquired so much of fame and repute as to demand a Club of its own, as well as a place in the Kennel Club Stud Book. Since that time, the march of the basset has, among connoisseurs who can afford the luxury of a new and somewhat expensive fashion, been a triumphant one. In 1883 there were but ten entries of these hounds in the Kennel Club Stud Book. In 1896 there were no less than ninety bassets entered at the Kennel Club Show.

Yet, although the basset has thus achieved a not inconsiderable triumph in a comparatively short period, he is still a somewhat scarce commodity, caviare to the general public. A certain number have seen him on the show benches, or walking abroad with his master; few have watched him at work in the hunting field. In appearance, the basset hound looks somewhat like a handsome foxhound - with long ears, deepish flews, and a somewhat old-fashioned type of head - set on extremely squat legs, the forelegs, especially, being much bent inwards. As to the conformation of the legs, they give, at first, the impression of this hound having some kinship with dachshunds and the old English turnspit. But, as a matter of fact, they are totally distinct. The dachshund is a terrier, while the basset is a pure hound of very ancient descent.

How long he has been bred in his present state it is impossible to say with anything like precision. By some authorities the basset, as found in France and Belgium, is placed in three classes:

1. Bassets *à jambes droites* (or straight-legged bassets).
2. Bassets *à jambes demi-torses* (with fore-legs half crooked).
3. Bassets *à jambes torses* (with fore-legs wholly crooked).

To these, again, three variations of coat are assigned, smooth, rough, and half-rough. The rough-coated variety is, by the way, known as the Griffon-basset. The crooked-legged bassets are in most favour, and are regarded as the best representatives of their race. They show a finer type of hound head, with the long pendulous ears, and other points laid down as desirable in this kind of hound. Bassets run in all colours, foxhound colour, blue-mottle, lemon-and-white, harepie, black-and-tan, and whole red. Sir Everett Millais, who studied the type most closely, favoured the tricoloured variety, that is, a hound with a tan head and a black-and-white body. This type is still much fancied. His well-known hound, "Model," weighed forty-six pounds, and had the following measurements. Shoulder height, twelve inches; length, from tip of nose to setting on of tail, thirty-two inches; height from ground, between fore-feet, two and ¾ inches. The texture of the coat is described as that of a hound, by which one understands the modern English foxhound. [2]

In La Vendée, Luxembourg, Alsace-Lorraine, and other parts, where coverts are extensive, the rough-coated basset seems to be most in favour, but this variety is, as a rule, much scarcer than the smooth-coated hound. The basset is an independent, determined kind of hound. He prefers to take nothing on trust, but instead of giving tongue and joining in the cry of the other hounds, which have already owned the scent, likes to work out the line for himself and then raise his voice. He has an extraordinarily delicate sense of scent. On the Continent this race was, apparently, used very largely for shooting purposes, hunting the country for different kinds of game, and driving it to the guns posted in various positions. In the Ardennes, a bigger breed seems to have been used for driving wolves, boar, and roe; this is the rough-coated kind, previously referred to. But in various districts this useful hound was, and is, employed for all kinds of sport, including badger, vermin, and even truffles. A good truffle-hound is, of course, a real treasure. The basset is a most courageous beast and takes readily to the chase of wolf, which ordinary hounds are said to be not very keen about. It is even stated that a well-bred basset will hunt a wolf single-handed, which, considering his inferior size, must be taken as evidence of very high mettle.

When these hounds were first used for hunting hare in this country, it was quickly discovered that, although they had wonderful noses and were infinitely persevering, they had certain drawbacks which required correction. They are inclined, as I have shown, to dwell too much on the line, and are somewhat too independent, and they are rather easily frightened by the whip. Still, within the last ten years they have shown excellent sport. I find, from my "Field" lists of hounds, that in 1895-96 three packs of bassets were hunting, viz., the Walhampton, the Wintershill, and the Wolvercote. In the next season there were four, viz., The Walhampton, the Wintershill, the Delapre, and Mr. Moss's. In 1897-98 the Wintershill dropped out, and the Highworth were added to the other packs. In 1898-99 three packs remained hunting - the Walhampton, the Delapr, and the Highworth. In 1899-1900 the Walhampton apparently held the field alone, to be joined in 1900-01 by the Stoodleigh and the Knowlton. 1901-02 saw two packs again hunting - the ever-faithful Walhampton and Mr. E. H. M. Denny's, the latter hunting from Chiddingstone Castle, Kent - the Knowlton and the Stoodleigh having retired. The Knowlton, it is to be noted, were mastered and hunted by Miss Gladys Peto, to whom two sisters and a brother acted as whippers-in. During the season, 1902-03, the Walhampton and Mr. Denny's were joined by a new pack, the Reepham, hunting near Lincoln.

From these particulars it would seem that many people have tried hare-hunting with bassets for a short time, usually a season or two, and have then abandoned it. Whether they found that the sport was somewhat slow, or that these dwarf hounds required more time and patience in their education than they could afford to give them, it is beyond me to say. Probably both reasons led to their abandonment, after a brief trial. In some few instances, no doubt, the pack was started as a mere passing fad or fashion, the owner having acquired a few couples of these hounds and wishing to see how they would behave themselves in the field.

The Walhampton pack, as will be seen, have alone remained constant, season after season, to the sport which they inaugurated in 1891. They have been invariably mastered and hunted by the Messrs. Heseltine, Mr. Christopher Heseltine acting as Master, and Captain Godfrey Heseltine having usually carried the horn, except during his absence on service in South Africa.

Captain Heseltine has been good enough to send me particulars of the pack and accounts of some of their best runs; and the narrative seems to me so instructive, not only in reference to sport with bassets, but as regards hare-hunting generally, that I have thought well to print it, in its entirety. It will be noticed with what patience and care this pack has been trained and matured to a successful issue, and how disappointing, comparatively, were the first essays in hare-hunting during the season of 1890-91, when the hounds never killed a hare. It will be noticed, too, how much more readily even bassets can kill hares early in the season, i.e., in September, October, and the early part of November, than later on when hares are so much stronger. This is a point that is often forgotten by young Masters of harriers and beagles.

Here, then, follows Captain Heseltine's account of the Walhampton Basset Hounds:

"(1) The first couple of basset hounds we ever possessed were given to us by Captain Peacock (late M.F.H. Hertfordshire, Isle of Wight, etc.), in 1890, and with four or five couples we used to chivey about, but in April 1891, we purchased 9½ couples from Mr. T. Cannon, Junr., of Danebury, and commenced hunting regularly in the season, 1891-2, and I have a record of every day's sport from then till now. We commenced hunting badger in the New Forest in July 1891, and had several good hunts, both by moonlight and in the early morning, but gave it up for hare-hunting in September, and have never hunted any-

WALHAMPTON BASSET HOUNDS

WALHAMPTON BASSET HOUNDS
THE KILL

thing but hare since. In the seasons 1891-2, 1892-3, the hounds hunted during term time at Cambridge, having their kennels at Chesterton; the remainder of the season they hunted in the New Forest, and around Lymington. Since 1892-3, with the exception of the season, 1900-1, they have been regularly hunted by the writer in the New Forest and the neighbourhood of Lymington. The hounds are the joint property of my brother and myself. My brother is the Master of the pack, and I have always hunted them, with the exception of Nov. 1894, when my brother hunted them. At the present moment (December 1903) kennels are being erected at Canterbury, where I hope to hunt them till the end of the season.

"We have had as many as fourteen couples of puppies at walk, but the last two seasons we have been particularly unfortunate in not being able to breed half that number. I do not think I got more than four couples of whelps. In March 1896, we purchased the whole of the late Major V. Ferguson's pack of basset hounds (15 couples), from which we made a good selection; and in August 1896, Prince Henry of Pless presented us with the whole of his pack

170

from Germany, consisting of about 10 couples. And at various times since then we have purchased small packs, with a view to selecting some 2 or 3 hounds to add to our pack.

"Here is a short summary of our hunting seasons, with the number of hounds in kennel at commencement of the season:

"(2) The country in the New Forest is admirably suited to basset hounds, being moorland or large open woodland.

"The heather on the moor is not sufficiently high to stop these little hounds and invariably carries good scent. The country round Lymington is chiefly plough and banks. The country around Cambridge was chiefly plough, and fenland, which latter suited the hounds very well, if it had not been for the dykes. Deep ditches or stone walls are a terrible hindrance to basset hounds.

Season 1890-1 No record kept; hunted with 5 couples of hounds, but never caught a hare.

	No. of Hunting days.	No. of Blank days.	No. of Hares brought to hand.	No. of Couples of hounds in kennel at commencement of season.
Season 1891-2	47	2	9	10
„ 1892-3	54	4	17	12
„ 1893-4	42	3	11	14
„ 1894-5	43	1	14	13½

6½ brace of hares were killed this season in 27 hunting days. On fifteen days on which the hounds were taken out, they could do nothing at all owing to the frost-bound state of the ground; thus there were only 27 days in the whole season on which it was fit to hunt.

	No. of Hunting days.	No. of Blank days.	No. of Hares brought to hand.	No. of Couples of hounds in kennel at commencement of season.
Season 1895-6	38	2	19	14½
„ 1896-7	41	0	17	17½
„ 1897-8	34	1	12	17
„ 1898-9	32 (8 by-days)	0	16	17½
„ 1899-00	20	1	4	13

Hunting very irregularly; I was hunting the dog pack of the New Forest Foxhounds as well until Jan. 1900, when we both went to the war.

	No. of Hunting days.	No. of Blank days.	No. of Hares brought to hand.	No. of Couples of hounds in kennel at commencement of season.
„ 1901-2	24	2	8	19½

In 1900-1 these hounds did not hunt, owing to the South African War.

WALHAMPTON BASSET HOUNDS.

SEASON 1902-03

DOGS.

Eight years old	. . . .	1
Five years old	. . . .	1
Four years old	. . . .	1
Three years old	. . . .	4
Two years old	. . . .	1
One year old .	. . . .	4 — 12 dogs.

BITCHES.

Eight years old	. . . .	1
Six years old	. . . .	2
Five years old	. . . .	3
Four years old	. . . .	6
Three years old	. . . .	6
Two years old	. . . .	2
One year old	. . . .	4 — 24 bitches.
Total	. . .	36 hounds.

"S. Walker has been the kennel huntsman and whipper-in since 1891. The following is a summary of hounds for this season:

"(3) In the New Forest, during the months of September, October, and early part of November, given a scent, the hounds can bring a hare to hand in 50 minutes to i hour 20 minutes. After the middle of November till the end of the season, I have scarcely ever hunted a hare to death in less than 2 hours and it has much more often been 3 or 4 hours; it is very seldom that these hounds manage to kill a hare before she is so beat that you can pick her up yourself.

"They are very slow to take any advantage; sometimes they would rather throw their tongues than bite; in many cases beagles or even terriers would have killed a hare which has absolutely escaped from the jaws of the pack, because they are so slow to grasp the situation, or, more to the point, the hare.

"(4) I do not think that our kennel management differs in any degree from that of a pack of foxhounds, except that our hounds have biscuit with their meal during the hunting season, and that I only give them the soup from the horse-flesh and none of the meat; otherwise, the kennel management is the same. The floors of the lodging-houses are boarded with battens, 4 inches from the cement flooring, so that no hound can lie on the cement when shut in the lodging house.

"(5) I believe Major Croker and Mr. Miles B. Kennedy were two of the first ever to attempt hunting a hare with basset hounds, about 1886. There were no basset hounds in England prior to 1872, and Lord Onslow, the late Sir Everett Millais, and Mr. Krehl were three of their first admirers."

Six good days with the Walhampton Basset Hounds.
(From Capt. Heseltine's Diary.)

"On Saturday Sep. 24, 1892 (10½ couples), met, 11-30, Hill Top Gate, Beaulieu. Found immediately a three-part grown leveret; raced her for 25 mins., without a check, and killed her at Harley Pitts. Found No. 2 Harley Pitts, hounds ran away from us; they ran straight to the Nodes, which they skirted, sinking the valley thro 5 King's Hat Enclosure, crossed the high road; she jumped up close to Ipley River, and they ran a circle by King's Hat Enclosure. She squatted off a track and we had a long check.

"We had been running i hr. 10 mins. and the point was nearly four miles; a forest keeper poked her out, and 9 mins. later Radical rolled her over in the open in Dibden Bottom, running game to the very end. Who-Whoop!

"On Wedy. March 8, 1892, a blazing hot summer day, met for a by-day, 1-30 P.M. at the Kennels, Chesterton, Cambridge. The ploughs raised a dust cloud, as hounds ran over them; we found a hare at Chesterton at 2-30 P.M. and hunted her to death at 5-25 P.M. A small jack hare.

"On Monday Sep. 17, 1894 (10½ couples), met at Walhampton. Found on Warborne and ran her to ground; had her out and turned her down in the forest; she ran back to Warborne, and, after hunting her for 53 minutes, killed her.

"Found No. 2 on Warborne, and had 47 mins. without a check and killed her. Hounds rather tired, so sent Sam home for 2 couples left in kennel. Found No. 3 close to Bull Hill, ran her by Pilley Green, over Ditton Farm, and thro' Sheffield Copse to the forest, where Sam joined us with two couples of fresh hounds, and we had an excellent hunt and killed our hare in the middle of Beaulieu Heath. Time 1 hour, 3 mins.

"On Friday, Nov. 1, 1895, met, 10 o'clock, Hill Top Gate (13 couples). Found at 11-15 close to Harley Pitts; they ran over the burnt ground and on to the cultivated land at Hythe Cross Roads down to Butts Ashe; hounds were running hard and they packed like a flock of pigeons; they never left her in covert and hunted her back to Hythe Cross Roads. Christopher viewed her away, leaving the Nodes on their left; they sank the valley, but on rising the opposite hill, hounds were at fault on heather, burnt ground, but we viewed her making for Ipley.

"I lifted them and they hunted beautifully past King's Hat Enclosure, which they left on their left, up the high road, and across Ipley Farm, running parallel to Ipley River; we reached the Decoy Farm, and viewed her ' tit-titupping ' on to the forest moor again; she made a sharp double, and hounds were at fault, but I fresh found her on the river bank, where it runs below the L. & S.W.Ry. at the head of Mattey bog, and hounds being on excellent terms with her, hunted her to death, close to Deerleap Enclosure, at 2-20 P.M., nearly five miles as the crow flies, from Butts Ashe, after a slow but good hunting run of 3 hrs. 5 mins.

"On Jan. 31 (Friday), 1896, met at Shirley Holmes Station, n o'clock, a by-day. A cold, cloudy day, wind N.W. very slight. Immediately we began drawing just above Shirley Holmes, hounds began to puzzle out a line, but we never got on terms with our hare, and a road beat us. Time 1 hr. Found No. 2 at Marlpit Oak and had 30 mins. very fast by Set Thorns, Hincheslea, to Sway, where I think a man with a long dog accounted for our hare.

"The hunt of the day was yet to come; we found a hare at 3:30 P.M. at Boldre Grange, in a fallow field; they ran fast to Batramsley Cross Roads, bearing left-handed through Mead End and Rope Hill, and back to St. Austins to Boldre Grange, thro' the wood, and drove her out the bottom end of the covert. They swam the Lymington River below Hey wood Mill, and scuttled best pace by Boldre Church; I held them forward with a long cast up the road, until they hit it off at a gateway, and had to run but slowly over sheep-stained ground. In Sheffield Copse we fresh found her, and on the Forest scent began to improve; bearing left-handed they hunted beautifully by Greenmore, and so to Stockley Cottage; our hare had now run the road (Beaulieu and Brockenhurst), but Resolute, Stella, Minstrel, Dauntless and Coquette revelled in the enjoyment of an undeniable scent, as they hunted it down the road for over a mile. When nearly opposite the head of Hatchet Pond, Gaston's reassuring chime led us over the moor once more; it was now almost dark, and by the time we were running round the head of Hatchet Pond it was dark; but they were not to be denied; they ran with increasing music, or was it the stillness of the evening which made the cry so sweet. They ran yet faster as they neared Blackwater bog; I thought I saw her just in front of them, but it was so dark I could not be certain; the pace meanwhile improved. From Hatchet I had run my very best and had only just succeeded in living with them; no one was with me except a young farmer, who joined me at Sheffield Copse. Close to Pilley Green, I saw without a doubt a hump-backed spectre against the brighter light caused by the reflection of a pond in the heather; so did Raglan and Gas ton, and with a fresh chorus and crash of music six couples were straining for her blood, and pulled her down in the middle of the pond at 5:45 P.M. The best hare-hunt I have ever seen in my life; 2 hrs. 15 mins. and a big point.

"On Monday, Jan. 10, 1898 met, 11 o'clock, at Efford, Lymington, and found a hare close to Vidle Van Farm; bearing right-handed, they crossed the Milford Road just below Keyhaven, and hunted slowly over 2 rivers, by the golf-links, and down to the sea, left-handed down the Stour beach, nearly to Hurst Castle, when up she jumped and immediately took to the sea. She swam nearly 500 yards before she turned back against the current and landed on the beach again, where hounds killed her. Time, something over an hour.

"All these days, which I have taken out of my hunting diary, have ended successfully with blood; and there are many more, which I have enjoyed equally well, that have not, but I have not the time to write, nor you the patience to read more.

"The day - Jan. 31, 1896 - is the best thing of its sort I have ever seen."

These most interesting notes prove very conclusively that hare-hunting with bassets can, if properly managed, yield very fine sport. The Walhampton Master is fortunate in being able to get puppies walked in his surrounding country. A puppy show is annually held, and, in addition to other prizes, since 1897 a Record Reign Challenge Cup, to be won twice before becoming the absolute property of any walker, has been established for the benefit of those undertaking the temporary care of young hounds. It remains to be said that the Walhampton bassets have been as successful on the show benches as they have in the field. Several of the present pack have been distinguished at the Kennel Club Show, Crystal Palace.

In addition to the packs I have before referred to, I believe that, here and there, a little hunting is attempted with a few couples of bassets; these are probably not thought worth while including in the annual lists of hounds. That for the first season or two not much sport may be expected with a new pack has been demonstrated by Captain Heseltine's experiences. But with any new pack of hounds, whether in pursuit of fox, hare, or otter, the same difficulty must be experienced until the huntsman has learnt his craft. The late Rev. John Russell, the famous hunting parson of North Devon, has left on record the ill success of his first season or two with otter hounds. He got together a pack, but could do nothing with them. "I walked," he says, "three thousand miles without finding an otter; and although I must have passed over scores, I might as well have searched for a moose deer." However, he presently got hold of a hound that understood the business, and by its means educated his scratch pack to proper hunting-pitch. In his next two seasons he tells us, he scored "five-and-thirty otters right off the reel." Now, this is the experience of a man who had been entered to hunting from his earliest boyhood, and not of a raw hand, who had never seen hounds handled before. It is not surprising, bearing this precedent in mind, that Masters of basset hounds or beagles, who have hitherto had small experience of hunting hare, or of the management of hounds, should find themselves unable to show sport or obtain blood as often as they could wish. There is no royal road to hunting; a man can only learn the business by long and sometimes rather painful experience, and by constant application and a steady determination

174

to master the mysteries of a most difficult yet absorbing form of sport, at any cost of time and trouble. Just before I wrote this chapter, a gentleman sent to the *Field* the following letter, which, it seems to me, illustrates very well the points I have been discussing:

"Sir, - I have this season been hunting a small pack of basset hounds, and although we have had some excellent runs, and the hounds when on a good scent are absolutely impossible to stay with, our number of kills has been very small. I do not know much about beagles, but have one-and-a-half couple, which I hunt with the basset hounds, and they (the beagles) are not any faster than the bassets, and certainly do not stay as well. I see, however, every week in the papers accounts of kills by beagles in England, and I cannot understand why they should get into their hare so much oftener than we do. Is there very much difference in the English and Irish hares, for, if so, perhaps this would account for it? Perhaps some of your readers, who are interested in foot-hunting, would be good enough to throw some light on the subject. I may add that the country I hunt in is mostly pasture, with very large fields and fences." [3]

It is, I think, almost certain, that this gentleman owed his lack of that crowning triumph and supreme test of a run the kill to the great and sufficient reason that he and his pack were probably not well practised in hare-hunting. If the same pack were hunted next season, it is almost certain that, after the experience they had thus painfully acquired, they would begin to kill hares. Even the Messrs. Heseltine did nothing in their first essays; yet in the following season they began to get blood and so moved forward by degrees from success to success. Bassets are proverbially poor catchers of a hare at the end of a run, and it is in the last phases of the chase, just when she is getting most beaten, that the hare practises all those wonderful tricks and stratagems which are found so puzzling even by practised huntsmen. As to Irish and English hares, it may be stated with confidence that English hares are at least as stout as those of the Sister Island. Most men who have hunted with both would be inclined to yield the English hare the superiority in this respect.

It is difficult to understand the writer's assertion that his beagles are no faster than bassets. Unless the beagles are very small indeed, it is, I think, the experience of most sportsmen who have tested the question that the average beagle is considerably faster than the short-legged, long, and heavy-bodied basset.

Before concluding this chapter, it may be not out of place to mention the value of the points of a basset hound, as now recognised for judging.

	Points
Head, skull, eyes, muzzle, and flews	15
Ears	15
Neck, dewlap, chest, and shoulders	10
Fore-legs and feet	15
Stern	10

[1] "Bassets, their Use and Breeding."
[2] For further information on the basset, the reader may be referred to the works of Mr. Hugh Dalziel and Mr. Rawdon Lee on British dogs, and to Sir Everett Millais' book on this hound.
[3] The *Field,* Feb. 14, 1903, p, 234.

Chapter Nineteen - The Future of Hare-Hunting

THE future of hare-hunting, a sport which, eighty years ago and less, when fox-hunting was rising to its zenith, was being laughed out of fashion, is now safe enough. There have been pauses in the quiet tide of popularity, which, during the last score of years, has been running steadily in favour of this ancient and most interesting sport. The Ground Game Act seemed for a time likely to threaten disaster to hare-hunting, but, happily, the dangers of that dubious piece of legislation have been and are being surmounted; and, with the exception of certain districts, usually where small holdings prevail, Sir William Harcourt's Act has no longer quite the terrors it used to possess. After all, the preservation of hares rests mainly with the farmers, and farmers are more often than not, where they are properly approached, excellent friends to hare-hunting. It is certain that many of them, thanks to the causes to which I have referred heretofore, are, nowadays, even more inclined to be friendly to harrier-men than they are to fox-hunters.

The too great popularity of fox-hunting seems, at the present time, in what are known as the fashionable countries, to threaten the very existence of that sport. Too many people now wish to hunt, and it is impossible to accommodate them all. With every desire to be friendly to the sport which they and their forefathers have supported for generations, the tenantry of this country cannot, in these hard times, be expected to extend the same hospitality as of yore to hundreds of strangers, the greater part of whom they scarcely know by sight, and who care no more for the man, over whose land they ride, than they do for his bullocks. The thing is reaching an impossible development, which, as all sensible men are aware, can end only in one way. The tenant farmer will welcome fields of a reasonable number, but he will not for long continue to put up with the disorderly and often unmannerly crowds that now ride in hundreds over his land, without giving him so much as a thank-you, or a "by your leave." The following letter, which appeared in the *Field,* of February 21, 1903, very well illustrates the scenes of disorder and lack of all hunting decorum which now too often occur with foxhounds in favourite hunting countries:

"SIR, The over-riding of hounds referred to by your correspondent of the Warwickshire Hunt in the issue of the 7th inst. is one which has, with some packs, grown to such an extent as to render the hunting-field almost a pandemonium.

"With one fashionable Hunt, where the fields range, on an average, from 200 to 300, the position of affairs is this: The holloaing of a fox away, instead of being, as it should be, merely a signal for hounds to come out of covert, is, of course, as has always been the case, taken as one for the field to break away, with the result that in almost all cases, particularly where the covert is thick and big, about four couples of hounds get away; then come the foremost brigade, then a few more hounds, then another strong body of the field, with the remainder of the pack picking their way through a mob of galloping horses. The result is that the Master is hoarse with shouting, and the leading hounds are so pressed that, if it be at all a bad scenting day, up go their heads, and the field is then found in the position of a half-moon, the two horns being in advance of the leading hounds, while the rest of the pack are scattered all abroad. It is impossible for the Master to be here, there, and everywhere at once; and it would be in the interests of every one if a rule were enforced that for the future the holloaing of a fox away is to be treated as a call to the hounds only, and that none of the field are to move until the Master's or whipper-in's whistle goes, which, in the majority of cases, would not be until the last hound was out of covert. If the present state of affairs with some Hunts goes on much longer, we may probably see from some determined Master a repetition of the action of the Master of the Quorn some few years ago, when he took hounds home in consequence of the over-riding that went on in defiance of his authority. It is invidious to make distinctions, but I am sorry to say that the chief offenders are often men who, from their position in the Hunt, ought to set a better example.

"W. B."

When this sort of conduct is a matter of common practice, it cannot be denied that fox-hunting must be in a bad way indeed. That gross over-crowding and unmannerly conduct have reached a climax is made clear by the new regulations of the Pytchley, Warwickshire, and North Warwickshire Hunts, under which all people hunting with those packs, other than owners or tenants of land and subscribers, are now to be capped £2 per head per diem when they appear. Whether even this remedy will suffice to purge the evil may well be doubted; it is to be feared that even more drastic measures may have to be enforced.

With harriers no such scenes or such remedies are at present dreamed of. The sport, having quietly regained its former favour, goes peacefully on its way, undisturbed by the din, the turmoils, and the anxieties of modern fox-hunting. Long may it so continue!

This book has not been written with any view of enhancing the popularity or increasing the fields of present packs of harriers. The writer is the last person in the world to wish to see this sport visited by the misfortunes of fashionable fox-hunting. But it may be pointed out that large districts in England, Wales, and Ireland are to be found, where at present harriers or beagles are unknown, and where, given the right conditions and the right men, hare-hunting in a modest way might give pleasure to many a countryside. [1] Where farmers cannot see their way to accommodating a pack of mounted harriers, they would, I am convinced, often be glad to see foot-harriers or beagles over their land. That this is the case has

[1] A reference to the chapters on the various packs of England, Wales, and Ireland, together with the list of beagles in Appendix D, will, with a simultaneous perusal of a map of Great Britain, convince the reader of this fact.

been made abundantly clear in the last twenty years by the great increase in the number of beagle packs now hunting. It is in this direction, especially, that I anticipate a considerable change for the better in many parts of the country, which are yet unblessed by the cheery note of the hare-huntsman's horn and the beautiful cry, so welcome in a winter landscape, of his harriers or beagles.

In opening up negotiations with landowners, farmers, and Masters of neighbouring packs of foxhounds, there are, of course, a good many initial difficulties to be overcome. It is necessary that the embryo Master and huntsman as huntsman he probably will be should have a fair knowledge of the sport he intends to pursue, a good address, and stability. Pleasant manners go very far indeed, especially among farmers and their women folk at the present day, as indeed they always have done and always will do. The days are gone by when some well-descended lout, or Tony Lumpkin, could hope to establish himself at the head of a pack of hounds. Even Somervile, as far back as 1735, well recognised the profit of a good address. Here are his words on this very subject:

> "Well-bred, polite,
> Credit thy calling. See! how mean, how low,
> The bookless saunt'ring youth, proud of the skut
> That dignifies his cap, his flourish'd belt,
> And rusty couples jingling by his side.
> Be thou of other mould; and know that such
> Transporting pleasures were by Heav'n ordained
> Wisdom's relief and Virtue's great reward."

These last two lines are, perhaps, a trifle high-flown the poet's licence must always be allowed for but Somervile's admonition is a perfectly true one, well to be remembered by all sportsmen.

But, perhaps, some of my readers may say: "We have no hares left in our country and it is impossible to get them up again." I doubt the impossibility of raising a fair stock of hares in almost any country, given the goodwill of some few of the farmers, a thing surely not incredibly difficult of achievement. I have shown in earlier chapters how prolific hares are and how rapidly they increase. Even in districts practically depleted of these animals, a fair head could be raised, in the course of a season or two, by turning down a few couples. With even a moderate amount of preservation, it is astonishing how almost inordinately plentiful they will speedily become. It is rather curious that at the present day hare-warrens are so neglected. In Beckford's time they were evidently common, and many squires trapped hares and made use of them for turning down, or for sport, as required. One would not, of course, advocate hunting or coursing trapped hares, but warrens might well be utilised for the purpose of increasing the stock in other places. The warren was paled in. It usually consisted of a wood of twenty or thirty acres, cut in places into various walks. Traps were constantly set for stoats, weasels, and polecats, and no dog was ever allowed within the enclosure. Parsley was recommended to be planted, as giving hares strength and keeping them at home. It is certain that they are very fond of this vegetable.

When hares were required they were duly trapped, the traps being placed at the meuses, but only set when hares were wanted. By this means the animals became accustomed to them and were readily taken when required. It was recommended that the traps should be made of old wood, and even then it took time before the hares became accustomed to them.

Other metises were directed to be left open, lest hares should become alarmed, or disgusted, and so forsake the place. Where traps were set, the meuses were of brick. When hares became very shy of the traps and could not be readily caught, it was sometimes found necessary to drive them in from the outside where they were often thickly congregated with spaniels. This was, of course, a method seldom resorted to.

"The number of hares that a warren will supply," says Beckford, "is hardly to be conceived. I seldom turned out less, in one year, than thirty brace of traphares, besides many others killed in the environs, of which no account was taken." He adds an amusing anecdote. "I had once some conversation with a gentleman about the running of my trap-hares, who said he had been told that catching a hare, and *tying a piece of ribbon to her ear,* was a sure way to make her run *straight.* I make no doubt of it," he adds, "and so would *a canister tied to her tail.*" Hare warrens, then, where hares are scarce, might surely, be cultivated at the present time, as they were by country gentlemen in those fine old hunting days of the Georgian period. For turning down, they would be of invaluable assistance.

But of the future of hares in this country, or of the right sort of hounds to hunt them, I, for one, have no fear. One's only dread is, that at the present rate of increase in population, and of the growth of towns and cities, large portions of England will be, within the next two hundred years, rendered impossible for hunting. Already infinite mischief is done by the enormous manufacturing towns in various parts of the kingdom. Go to Yorkshire, and walk through the country within seven miles of Leeds, Sheffield, and other great centres of industry, and note the ravages of smoke and soot upon the vegetation, and the filth that is deposited everywhere. It makes one despair sometimes for that rural England of which we have for ages boasted and still continue to boast. The very gunners, shooting within hail of these great cities of toil, find the moors even black with soot. What is to be the end of it all? Is this country to be gradually destroyed, and the state of man in this island reduced to the condition of a mill-horse or a mine pony, toiling, poor creature, endlessly, hopelessly, amid the most dismal of all conceivable surroundings? Is the life of man to be sunk to such depths of despair and blackness? If so, perish our so-called civilisation! A return to the wild, natural freedom of the pure savage would be infinitely preferable. England is rich, the envy of the world; but surely her richness and her prosperity will have been dearly purchased, if her smiling fields are all to be reduced in turn, mile by mile, acre by acre, to the level of the deserts of the Black Country, the hideous brick wastes of the East-End of London, or the hopeless, squalid, endless rows of streets upon the outskirts of some of our great manufacturing towns! These things will not come in our time; but the day, apparently, is approaching when great parts of England will, to the lover of nature, the man of the open air, be impossible places to live in.

Still, thanks to the fact that the east, the west, the south, and some other portions of this country, have not been invaded by the blight of manufactures and minerals, there remain, probably for another hundred or two of years, large areas where nature will still show her face in its fresh and natural beauty, where the wild flowers can awaken each spring, the woods deck themselves in verdure uncontaminated, and the wild creatures find their resting-places. Here the hare-hunter will, let us hope, for generations yet to come, pursue his quiet sport, taking his hounds into the field with each succeeding October, and for five months of the year awaking the echoes of hill and moor and valley with the thrilling note of his horn and the inspiring cry of his hounds.

Fox-hunting as it is now pursued in many localities, has apparently to endure a crisis. There are many signs that this crisis is not long to be delayed. As an admirer of fox-hunting, I can but be concerned with the changes for the worse that have in too many places overtaken this fine sport. In the year 1893 there died in Warwickshire an old relative of my own, at the great age of ninety years. She had been bred up all her life among fox-hunters, and was old enough to remember the time when Squire Corbet hunted the whole of the Warwickshire country, north and south. Squire Corbet reigned from 1791 to 1811, one of the most glorious periods of hunting in that shire. I remember well the old print of Mr. Corbet, on his white horse, cheering his hounds out of covert, which used to hang in my aunt's dining-room.

This old lady lived to see the days of over-crowded fields, of barbed wire, of the decline of the farming interest; yet the memories of Squire Corbet and his hounds remained fresh in her mind to the end of her life. She was born in 1803, her mind was, to the last, unimpaired; she remembered well the bitter winter of 1812 and Napoleon's terrible Russian campaign; and from her I drew, from the days of my youth, many a picture of old English country life. Even in my own time, I have seen many changes for the worse in fox-hunting. I can well remember, as a lad, the Warwickshire, Bicester, Pytchley, and Grafton countries, when not a yard of wire existed throughout the length and breadth of those splendid fields and pastures. Fox-hunting, I am afraid, has to undergo a purge; how it will emerge from the ordeal remains to be seen. At present, it seems that, in the best and most popular countries, only the man of the longest purse can survive, a consummation not, perhaps, the most desirable in the world. As for the man of small means, who loves fox-hunting, he must either betake himself to the unfashionable countries - where, after all, some of the best sport is nowadays often to be found - or condescend to harriers.

For harriers I see no such symptoms of crisis. Rather, as I have said, I believe, in its quiet way, the sport is destined to go on and prosper, so long as portions of England remain sufficiently rural. That it may continue to do so must be the wish of every true lover of sport and of wild life. It will be a bad day for Britain, indeed, when her field sports are brought to an end. In these days, when our country is the object of envy, hatred, and malice to more than one Continental power; when her wealth and her success attract the fiercest scrutiny and the most savage desire; it is in the last degree necessary that her manhood should, by every means in their power, prepare themselves steadily and pertinaciously for that great combat which, sooner or later, must be our destiny. The man who keeps himself fit, and active, and hardy, whose eye is clear, whose muscles are toughened, whose courage is high, and whose nerve is steady; who can ride, run, shoot, swim, march long distances, and knows something of the country and the life of the open air, must always be, inevitably, far more valuable to his country than the man soddened by town-life, enervated, soft, purblind, and emasculate. Any out-door sport or pastime, be it hunting, athletics, football, cricket, or any other form of exercise and training, must of necessity be invaluable to such a civilisation as ours; and these recreations will, I am convinced, be, in the long run, the saving of our manhood and of our country. Hunting, then, in any form, whether it be fox-hunting for the rich man, or hare-hunting with harriers or beagles for the man of moderate means, is surely to be encouraged by all means, by those who wish well to their country. Indeed, it may be hoped and believed that hunting never will die out of these islands so long as England possesses pure air, open country, stout hares, and wild foxes. I believe that if mounted men were ever driven from the field by barbed wire, or other atrocities, some kind of hunting, whether with fox or hare, would still be pursued on foot, so irrepressible and inborn is the natural instinct of the chase in most men of British blood. And if one might hazard a prophecy - far distant may be the day of its fulfilment! - it is this, that when the last fox has been extirpated from wild Britain, when the last mounted hunter has leaped his final fence, or fallen a victim to barbed wire, some faithful remnant of our descendants may yet be found following the hare on foot, hunting her down in the ancient manner of their forefathers with beagle or harrier.

If there should, unhappily, come a time when hunting of any kind is brought to an end within our borders, I am by no means certain that many of our descendants may not be found settled in other and wilder countries, or passing to and fro by some rapid means of communication at present unknown to us, still pursuing those field sports in which their hardy ancestors so much delighted. Various parts of remote Europe, or of yet remoter Asia, Africa, or America, may, in centuries to come, still continue to be used as hunting-grounds, when much of western Europe is overlaid with bricks and mortar, and overhung with its hideous canopy of smoke. It is by no means a wild stretch of fancy to imagine that such may be the case. Thousands of our countrymen already go abroad for their sport; and, as England becomes more overcrowded and communication more rapid, tens of thousands will betake themselves to yet remoter fields. I do not say that in all these countries good hare-hunting or good fox-hunting will be obtained off-hand. In South Africa, for instance, where immense wastes of veldt will afford playgrounds and sporting-fields for centuries to come, the indigenous hare of the country is not a good one for hunting, as we understand hunting at home. He has a nasty habit of going to ground, and, although I have followed English foxhounds on horseback, in rousing chases after the jackal and small antelopes of Bechuanaland, I should be sorry to have to hunt any of the various species of South African hare with a pack of harriers or beagles.

Many a laughable course have I viewed across the veldt from the back of my pony or the fore-kist of my waggon, as our mongrel pack of waggon dogs raved frantically after some errant hare; but I doubt very much whether much fun would be obtained in any other way. The beast would most surely go to earth in half a mile or a mile, and a fresh find would have constantly to be undertaken. Hares, however, are easily acclimatised, and our English species already flourishes in New Zealand and elsewhere. When the merry British hare-hunter has been driven from his own island, he can surely betake himself to fresh woods and pastures new, and pursue his beloved sport on some Asiatic Steppe, or Tundra, or over the wild Karroos and rolling uplands of South Africa, or amid the green pastures of New Zealand or the plains of Australia. I, for one, will never believe that the British hunter, whether he favours fox, hare, or stag, will relinquish his sport, because, forsooth, his island has grown too overcrowded for him. Rather do I believe that if the last remaining portion of the globe open to him for hunting consisted of the wet wastes of the Falkland Islands, or the dreary desolation of Tierra del Fuego, he would still repair thither and try his luck.

However, although some of these expectations and possibilities may actually lie within the bosom of the future, at present there is no instant necessity for the average man of British blood to be looking quite so far afield. I hold with confidence that, in our time and for a good many generations thereafter, he will be able to pursue his favourite method of hunting in much the old way. And especially do I anticipate that the hare-hunter is destined, for may a long year yet, to meet, as he and his forefathers have met for centuries, on some quiet village green, or by the timeworn walls of some ancient manor-house, to greet his friends just in the hearty old way, to listen with enraptured ears to the sound of the deep-tongued harrier, to view the hare speeding from her form, to hear, as the pack first opens upon the line, that burst of hound melody which never yet failed to stir the heart of youth or age, of man or woman, and to watch with never failing ecstacy the passage and the working of the hounds, as they puzzle out the infinite mazes woven by one of the cleverest and most resourceful creatures ever known to the lover of the chase. These sights and sounds, these exercises, so dear to the follower of hare-hunting, are destined, I fully believe, to endure in British fields for many and many a winter day yet to come, and to cheer the heart, clear the brain, and toughen the fibres of many a sportsman of the right British blood.

Bearing these things in mind, I do not think that I can close this volume more fittingly than with a motto taken from an old translation from the third Georgic of Virgil:

> "Hark away,
> Cast far behind the ling'ring cares of life.
> Cithaeron calls aloud, and in full cry
> Thy hounds, Taygetus. Epidaurus trains
> For us the generous steed; the hunter's shouts,
> And cheering cries, assenting woods return."

Appendices

Appendix A - The Hunting of the Hare

With her last Will and Testament. As 'twas perform'd on Bamstead downs By Cony-catchers and their hounds. To a pleasant new Tune: "Of all the Sports the World doth Yield."

OF all delights that Earth doth yield,
Give mee a pack of hounds in field;
Whose echo shall throughout the sky
Make *Jove* admire our harmony
   and wish that he a mortal were
   to view the pastime we have here.

I will tell you of a rare scent,
Where many a gallant horse was spent
On *Bamstead-Downs* a Hare we found
Which led us all a smoking round;
   o're hedge and ditch away she goes,
   admiring her approaching foes.

But when she found her strength to wast
She parleyed with the hounds at last:
Kind hounds, quoth she, forbear to kill
A harmless Hare that neer thought ill,
   and if your Master sport do crave
   I'll lead a scent as he would have.

HUNTSMAN

Away, away, thou art alone,
Make haste, I say, and get thee gone,
Wee'l give thee law for half a mile
To see if thou canst us beguile,
   but then expect a thund'ring cry,
   made by us and our harmony.

HARE

Now since you set my life so sleight,
I'll make black sloven turn to white:
And Yorkshire Gray that runs at all
   I'le make him wish he were in stall, or Sorrel he that seems to flye,
   I'le make him supple e're he dye.

Let *Barnards* Bay do what he can,
Or *Barrons* Bay that now and than
Did interrupt mee on my way,
I'le make him neither jet nor play,
   or constant *Robin* though he lye,
   at his advantage, what care I.

Will Hatton he hath done mee wrong,
He struck mee as I run along,
And with one pat made mee so sore,
That I ran reeling to and fro;
   but if I dye his Master tell,
   that fool shall ring my passing bell.

HUNTSMAN

Alas poor Hare it is our nature,
To kill thee, and no other creature,
For our Master wants a bit,
And thou wilt well become the spit,
   he'll eat thy flesh, we'll pick thy bone,
   this is thy doom, so get thee gone.

HARE

Your Master may have better chear,
For I am dry, and butter is dear,
But, if he please to make a friend,
He'd better give a puddings end,
   for I being kill'd the sport he'l lack,
   and I must hang on the Huntsman's back,

HUNTSMAN

Alas poor Hare we pity thee,
If with our nature 'twould agree,
But all thy doubling shifts I fear,
Will not prevail, thy death's so near
   then make thy Will, it may be that,
   may save thee, or I know not what.

(The Hare makes her Will)

Then I bequethe my body free,
Unto your Masters courtesie:
And if he please my life to grant,
He be his game when sport is scant:
   but if I dye each greedy Hound,
   divides my entrals on the ground.

- - - -

Item, I do give and bequeathe,
To men in debt (after my death
My subtle scent, that so they may,
Beware of such as would betray,
   them to a miserable fate
   by blood-hounds from the *Compter-gate.*

Item, I do a turn-coat give
(That he may more obscurely live)
My swift and sudden doublings which,
Will make politick and rich,
   though at the last with many wounds
   I wish him kill'd by his own hounds.

Item, I give into their hands,
That purchase Dean and Chapter lands,
My wretched jealousies and fears,
Mixt with salt of Orphans' tears,
   that long vexations may persever,
   to plague them and their heirs for ever.

Before I dye (for breath is scant)
I would supply mens proper want,
And therefore I bequeath(e) unto,
The Scrivener (give the Devil his due)
   that Forgeth, Swears, and then forswears
   (to save his credit) both my Ears.

I give to some Sequestred man,
My skin to make a jacket on:
And I bequethe my feet to they,
That shortly mean to run away,
   When truth is Speaker, False-hood's dumb,
   Foxes must flye when Lions come.

To Fiddlers (for all Trades must live)
To serve for strings, my guts I give:
For Gamesters that do play at rut,
And love the sport, I give my skut:
   but (last of all in this sad dump)
   To *Tower-Hill* I bequeathe my Rump.

HUNTSMAN

Was ever Hounds so basely crost,
Our Masters call us off so fast,

That we the scent have almost lost,
And they themselves must rule the rost,
   therefore kind Hare wee'l pardon you,
   Thanks gentle Hounds, and so adue.

HARE

And since your Master hath pardon'd me
I'll lead you all to *Banbury*,
Whereas *John Turner* hath a Room
To entertain all Guests that come
   to laugh and quaff in Wine and Beer
   a full carouse to your Careere.

May, 1660.
Roxburghe Ballads.

Appendix B - Lists of Hound Names

I. *From Beckford's "Thoughts on Hunting," 1780*

DOGS	BITCHES	
		Boaster
		Boisterous
Able	Accurate Active	Bonnyface
Actor	Actress	Bouncer
Adamant	Affable	Bowler
Adjutant	Agile	Bragger
Agent	Airy	Bravo
Aider	Amity	Brawler
Aimwell	Angry	Brazen
Amorous	Animate	Brilliant
Antic	Artifice	Brusher
Anxious	Audible	Brutal
Arbiter		Burster
Archer	**DOGS**	Bustler
Ardent		
Ardor	Bachelor	**BITCHES**
Arrogant	Baffler	
Arsenic	Banger	Baneful
Artful	Barbarous	Bashful
Artist	Bellman	Bauble
Atlas	Bender	Beauteous
Atom	Blaster	Beauty
Auditor	Bluecap	Beldam
Augur	Blueman	Bellmaid
Awful	Bluster	Blameless

187

Blithsome
Blowzy
Bluebell
Bluemaid
Bonny
Bonnybell
Bonnylass
Boundless
Bravery
Brevity
Brimstone
Busy
Buxom

DOGS

Caitiff
Caliban
Capital
Captain
Captor
Carol
Carver
Caster
Castwell
Catcher
Catchpole
Caviller
Cerberous
Challenger
Champion
Charon
Chaser
Chaunter
Chieftain
Chimer
Chirper
Choleric
Claimant
Clamorous
Clangour
Clasher
Climbank
Clinker
Combat

Combatant
Comforter
Comrade
Comus
Conflict
Conqueror
Conquest
Constant
Contest
Coroner
Cottager
Counsellor
Countryman
Courteous
Coxcomb
Craftsman
Crasher
Critic
Critical
Crowner
Cruiser
Crusty
Cryer
Curfew
Currier

BITCHES

Capable
Captious
Careless
Careful
Carnage
Caution
Cautious
Charmer
Chauntress
Cheerful
Cherripur
Chorus
Circe
Clarinet
Clio
Comely
Comfort

Comical
Concord
Courtesy
Crafty
Crazy
Credible
Credulous
Croney
Cruel
Curious

DOGS

Damper
Danger
Dangerous
Dapper
Dapster
Darter
Dasher
Dashwood
Daunter
Dexterous
Disputant
Downright
Dragon
Dreadnought
Driver
Duster

BITCHES

Dainty
Daphne
Darling
Dashaway
Dauntless
Delicate
Desperate
Destiny
Dian
Diligent
Docile
Document
Doubtful

Doubtless
Dreadful
Dreadless
Dulcet

DOGS

Eager
Earnest
Effort
Elegant
Eminent
Envious
Envoy
Errant
Excellent

BITCHES

Easy
Echo
Ecstacy
Endless
Energy
Enmity
Essay

DOGS

Factious
Factor
Fatal
Fearnought
Ferryman
Fervent
Finder
Firebrand
Flagrant
Flasher
Fleece'm
Fleecer
Flinger
Flippant
Flourisher
Flyer

Foamer
Foiler
Foreman
Foremost
Foresight
Forester
Forward
Fulminant
Furrier

BITCHES

Fairmaid
Fairplay
Faithful
Famous
Fanciful
Fashion
Favourite
Fearless
Festive
Fickle
Fidget
Fiery
Fireaway
Firetail
Flighty
Flourish
Flurry
Forcible
Fretful
Friendly
Frisky
Frolic
Frolicsome
Funnylass
Furious
Fury

DOGS

Gainer
Gallant
Galliard
Galloper

Gamboy
Gamester
Garrulous
Gazer
General
Genius
Gimcrack
Giant
Glancer
Glider
Glorious
Goblin
Governor
Grapler
Grasper
griper
Growler
Grumbler
Guardian
Guider
Guiler

BITCHES

Gaiety
Gaily
Gainful
Galley
Gambol
Gamesome
Gamestress
Gaylass
Ghastly
Giddy
Gladness
Gladsome
Governess
Graceful
Graceless
Gracious
Grateful
Gravity
Guilesome
Guiltless
Guilty

DOGS

Hannibal
Harbinger
Hardiman
Hardy
Harlequin
Harasser
Havoc
Hazard
Headstrong
Hearty
Hector
Heedful
Hercules
Hero
Highflyer
Hopeful
Hotspur
Humbler
Hurtful

BITCHES

Handsome
Harlot
Harmony
Hasty
Hazardous
Heedless
Hellen
Heroine
Hideous
Honesty
Hostile

DOGS

Jerker
Jingler
Impetus
Jockey
Jolly
Jollyboy
Jostler

Jovial
Jubal
Judgment
Jumper

BITCHES

Jealousy
Industry
Jollity
Joyful
Joyous

DOGS

Labourer
Larum
Lasher
Laster
Launcher
Leader
Leveller
Liberal
Libertine
Lictor
Lifter
Lightfoot
Linguist
Listener
Lounger
Lucifer
Lunatic
Lunger
Lurky
Lusty

BITCHES

Lacerate
Laudable
Lavish
Lawless
Lenity
Levity
Liberty

Lightning
Lightsome
Likely
Lissome
Litigate
Lively
Lofty
Lovely
Luckylass
Lunacy

DOGS

Manager
Manful
Marschal
Markman
Marplot
Martial
Marvellous
Matohem
Maxim
Maximus
Meanwell
Medler
Menacer
Mendall
Mender
Mentor
Mercury
Merlin
Merry boy
Merryman
Messmate
Methodist
Mighty
Militant
Minikin
Miscreant
Mittimus
Monarch
Monitor
Motley
Mounter
Mover

Mungo
Musical
Mutinous
Mutterer
Myrmidon

BITCHES

Madcap
Madrigal
Magic Maggoty
Matchless
Melody
Merryglass
Merriment
Mindful
Minion
Miriam
Mischief
Modish
Monody
Music

DOGS

Nervous
Nestor
Nettler
Newsman
Nimrod
Noble
Nonsuch
Novel
Noxious

BITCHES

Narrative
Neatness
Needful
Negative
Nicety
Nimble
Noisy
Notable

Notice
Notion
Novelty
Novice

DOGS

Paean
Pageant
Paragon
Paramount
Partner
Partyman
Pealer
Penetrant
Perfect
Perilous
Pertinent
Petulant
Phoebus
Piercer
Pilgrim
Pillager
Pilot
Pincher
Piper
Playful
Plodder
Plunder
Politic
Potent
Prater
Prattler
Premier
President
Presto
Prevalent
Primate
Principle
Prodigal
Prompter
Prophet
Prosper
Prosperous
Prowler

Pryer

BITCHES

Passion
Pastime
Patience
Phoenix
Phrenetic
Phrensy
Placid
Playful
Playsome
Pleasant
Pliant
Positive
Precious
Prettylass
Previous
Priestess
Probity
Prudence

DOGS

Racer
Rager
Rallywood
Rambler
Ramper
Rampant
Rancour
Random
Ranger
Ransack
Rantaway
Ranter
Rapper
Rattler
Ravager
Ravenous
Ravisher
Reacher
Reasoner
Rector

Regent
Render
Resonant
Restive
Reveller
Rifler
Rider
Rigid
Rigour
Ringwood
Rioter
Risker
Rockwood
Romper
Rouser
Router
Rover
Rudesby
Ruffian
Ruffler
Rumbler
Rummager
Rumour
Runner
Rural
Rusher
Rustic

BITCHES

Racket
Rally
Rampish
Rantipole
Rapid
Rapine
Rapture
Rarity
Rashness
Rattle
Ravish
Reptile
Resolute
Restless
Rhapsody

Riddance
Riot
Rival
Roguish
Ruin
Rummage
Ruthless

DOGS

Salient
Sampler
Sampson
Sanction
Sapient
Saucebox
Saunter
Scalper
Scamper
Schemer
Scourer
Scrambler
Screamer
Screecher
Scuffler
Searcher
Settler
Sharper
Shifter
Signal
Singer
Singwell
Skirmish
Smoker
Social
Solomon
Solon
Songster
Sonorous
Soundwell
Spanker
Special
Specimen
Speedwell
Spinner

Splendour
Splenetic
Spoiler
Spokesman
Sportsman
Squabbler
Squeaker
Statesman
Steady
Stickler
Stinger
Stormer
Stranger
Stripling
Striver
Strivewell
Stroker
Stroller
Struggler
Sturdy
Subtle
Succour
Suppler
Surly
Swaggerer
Sylvan

BITCHES

Sanguine
Sappho
Science
Scrupulous
Shrewdness
Skilful
Songstress
Specious
Speedy
Spiteful
Spitfire
Sportful
Sportive
Sportly
Sprightly
Stately

Stoutness
Strenuous
Strumpet
Surety
Sybil
Symphony

DOGS

Tackler
Talisman
Tamer
Tangent
Tartar
Tattler
Taunter
Teaser
Terror
Thrasher
Threatner
Thumper
Thunderer
Thwacker
Thwarter
Tickler
Tomboy
Topmost
Topper
Torment
Torrent
Torturer
Tosser
Touchstone
Tracer
Tragic
Trampler
Transit
Transport
Traveller
Trial
Trier
Trimbush
Trimmer
Triumph
Trojan

Trouncer
Truant
Trueboy
Trueman
Trudger
Trusty
Trywell
Tuner
Turbulent
Twanger
Twig'em
Tyrant

BITCHES

Tattle
Telltale
Tempest
Tentative
Terminate
Terrible
Testy
Thankful
Thoughtful
Tidings
Toilsome
Tractable
Tragedy
Trespass
Trifle
Trivial
Trollop
Troublesome
Truelass
Truemaid
Tunable
Tuneful

DOGS

Vagabond
Vagrant
Valiant
Valid
Valorous

Valour
Vaulter
Vaunter
Venture
Venturer
Venturous
Vermin
Vexer
Victor
Vigilant
Vigorous
Vigour
Villager
Viper
Volant
Voucher

BITCHES

Vanquish
Vehemence
Vehement
Vengeance
Vengeful
Venomous
Venturesome
Venus
Verify
Verity
Vicious
Victory
Victrix
Vigilance
Violent
Viperous
Virulent
Vitiate
Vivid
Vixen
Vocal
Volatile
Voluble

DOGS

Wanderer

Warbler
Warning
Warrior
Warhoop
Wayward
Wellbred
Whipster
Whynot
Wildair
Wildman
Wilful
Wisdom
Woodman
Worker

Workman
Worthy
Wrangler
Wrestler

BITCHES

Waggery
Waggish
Wagtail
Wanton
Warfare
Warlike
Waspish

Wasteful
Watchful
Welcome
Welldone
Whimsey
Whirligig
Wildfire
Willing
Wishful
Wonderful
Worry
Wrathful
Wreakful

2. *From the Duke of Rutland's Hounds,* 1826.

Ajax
Abigail
Artful
Bender
Bloomer
Courtly
Carnage
Careful
Corsican
Contest
Chaunter
Chorister
Clencher
Columbine
Caroline
Cardinal
Cruel
Constant
Crimson
Danger
Damsel
Daphne
Gadabout
Gipsy
Gamble
Gratitude
Hoyden
Hernia

Hostess
Harlot
Joker
Jargon
Jewel
Jailer
Juliet
Jessamy
Joyous
Jealousy
Joyful
Luther
Limner
Lavender
Legacy
Ladyblush
Lady
Mindful
Merrical
Nabob
Niobe
Nectar
Nelly
Nimble
Nancy
Paragon
Pliant
Proctor

Primrose
Rhapsody
Ruby
Ragland
Ranter
Rebel
Redrose
Rocket
Rosalind
Rally
Ravager
Remus
Rosebud
Rummager
Racket
Roundly
Ruin
Rachel
Rambler
Ringwood
Regale
Rapid
Ruler
Rasselas
Remnant
Shifter
Sally
Syren

Sparker
Splendour
Stormer
Statesman
Sultan
Symmetry
Stranger

Songstress
Vulcan
Vestal
Vaulter
Valiant
Vixen
Virgin

Vengeance
Violet
Warble
Watchful
Waspish

3. *From the Duke of Beaufort's Hounds,* 1826

Affable
Aimwell
Archer
Amorous
Absolute
Bluster
Brusher
Boxer
Barrister
Bluebell
Bravery
Brilliant
Benedict
Baronet
Commodore
Costly
Columbine
Charmer
Doriment
Dreadnought
Dandy
Diomede
Darter
Dashwood
Diligent
Dauntless
Dorcas
Denmark
Dexter
Dalliance
Daphne
Dashaway
Driver
Dainty
Duncan

Dragon
Doxy
Duster
Destiny
Delicate
Dimity
Daffodil
Damsel
Emily
Elegant
Edgar
Empress
Edwin
Gaylass
Governess
Gainer
Guzman
Gladsome
Graceful
Gaiety
Gertrude
Grecian
Gossip
Garland
Gaudy
Honesty
Harbinger
Jasper
Jessamine
Jason
Jesse
Libertine
Lovely
Laundress
Lancaster

Lively
Latimer
Lightfoot
Nectar
Niobe
Nimrod
Plunder
Playful
Paragon
Prophetess
Platoff
Pontifi
Princess
Purity
Pastime
Partner
Pilgrim
Pugilist
Pillager
Pasquin
Parasol
Policy
Proctor
Pelican
Piper
Rival
Regent
Rifleman
Ranter
Ruby
Raffle
Racket
Rubens
Rustic
Ransom

Rampish
Rarity
Ruin
Ragland
Rallywood
Rutland
Rafter
Restless
Rapture
Rachel
Reveller
Rhapsody
Rosamund
Ravager
Relish

Sprightly
Tandem
Toilet
Tuneful
Vaulter
Vanity
Valiant
Vanguard
Victor
Vulcan
Vanquisher
Waterloo
Wellington
Whimsey
Wary

Wildair
Wonder
Workman
Wilful
Waverly
Wrangler
Wanton
Woodbine
Whirlwind
Whisker
Willing
Winifred
Warrior

4. *From Mr. Osbaldestone's Hounds (The Quorn),* 1826.

Active
Artful
Abelard
Auditor
Actress
Abigail
Archer
Amulet
Aimwell
Beatrix
Brevity
Bachelor
Baroness
Boozer
Blameless
Barbary
Brusher
Benedict
Bloomer
Crafty
Chorister
Clencher
Caliban
Caroline
Comely
Champion
Cruizer

Chaunter
Charon
Cypher
Charmer
Cobweb
Concord
Comedy
Careful
Curricle
Castor
Damsel
Drugger
Dromo
Dexter
Dalliance
Diomed
Dandy
Decent
Dairymaid
Emerald
Emperor
Farrier
Fallacy
Felony
Gossamer
Gratitude
Granby

Gaylass
Golding
Gilder
Gertrude
Hernia
Hermit
Hostess
Harlot
Harper
Horsa
Handmaid
Harpy
Harmony
Hardwick
Hasty
Heroine
Joyful
Jasper
Jewess
Jubilee
Jessamy
Junket
Jezebel
Jealousy
Justice
Joyous
Lunatic

Lively
Lightning
Lady
Lightfoot
Milliner
Mortimer
Margaret
Musical
Marmion
Nimble
Nancy
Orpheus
Ottoman
Oddity
Ornament
Piper
Prattle
Palestine
Pilot
Proctor
Promise
Pastime
Purity
Palafox
Prodigal
Pilgrim
Primrose

Pontiff
Placeman
Prizer
Phoebe
Prompter
Pangloss
Patience
Rocket
Rasselas
Roundelay
Rosy
Rattler
Ruin
Rallywood
Rhapsody
Racer
Royster
Ransom
Rachael
Rosemary
Singwell
Singer
Sailor
Syntax
Sampson
Senator
Telltale

Trywell
Truelove
Tarquin
Vaulter
Volatile
Violet
Valentine
Vigilant
Vanquisher
Venus
Vengeance
Vanity
Victory
Vocal
Vicious
Varnish
Vagrant
Wilderness
Wonder
Welcome
Wanton
Witchcraft
Woodman
Whiterose
Woodbine
Woful

5. *From Mr. Musters' Hounds (The Pytchley),* 1826

Ambrose
Actress
Artful
Abelard
Archer
Active
Abigail
Amazon
Arthur
Adeline
Amulet
Airy
Boundless
Bouncer
Benedict

Bacchanal
Byblow
Brilliant
Bauble
Bravery
Bonnybell
Bachelor
Buxom
Collier
Champion
Careless
Columbine
Crier
Charity
Castor

Cipher
Chancellor
Charmer
Celia
Cheerly
Caroline
Charming
Cardinal
Chantress
Crafty
Chanticleer
Chirper
Careful
Comedy
Conrad

Comely
Cottager
Carver
Doubtful
Dreadnought
Dairymaid
Dashaway
Duster
Diligent
Dexter
Dashwood
Driver
Desperate
Dalliance
Daphne
Forrester
Fortune
Fairy
Gulliver
Gaudy
Glory
Gaiety
Gaylass
Governor
Governess
Gamboy
Harlequin
Hermit
Harlot
Harmony
Hector
Hotspur

Harriet
Joyful
Justice
Jessamine
Jessica
Juliet
Judy
Lasher
Laughable
Monitor
Monarch
Matchless
Modish
Madrigal
Ottoman
Orpheus
Pilot
Porcupine
Prettylass
Purity
Playful
Pleasant
Pastime
Proctor
Painter
Rachel
Roman
Royster
Rival
Ruin
Riot
Racket

Ransom
Singwell
Speedwell
Sultan
Scornful
Stormer
Saladin
Stately
Symphony
Susan
Syren
Sailor
Songstress
Safety
Sportsman
Sanguine
Topper
Thetis
Vaulter
Vanquisher
Vanguard
Woodman
Willing
Wonderful
Wildboy
Watchful
Woodbine
Welcome
Wonder
Walter

Appendix C - Old Derbyshire Poem on the Great Run with Squire Frith's Harriers

[1]

(From "The Sporting Magazine" 1826)

Hark! Hark! brother Sportsman, what musical sounds
Through the valley do ring from the merry-mouth' d hounds!
No one in this land with Squire Frith can compare,
For chasing bold Reynard or hunting the hare.

When Phoebus peeped over yon high eastern hills,
And darted his rays o'er the lawns and the fields,
One eighth of December a mem'rable morn,
We chased bold Reynard with hounds and with horn.

With a staunch and fleet pack, most sagacious and true,
What a musical chorus when Reynard's in view!
No pleasure like hunting we mortals can know;
Then follow I hark forward, boys! yoicks! Tally-ho!

First for the Combs rocks swift as lightning he flew;
Tally-ho! was the word, we've bold Reynard in view!
The hills and the valleys re-echo all round
With the shout of the huntsman and the cry of the hound.

The cunning old trotter no covert can find;
Our staunch dogs pursue him as fleet as the wind:
For all the strong holds we had stopped up secure,
And crafty old Reynard the chase must endure.

There's Pedlar and Ploughboy, two dogs of great fame,
And Primrose and Connylass, and Conqueror by name,
Old Bellman and Bowman, Ringwood, Rally-ho,
With Lily and Lady, and little Dido.

Squire Frith is well mounted upon a swift steed,
Black Jack! there are few that can match him for speed;
The Squire and his huntsman no horse-flesh will spare,
When chasing bold Reynard, or hunting the hare.

For Macclesfield Forest the felon did fly,

Through Tagsneys and Crookyard and unto Langly,
Through Chalvecross, Gracely Woods, and Swithingly,
At his brush close did follow the hounds in full cry.

Near to Gawsworth and Horsley he came back again,
'Twas speed that prolong' d his life, it was plain;
Near forty long miles the old trotter did run,
And we kill'd him at Cloud's Hill, near to Congleton.

Here's a health to all hunters of every degree.
All jolly good sportsmen wherever they be!
In a full flowing bowl, we will drink a health all,
To that great and true sportsman, Squire Frith, of Bank Hall.

[1] There appear to be two versions of this poem: the other, taken from *The Reli-quary*, vol. i., 1860-1, p. 243, having been kindly forwarded to me from Derby-shire. There are some few differences, but, on the whole, the versions are much the same. I have printed the older rendering.

www.ingramcontent.com/pod-product-compliance
Lightning Source LLC
Chambersburg PA
CBHW051824040426
42447CB00006B/361